JAMES TAYLOR'S

JAMES TAYLOR'S

ON and OFF the MIDWAY

James Taylor *and* Kathleen Kotcher

THE LYONS PRESS

Guilford, Connecticut

An Imprint of The Globe Pequot Press

Library of Congress Cataloging-in-Publication Data
Taylor, James (James Robert), 1950-
    [Shocked and amazed]
    James Taylor's shocked and amazed : on and off the midway /
James Taylor and Kathleen Kotcher.
      p. cm.
    Includes index.
    ISBN 1-58574-707-6 (pbk. : alk. paper)
    1. Sideshows--United States. 2. Circus performers--United
States.   I. Kotcher, Kathleen. II. Title.
GV1835.5.T39 2002
791.3'5--dc21

2002011298

To Rebecca, Anna, Ivan, Frank, and Cindy
Who always encouraged us
Without quite knowing why.

CONTENTS

Introduction: A Showman's IOU

First, I've got to say that—for a guy who's had no circus, carnival, or performing arts background, at least not in my youth, anyway—I feel pretty lucky to have gotten as far as I have with the business. I'm the guy who was never "with it," whose parents never took him to shows (other than movies), whose friends find my interest in "the other entertainment" about as freaky as they've always thought *I* was. Second, well, this isn't going to take a second. I've learned *that* much from the showmen I've interviewed, visited in their homes, hounded from lot to lot, and generally annoyed to the point where they finally revealed to me a secret I never expected. But I'll get to that. In a second.

Around 1992, when my "real" father had been dead for about four years, my mother gave me a priceless gift: a new father. Not to disparage Dad—a man with whom, I'm sad to say, I often felt I only had blood in common—but my mother's boyfriend, Jerry Farrow, was something else entirely. Jerome (as my mother called him when she was p.o.'ed) was carny to the core. He'd been with it since he was in his teens, when he hooked up with Prell's Broadway Shows, running the only pony ride that ever played with old man Prell. Jerry was also a premier dealer in horseflesh, though not as a horse murderer (as he called those who sold the old nags as meat or glue-on-

> **Around 1992, when my "real" father had been dead for about four years, my mother gave me a priceless gift: a new father.**

the-hoof). He was one of Maryland's prime auctioneers of farm stock, horses in particular. And I thought he was the most hysterically comical human being I'd ever met. Sorry Dad, but Jerry was the father I never had, a man whose entire life was a performance though he never owned a show, who seemed most alive telling the wild tale, the man with whom I clicked like the alcoholic does the first time he ever knocks back a drink. I suppose that's a bit heavy-handed, but as Jerry put it to me once (and you'll have to pardon the language), "You're a bullshitter, but I like bullshitters."

I knew what he meant. Whenever I moaned about money, he always told me I was made of money. Whenever I said I was working myself into the ground, he'd tell me I loved it. This, of course, from the man who worked until the day he dropped and who, though times toward the end were lean for him, paid off an $80,000 mortgage in just a couple seasons because he couldn't stand to have the debt. After he passed away, my mother told me Jerry had always said that, one day, I was going to be worth a lot of money, that I had it written all over me. Leave it to a showman to be both right and wrong, to confuse relentless momentum (my m.o. and his) with bankability. And God love him for it. Of course he was right and wrong about something else: He told me I could just approach showmen cold for the interviews, the stories, the "jackpots" I wanted for my impending *Shocked and Amazed!* "They'll know you're legit, and it'll be okay." He was right about the "legit" part. I'm not sure he was entirely right when he said it would be "okay."

But let me digress (because no one would recognize me if I didn't). I shouldn't give Jerry all the credit, even though I'll give him that lion's share he deserves. You see, I've been told the very meaning of life itself by the King of the Sideshows, had it questioned by the Original Human Blockhead, and had it confirmed in spades by the World's Only Living Half Girl. I've had the grande dame of the Gorilla Show tell me what I should do for the rest of my life, been told by the Greatest Showman in the World what happens to showmen in the afterlife, and been shown life's most monumental regrets by a true sideshow captain and the last century's only true Monkey Girl. I didn't create this little road show my life has become—part show publisher, part museum director, part sleepless lunatic, and full-time drummer for the show business—just to watch old-timers die. I got into the endless interviewing, the plodding from midway to midway, the fighting with printers and media and landlords and an ofttimes blissfully ignorant public for one reason: posterity.

But lest you think it's all altruism or selflessness at my end, let me tell a little story. Call it another digression if you like. Jerry Farrow wasn't a showman in the carny sense—he was a jointee, a concessionaire, a ride owner—but for a brief time early in his career he flirted with it seriously enough to nearly get arrested. It went something like this: Always liking monkeys, Jerry got himself a monkey show. Menagerie, monkey speedway, what have you, he knew enough to pick up the monks at the end of the season, when the previous owner had tired of, or—more likely—been driven bankrupt by them. By Jerry's reckoning, there were a dozen or two assorted sizes and types, all wild as, well, monkeys. Scheming and plotting on their owners, no doubt, those past and those present.

Unfortunately for Jerry, he never thought that his barn, locked high and low and plenty roomy, would be anything but ideal for them. I wanted to tell him (many years too late for an event that took place years before I was my parents' little monkey), "Jeez, Jerr, they were *monkeys*; what were you *thinking*?" Of course, it didn't take long before the ringleader, Jimmie—a huge monk whose name I've changed here to protect the innocent—figured out how to pull a Houdini from that old barn at Jerry's winter quarters just south of Baltimore. And it took Jerry just long enough to discover his misfortune before the whole tribe was running rampant throughout the Glen Burnie area. Picture this: a semi-rural community just south of town, the whole landscape dotted with the beginnings of suburbia, still bucolic though carved in half, east from west, by the newly highwayed Route 2, a scattered cow amid the corn and scattered split-levels, kids' toys and picnic tables amid farm tractors, and in that mix a few dozen monkeys hurling planters and up-ending barbecue grills, running the kids screaming before terrified mothers. Yeah, Jerry didn't like the picture much either, but the Baltimore *Sunpapers* and the now defunct *News American* sure did.

In the days before PETA and the animal rights movement, this was more media fun than ELEPHANT ESCAPES CIRCUS AND TRAMPLES USED CAR LOT. Unfortunately, fun for the *Sun* was less than fun for the Baltimore County police. For the next days, bordering on a week, the local cops, Barney–Fife style, shot monkeys out of trees throughout South Baltimore. The last to go, of

Huge and wily, he ducked the cops as long as he could, but eventually he ended up plugged like the rest of them.

course, was Jimmie. Huge and wily, he ducked the cops as long as he could, but eventually he ended up plugged like the rest of them. Shot dead because it was easier for the cops than calling in the zoo or Jerry. And you can bet when Jerry got word that big Jimmie had been shot and laid out at the local station, well, Jerry didn't go to ID the remains.

Fast forward to the next season. Jerry is on the road, as are all good outdoor amusement business folk everywhere. And into his pony ride runs one his boys with a message of frightening significance: "Big Jimmie's back! I just saw his show down the midway, big as life!" Well, Jerry couldn't let that go. When he had a few minutes, he took himself down to the other end of the lot, and there it was, sure enough, with a long line of paying customers: the Horrors of the Jungle! show (or whatever it called itself; memory fails at the moment and Jerry's not here to contradict this end of the story). And in that show stood Jimmie, just as large as the life Jimmie had once had. Of course he wasn't much alive at that point, but it was a fine job of stuffing he'd been put through after the Glen Burnie police shot him so many months before. The overall horrifying effect of the stuffed monk was heightened

Introduction

by the pint of red paint—bright as any stop sign and slathered all over the ape's mouth and hands—which stood in for the blood Jimmie didn't have to bleed anymore and for the blood of his hapless victims—the jungle mannequins lying at the ape's feet. The jungle screams and the jungle drums pounded and blared from the grind tape as Jerry left the show. Finding the owner, he asked him how the spot was going, told him of his own connection to the attraction, assured the showman he wasn't there to beef but to check out how Jimmie was doing. And, of course, Jerry was told what I've been told by countless showmen about such things: Jimmie was making more money dead than he did alive.

As wild, wacky, and, some might say, outrageous as that story is, and however much that type of tale might have inspired me to look into the business, I hope it's not really the verdict on the business: making more money dead than alive. I realize, though, that it could well be. The past couple of years have seen transpire another thing that drove me to this wild project of mine: I've watched as—one by one—the show business's old-timers have passed on, gone to that "big lot in the sky," as those of a religious bent would have it. Half girls, monkey girls, purveyors of athletic apes, human blockheads, keepers of two-faced cows— they've all gone.

Half girls, monkey girls, purveyors of athletic apes, human blockheads, keepers of two-faced cows— they've all gone.

Oh, there's still the old timer or two kicking it around, still cuttin' up jackies, but even they'd admit that the truly *old* old timers—from that classic era between the World Wars—just aren't around to say their piece. Having said that, though, of course you've got to know that my phone rings off the hook anymore, with everyone looking for the "old freaks," "that town in Florida where all the sideshow people live," "that place with more human oddities per square mile than anyplace else on earth." It's pointless to tell them that the business was bigger than just the freak acts, bigger even than what they imagine that town—Gibsonton—was in its heyday. And frighteningly, it often seems pointless to even argue with them that the old-timers aren't there to bother—as I bothered them for years and years. Just the other day, for example, I was contacted by an arts director from a European festival which, this year, is themed around the "sideshow"—well, a European's idea of the American sideshow. And, of course, he owns a copy of Tod Browning's cult classic *Freaks* and the Siamese twin Hilton Sisters' terribly bad film, *Chained for Life*. And, of course, he's read Dan Mannix's *Freaks—We Who Are Not As Others* and, I suppose, Katherine Dunn's *Geek Love*. And, equally, of course, he wants to come to Gibtown.

Honestly, it exhausted me to explain to him that he was looking for ghosts or his own dreams or, well, something about as honestly freakish as an old time ghost show and just about as long gone. How could I tell him that—wanting what he wanted—there simply wasn't any *there* there, not in Gibtown and not on any midway, not now and maybe not ever. The allure of the midway for most of us rubes was never any deeper than the glow of the countless bulbs shining from the carnival joints, rides, and shows in the evening twilight of autumn.

I knew that sad truth before I began this *Shocked and Amazed!* adventure and before I co-founded the American Dime Museum in Baltimore, the only museum devoted to the novelty and variety exhibition business. I knew that the showmen would be just people—albeit amazing ones, as often as not—with their own worries and fears and foibles and perhaps not one ounce of the pizzazz offstage that they had to affect onstage. Their tales, I figured from the beginning, would be a wild mix of truth and "truth," and in their telling I'd be tested, not for my gullibility—though that's always in there, too—but for my ability to enjoy the inherent and central truth in any good story: its ability to entertain and make you remember.

You see, I told you we'd get back to posterity. I'm a little ashamed to admit that I've sought my own in the midst of chronicling for future generations the showmen of the 20th and 21st centuries. I'm equally embarrassed to be courted for my "knowledge" of the business, a business in the face of which—in my humble opinion—I'm a total rube, though one who's truly "for it." I watch and listen to showmen and fans of the business rattle off significant dates and fairs, plot routes long played, all this as some might play bridge, and I just have to smile and nod, like I have a clue what's going on in those discussions.

No, those things—those circus and carnival sideshow minutiae, those literal nuts and bolts of the business—those things stick with me not at all, and that's not really "okay" with me. But those details weren't the reason I began my own half-way version of trouping behind the countless showmen I've followed: It's been my need to play the James Boswell to all those Samuel Johnsons of the midway, those carnival showmen who *are* the carnival, after all. It's been my need for visibility in the midst of a life that guarantees invisibility for most of us over time, and my belief that the showmen in this world I've investigated (and will continue to pursue) should be guaranteed at least that as well. The world they've long entertained owes them that much.

> **The allure of the midway for most of us rubes was never any deeper than the glow of the countless bulbs shining from the carnival joints, rides, and shows in the evening twilight of autumn.**

Frank Lentini, the human tripod, as a youth.

Amazing Feets

When I asked Jeanie Tomaini, inarguably the most famous living half girl (billed in her day on the shows, of course, as "The World's Only Living Half Girl"), what was the most amazing act she ever saw on the midway, without a moment's hesitation she told me, "Oh, Frank Lentini. He had three legs and you know he could kick a football the whole length of the show with that leg." And Jeanie's not the only person who'll bring Lentini's name up, either. He was certainly one of the premier sideshow attractions of this century, a savvy show owner as well, and it's a rare book on the subject of carnival shows that doesn't mention him. A lot. What follows is an assortment of his pitch—original text and images as well. See. Jeanie told you he was an amazing piece of work.

The life history of a Francesco A. Lentini

I am the subject of the present sketch. I was born in Rosblini in the province of Siracusa, Sicily, in the year 1889. I am of a family of twelve children (seven sisters and five brothers, who are all ordinary appearing people, there being nothing unusual in their personal appearance or physical characteristics).

Indeed careful investigation does not reveal any peculiarity in any of my ancestors either on the maternal or paternal side of my family.

I am often asked the question. "What is the cause of my strange condition?" I have appeared before the leading medical world in Europe as well as in the United States, and the only cause that they can give me is that my mother was to have given birth to twins but at a certain period some of the cells holding one of the bodies ceased to develop so that my mother gave birth not to two children, but more than one, yet not two.

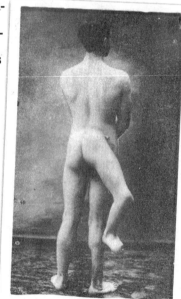

FRANK A LENTINI

The only man in the world with 3 legs 4 feet 16 toes 2 bodies from the waist down Operation impossible doctors claim would cause death or paralyze my entire body 3rd limb connected to spine   THANK YOU
Please show this photo to your friend

Frank Lentini bares all in this early pitchcard.

1

Up to the age of six I was able to extend the third limb so that it was possible for me to reach the floor with it, but was never able to use it for walking purposes, but strange as it may seem at the end of the sixth year my body started outgrowing the third limb, so that at the present time you will notice that it is six or seven inches shorter than the two limbs that I stand on. And furthermore, you will notice, that none of my limbs are alike—yet, I have three and yet, haven't a pair.

Often people look at me and pass the remark, "Isn't that too bad!" But I am here to tell you that there are lots of people in the world who are a great deal worse off than I am. Who have far less to live for, and who have but a fraction of the pleasure that I get out of life.

When I grew to the age when boys are allowed to go out of doors to play it was then that the realization came to me of my unusual peculiarity, and naturally, I grew a little despondent about everything. My parents were fairly well-to-do and I have every comfort and was not neglected, but I began to grow unhappy, nevertheless.

But one time I was taken to an institution where I saw a number of blind children and children who were badly crippled and otherwise mistreated by fate, and then and there, I realized that my lot wasn't so bad after all. Even though a child, I could appreciate the fact that I was possessed of all my faculties and senses. I could hear, talk, understand appreciate and enjoy the beauties of life. I could read and they couldn't. I could talk to my friends, but some of them couldn't because they were dumb. I could hear and enjoy beautiful music, while some of them couldn't because they were deaf. I have my mental faculties and began to look forward to my education, and some of them couldn't because they were idiots. The visit to that institution, unpleasant though it was because of the misery that I saw, was the best thing that could have happened to me. From that time to this I have never complained. I think life is beautiful and I enjoy living it.

When I was quite young my family moved to America. Wherever we went I was, of course, considered a curiosity and while at first their

FRANCIS LENTINI
THREE LEGGED BOY

PHOTOGRAPHS COPYRIGHTED BY CHAS. E. RIDENOUR, EDENA STUDIO, 808 ARCH ST., PHILA.
ALL RIGHTS RESERVED AND REPRODUCTIONS POSITIVELY PROHIBITED.

A young Francis Lentini demonstrates he has more than enough legs to stand on.

curious, critical gaze was considerably embarrassing, I gradually became used to it. It was natural for everyone to suggest to my parents that I be put into the show business, but my father said, "No," emphatically—at least until I should have gained an education. He said he could foresee eventually that I might travel, but that he would not allow it until I had the benefit of an education.

I am often asked the question if I know of any other case of my kind, of anyone being born as I am. Yes, I knew of two three-legged cases, and two four-legged cases—the three-legged being males, and four-legged being females—but none of these had a normal extra lower limb. And none had control of their extra limbs, and in fact they had all they could do to get around on their normal lower limbs. Only one of these lived to an old age. And that was Mertle Corbet, the four-legged woman.

No, my limb does not bother me in the least. I can get about just as well and with the same ease as any normal person—walk, run, jump; ride a bicycle, horse; ice and roller skate; and drive my own car. I can swim— one advantage I have over the other fellow when I swim is that I use the extra limb as a rudder. I am sometimes asked how I buy my shoes. Well, here's how: I buy two pairs and give the extra left shoe to a one-legged friend of mine who had the misfortune to lose his right leg, so you see every

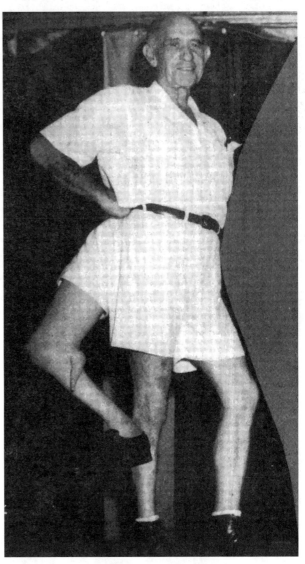

*Frank Lentini
in his later years.*

time I buy a pair of shoes I really do a good deed along with it. Another question often asked is "Does the extra limb bother in sleeping?" It does not: I can lie on my back or either side of my body without any hardship or loss of sleep.

Of course, it was a great shock to my parents that I was born as I was, but when they found that I was perfectly normal every other way they, too, began to be philosophical about it. I have been traveling for the most part of my life and must say that I enjoyed it very much.

Amazing Feets

Ward Hall enjoys a light snack.

KING *of the* SIDESHOWS

If you want to climb the highest mountain, you go to Mt. Everest. If you want to talk to the King of the Sideshows, you talk to Ward Hall. Around longer than virtually anybody in the business, involved in just about every aspect of it as well (and in a lot of attempts to break the barriers between sideshow and mainstream venues), it's little wonder that his name ends up on every showman's and performer's lips if you talk to them long enough. Grind shows? "You talked to Ward Hall?" Freak shows? "You oughtta talk to Ward Hall." Sideshow history? "Ward Hall was on *Nightline* for that. You seen him yet?"

When I first spoke to him, it was by phone, at the start of my work on *Shocked and Amazed!* During our brief conversation to set up an interview, he pretty much told me that sideshows, especially freak shows, were a thing of the past and that I should be writing my book in a library somewhere. Knowing this was not the way to start my book, I told him I'd like to see and talk to him anyway. I suppose that at that point, I sounded to him like every other nitwit writer who ever thought he'd spook his editor with some Halloween or July 4th tomfoolery.

The Florida Citrus Festival and Polk County Fair in Winterhaven, Florida, where I met Ward in person, was another matter entirely. The World

of Wonders show was there, as Hall had said his show would be, in all its glory, a massive banner line across its face as in the days he'd told me were long gone. And if it harked back to an era now past, at least it did so with the flash you'd expect. Ward Hall or some other "professor" wasn't working the front, out on the bally platform giving the gathering crowd the spiel, tossing them some morsel from one of the performers (maybe a quick sword swallow, a blast from the fire breather at twilight), getting ready at just the right moment to go from their bally to the grind and, thereby, turn the tip. There was, though, a mysterious figure, its head covered in a black cloth bag, sitting out front, a silent lure to the passing fair goers to step right up. And of course, "Little Pete" Terhurne, the dwarf performer who's been with Hall four decades, a performer who's nearly a 10-in-1 all by himself, little Pete was acting as ticket seller.

Ward Hall and late partner Harry Lewis.

The days of multi-act, multi-performer shows at nearly every carnival, the old 10-in-1 shows, may be gone. Certainly, Ward Hall thinks they are, killed as much as anything by the economics of the carnival and fair lots themselves. As he told me over the phone that first time we spoke, he wasn't mounting the huge shows with massive overhead he used to put together. His current show is more of a museum, which is how he has the World of Wonders billed on the banner line, an outrageous mix of gaffed and for-real taxidermied freak animals, Egyptian giantesses, wax museum fixtures, live pythons. He told me that at least with a museum he didn't have to pay the mannequins. Truth be known, Ward and his longtime partner in the business, Chris Christ, still had the show on the road and still had some performers working the World of Wonders in the '94 season in spite of the difficulties.

During our first talk, Hall's stories of the business started where many a discussion with showmen and performers starts, how you just can't win. I don't remember whether I asked him how his current show was going or what, but he cut real quick to 1977 and the Lake County Fair in Illinois when he played the spot with a pickled punk show, a common carnival show over the years, a display of fetuses in jars. He told me he'd played that spot numerous times without incident, but politics was to change that.

WH: It was 1977 playing the Lake County Fair in Illinois, which I played numerous times and they had a new law that was going into effect eliminating the job of county coroner and replacing them with medical examiners. The fellow who had been the county coroner for twenty some years was going to lose his job, so he was going to run for sheriff. And he needed something to get him publicity so they came down and raided the freak baby show and arrested my partner Chris Christ.

The charge was illegal transportation of human remains. The idea is that you can't just go out and pick up a dead body and take it around unless you're a mortician. The county coroner wanted to get publicity, but he didn't know how much publicity he was going to get out of it and neither did we. It was a little local thing, but all of a sudden it hit the wire services, so it went all across the country. I had that show the year before at the Ohio State Fair in Columbus. I had it at the Illinois State Fair . . .

S&A: And nobody said anything about it?

WH: No. Had it all over the country. Big fairs. Now, all of a sudden, the newspapers are calling the fair board. Now, at one point in this procedure, we could've pled guilty and paid a hundred-dollar fine and the whole thing would be forgotten, but we weren't guilty of doing anything wrong and we weren't about to have that record of guilt. So we fought it. And it cost us a lot of money because it took several trips back there and it went to court. Now, we had the show at the Illinois State Fair and the other fairs in Illinois. The original freak baby show, or as they call them in the business, pickled punk shows, was in 1933–34 Chicago World's Exposition. A guy by the name of Lou Dufour had it. One of the biggest exhibits of freak unborn babies is at the Soldiers and Sailors Museum in Chicago, and at the moment we were exhibiting in Lake County, the King Tut exhibit with its remains was also in Chicago.

S&A: So much for your display of human remains.

Ginger Donahue demonstrates her love for snakes while Ward Hall mans the ticket box.

WH: So finally the judge ruled that these were *not* corpses; they were fetuses: They had never been issued birth certificates, therefore, there were no death certificates, therefore, it was legal to have then. But in the meantime they had confiscated the babies. Fortunately, we already had molds of them sitting at the rubber factory. We were only out of business with that show for a week, then we had the bouncers. *Now* I'm going to show you how you *cannot* win no matter what you do. I had had that show at the Ohio State Fair and numerous other fairs in Ohio. Ohio has a sixteen-page booklet that gives all the rules and regulations and state laws pertaining to the operation of sideshows and carnival shows at state fairs in Ohio. Very specific. You cannot have a picture on the front that shows blood. You cannot have a torture show. You cannot have a girl show. You cannot have a show where anyone dances under a tent (which means I could not take the Bolshoi Ballet and legally present it in the state of Ohio if it's under a tent). You can't have a ticket box over four feet high. You can't have a show within a show for an extra charge. So the people know that what they see advertised is exactly what they're going to see.

S&A: So you're moving with the bouncers at this point. Did you ever get the babies back?

WH: No. I never asked for them back. I didn't need them anymore. At least I *thought* I didn't need them. But I'm coming to that. So I just closed the show for the season. Now, the next year, we're opening the show, the first spot, at Canfield, Ohio. We had it all set up the opening day of the fair and I'm waiting for the inspector because every show has to be inspected. At any given time there's fifty, sixty people standing out in front of the show waiting to go in. Well, the inspector finally got there at four. He's a very nice gentleman. I'd known him for a long time. And a man by the name of Henry Valentine was running the show for me at that time. So when the inspector came in, the first thing Henry said was, "Hello, Mr. (So and So)," and he opened one of the bottles and took out the baby and said, "You see, these are legal. These are all rubber." And the inspector said, "Well, Henry, when Ward was here before he always had the real ones. Haven't you got the *real* ones?" Henry said, "No, no, we replaced them all with the rubber ones." And he said, "Oh, Henry, the law is very specific. You cannot have any made-up freak. Now if you had the *real* ones there'd be no problem. You'd get the license, but I can't license these because they're fake." Now, when we got the show snatched, we hit the wire services. Preliminary hearing, wire services. The hearing, wire services. And then the county coroner, his name was Mickey, did one more shot. They lined up twelve, fourteen little coffins. And he had a priest, a minister and a rabbi and Mickey standing there with the coffins at the cemetery having the burial for the carnival babies. This hit the wire services and came out during the New Orleans carnival trade con-

vention and the new Orleans paper carried a picture of the burial about four columns by eight inches. He got more press than he ever wanted, really, out of this thing. But he did get elected sheriff and we've been back and played the fair several times with sideshows since then, and it's, "Hi, Mickey." "Oh! Hey, glad to see you." Everything is fine. But Mickey died two years ago. He was a good guy. He just did what he was doing. He did his bit.

S&A: To get to another subject, you guys caught some heat down in Florida over Stanley "Sealo" Berent, and I think, "Little Pete" Terhurne and their being on display, didn't you?

WH: There was never any heat. Never any heat. Let me explain this. In 1921, I can't tell you exactly, or 1923, a law was put on the books in the state of Florida, I can almost quote it verbatim, "It shall be prohibited to exhibit for profit any human being that is deformed, malformed or disfigured. To present or to promote such an exhibition shall be punishable with a $1,000 fine and/or a year in the state penitentiary." Nobody in the business was even aware this law existed.

Stanley "Sealo" Berent fought for his right to bare arms in Florida sideshows.

S&A: You mean the shows are going on and nobody's even doing anything about it, even with this law on the books?

WH: *Nobody* knew it and everybody had been working in Florida all

King of the Sideshows

The masterminds behind the World of Wonders: Ward Hall and Chris Christ.

these years. During the Manatee County Fair, there was an article in the *St. Petersburg Times* about a frog girl show (which was not mine) and it quoted this law. This was the first time any of us ever knew about it. So our immediate reaction was these people live in Florida, they own property in Florida, they pay their taxes in Florida, and yet they would not be able to work in Florida. So we decided we ought to do something about it. So my company, which was World Attractions, Inc., with Stanley Berent—Sealo, the Seal Boy—and Pete Terhurne, we wanted to get this thing cleared up. My attorney at that time was a man by the name of Royal Flagg Jonas out of Miami Beach. Very good attorney. Roy wanted to do this because he knew this case was so unusual that it would put him in the book of precedents, which it did. Roy had formerly been the mayor of North Bay Village, Florida, which is the 79th Street causeway between Miami and Miami Beach, so of course he knew the police there and everything, so he applied for a license for a freak show for North Bay Village, with the understanding that the chief of police was going to turn down the application for the license on the basis of this law. So now we had somebody we could sue. Now at that time, Richard Gerstein was the state's attorney for Dade County and it was going to be tried in a Dade County Court. And Richard Gerstein, also a very fine gentleman, was a member of the Miami Showmen's

SHOCKED AND AMAZED!

Association, and he agreed that he would fight this because normally with something like this, they'd say, "Oh well, just throw it out of court." But we needed to go to court and we needed to lose. So we went into court in Dade County and we lost the case which now gave us the privilege of going to the Court of Appeals. Now in the Court of Appeals, again we lost, which was what we had to do. This went on 'til we got to the Supreme Court for the State of Florida.

S&A: So how did they rule?

WH: There are six justices and to make sure that it couldn't be contested later, one judge voted for the law, the others voted on our part. That way it can't be contested. As I understand it, a unanimous decision can be contested in the federal courts. Of course, nobody wanted to contest it anyway. So at that point, the law was stricken and removed from the books. But it's not over yet.

S&A: It never seems to be over.

WH: The next year, I had a unit and I had just closed the season at the Texas State Fair and had got home. The other unit was at the fair in Tallahassee. Henry, who had the thing with the baby show and couldn't get open because they were rubber, he was in Tallahassee. We had Dolly Reagan, the Ossified Girl; and Dick Brisben, the Penguin Boy. The sheriff came down accompanied by the television news cameras and so forth. And they made a big thing about closing up the sideshow because of this law. They didn't want to put anybody in jail, but the sheriff said it was illegal and it couldn't operate. They shut it down. Dolly was our MC. This will show you how ridiculous this is. They said Dickie can't work at all; Dolly can MC the show, but in such a way that her body would not be seen. They had to wrap a sheet around her so only her head was sticking out!

S&A: You should've just had her do Spidora.

WH: Yeah! Henry immediately went to the phone and called me. And he

What are you looking at, dummy? Inside the wondrous World of Wonders.

says, "I thought we had this straightened out." It was ruled that it was a discriminatory law, discriminating against handicapped people who are making an honest living. So I said to Henry, "Go down to the carnival office, and tell Mr. Kaufmann," (who owned the carnival). I was lucky. I had got home and was sitting at my desk and I happened to have the whole court decision right in front of me. So I said, "Here's the number of the case, the date it was tried, etc. etc." So he went down to the office, but Mr. Kaufman wasn't there; he was out of town.

So Henry said, "Now what should I do?" I said, "Go to the fair office." And I can't remember the lady's name—she was the manager of the fair, and also the secretary of the Florida Association of Fairs and Exhibitions. And because this was a statewide thing, I had kept her informed of every step, so she was well aware of it. So now the fair had opened on Friday night and we got closed and now it's late Saturday morning. And Henry went over to the fair office and she said, "Oh yes, Mr. Valentine, I am well aware of that and, yes indeed, that was stricken from the books. And they can't do that to us!" So she got on the phone and called the fair's attorney and got him off of the golf course.

S&A: I guess he was not amused.

WH: Well, he was amused, because the Saturday morning's paper had come out about how the sheriff had closed this illegal freak show and—of course—it was on television because they had been there with the cameras. It made the 11 o'clock news! So now they got down there and they called the sheriff. What it was, the sheriff still had an old law book and somebody had called and made a complaint about the show and cited the number of the old law and he looked it up and sure enough it was in his book and he wasn't aware that it had been stricken. So now the next day, the headline comes out, "Leon County Sheriff Doesn't Even Know What Laws He's Supposed to Enforce." That didn't do us any good either because this put mud on the face of the sheriff. But of course they came down, they apologized, and the show opened right back up.

Ward Hall and Bindlestiff Family Cirkus member (and sometime World of Wonder attraction) Keith Nelson.

S&A: So how was the sheriff afterward? Was he pretty decent about everything in spite of the bad press he got?

WH: Oh certainly! Oh yeah.

S&A: And in the years after, you didn't have any other problems with that sort of thing? You kept playing the spot?

WH: This is the first year in many years I haven't played it.

S&A: In terms of performers, the Galyon Brothers, the Siamese twins, are pretty amazing. Are you still in touch with them?

WH: I have not talked to them for quite some time. But they were never with my show. They had their own show. We put together the people for a motion picture called *Being Different*.

S&A: So you put together all those people? *Being Different*'s a hell of a documentary.

WH: But that was the only time that the Galyons ever worked for me, because they had their own show, which their father managed. It was a trailer-mounted show. The people walk up and they look in the window and see the boys sitting there watching television or something. The greatest attractions I ever had were Emmitt and Percilla Bejano—the Alligator Man and the Monkey Girl; Schlitzie the Pinhead; and the various giants. I've had several giants over the years. Johann Petursson only worked for me once. Johann came over to this country in 1948 for the Ringling Circus. He was with them for about two–three years and then he went to work for Doc Saunders who framed a big sideshow that went to Canada. And he was with Doc, I think, only one year. And then he went to work for Glen Porter and he was with Glen several years and then he wanted to have his own show, so Glen helped him to build his own show and Glen booked it for him for awhile. He made a lot of money and he had his own show for many, many years until he retired. He had been in retirement for some years and in 1973, I believe, I got him to come out of retirement to work the Ringling show in Washington, DC. Now, Johann was a good friend of mine. I liked Johann, I always did, but I also knew Johann could be a little temperamental. So even though in my contract I was

Johann K. Petursson, Iceland, Tallest Man in the World in Viking Costume

Johann K. Petursson, the biggest giant.

to have only one giant, I got a second giant, a big, tall boy by the name of Tyrone Reeder, and we had him made some beautiful, Arabian-style wardrobe, and I had a big headpiece that I bought out of the Folies Bergere with pheasant feathers. It was an Egyptian thing that stood four feet high on its own. So we had individual stages for the acts, the old circus style. I put Johann on one side, and directly across, facing him, was Tyrone. And it turns out that Johann and the other giant both loved to play chess. So they became good buddies because between shows they played chess all the time. And I don't know what happened; I'd give a thousand dollars to have it back, somewhere it got lost, or I gave it to somebody or something, but I had a picture and it was the only time that I know of that Johann ever allowed such a thing, I had a picture of him and Tyrone together.

Ward Hall uses his golden gift of gab to gather gangs of gawkers.

S&A: That's sad. You'll never get another chance at a shot like that. So the show opened pretty well?

WH: On opening night, Milt Robbins was my inside lecturer and he was going to take the crowd to Johann's platform next and he saw this well dressed gentlemen walk up the steps onto Johann's platform. So he went over; he was going to stop him. But then he saw that they greeted each other and the man sat there with Johann for the next hour, as long as the sideshow was open, and it turned out he was the ambassador for Iceland. They had been schoolboys together!

S&A: I guess that was one of the first times Petursson had seen anyone from the old country in a long time.

WH: A long time. But Johann, of course, he was old and had his ailments by then and there was one point there where we had some newspaper people and they wanted to interview Johann. Chris Christ went over and told Johann, "These people want to do an interview." "I don't want to talk to nobody. Don't want to talk to them." So Chris said, loud enough so Johann could hear, "Fellas, you don't want to talk to him. You want to talk to the big giant, don't you? Come right over here, because he's the smaller of the two and you want to talk to the big giant." And Johann turned around and goes, "Chris! Chris! Come over here! I talk to them!" But Johann was a great attrac-

tion. I had worked with him on other shows, and when he was younger *Old MacDonald had a* he had a great sense of humor. A wonderful person. He used to love to *farm, Ee i ee i—Oh* tease. We had a lady sword swallower who worked for me for quite *my goodness!* awhile, her name was Patricia Zerm—Lady Patricia. And she was, I think, the first one to swallow a neon tube in her act. She always wore beautiful gowns. It was a beautiful act. We were working the Tampa Fair and Johann was there and so was Pat and she used to tease him. She would chase him and it was so funny to watch this great big giant running away from this little woman. On the King Bros. Circus, the band leader, Phil, who also worked for me later as an inside lecturer, was married to Christine, the Alligator Skin Girl. And it was in the winter time. The show hadn't opened yet and they were visiting one day and in jest Johann said to Phil, because Phil was a feisty little guy, he said, "You know, Phil, this country ain't no goddamn good." "What do you mean?! What do you mean this country's no good?!" "Well, I been here already for five years and I only save $50,000." "Why you big son of a bitch, you should've stayed in Iceland! You wouldn't have fifty friggin' cents!"

S&A: You were talking earlier about Emmitt and Percilla Bejano. It's sad, but the picture that's painted of many of the sideshow and freak show marriages is one of marriages for publicity. But Emmitt and Percilla have been married longer than ninety-nine percent of the married population.

WH: We gave them a fiftieth wedding anniversary at the Showmen's Club. And Phil Dotto and Christine, the Alligator Skin Girl, were married until they died. Another great attraction who worked for me, and a wonderful, wonderful man, was Bill Durks, the Three-Eyed Man, and he was married to Mildred, the Alligator Girl. She died; he never remarried. And you could go on and on. The Davenports, the two midgets; Cliff and Mamie King, the midgets; Sandra Reed, Lady Sandra we called her, the albino sword swallower. She married on my show to Harold Spohn, the fat man. And when Harold died, it just devastated her to the extent that she quit the business and has not worked since then.

S&A: It's pretty obvious that loyalty's not an unknown virtue to show folk. The people you have left have been working with you for a long time, haven't they?

WH: Little Pete is in the ticket box. I'd have to ask him: this is either his thirty-ninth or fortieth year. So he probably won't stay: He's very unreliable! Jimmy Long, the fella I asked to get the chair for me a few minutes ago is my boss canvassman, this is twenty-seven years for Jimmy. He's made me a very religious man: I pray for him everyday because if anything happens to Jimmy, I'm just going to leave the show sit because I wouldn't know how to put it up or tear it down or drive the truck. And Bruce Snowdon, "Harold Huge," has been here for twelve years. Hi! [a kid comes up to Hall]

Keith Nelson puts a little iron in his system while contortionist Daniel Smith looks on from inside his box.

Kid: Where's the Tasmanian Terror at?

WH: The Tasmanian Terror? Look over there, now wait a minute, come here, not the little box, but the one next to it with the light in it. That's the Tasmanian Terror. Took it out of there and put it in the big box because it grew too big for the little one. [kid goes off to see Terror] You hear funny things you know. Years ago, one woman was in the baby show and she said, "Do you have to get bigger bottles for them as they grow?" And another one came in and she said, "Oh, it's so sad those babies in those bottles." She said, "How do their little souls get out of there and go to heaven." But one of the greatest was when I had a medieval torture chamber. And this very sweet old lady came up to the ticket box and said to our lady ticket seller, "Miss, how long do you have to wait?" And my ticket seller said, "Oh, you don't have to wait. You can walk in right now and see it." And she said, "No, I mean how long do I have to wait once I get in there?" Well, you don't have to wait. It's going on right now, you just walk through." "I don't think you understand. Do you have chairs that I could sit down while I wait." "Wait for what?" She says, "Well, how long does it take for one of them to die?"

S&A: Getting back to the loyalty of your people and those working the shows, that loyalty really contradicts the charge you always hear about sideshow performers being exploited. I've read some things that were pretty cruel to showmen in that regard.

WH: One gentleman made the statement that I was "the pornographer of the handicapped." That offends me. These writers set themselves up as authorities on the sideshow business. And yet they get their research about sideshows while sitting in an air-conditioned library reading books. I doubt they ever had to help load a sideshow tent when it was wet and cold and pouring down rain and had to get behind a truck and try to push it off of the lot because it was stuck. I'm sure that they never had to take a fat lady to the hospital in the middle of the night and sit in the waiting room of the emergency ward for six hours to find out if she was going to be okay. I'm sure they never even attended the funeral for one of these people. I exhibited freaks and exploited them for years. And right now you are going to exploit these people. The difference between Ward Hall and you is when Ward Hall exploits these people, I pay them very well to do so. These authors, newspaper columnists, and television companies don't pay them a frigging penny. Nobody is forcing them to be in show business. It's the same old thing, especially in television. How many of these handicapped people do you have anchoring the news on television? How many do you see performing in your sitcoms? They want to be actors. They want to be in show business. This is their only outlet. I had a call from a company in New York and they wanted to bring a crew down here and film a music video with a rock group with the sideshow in the background. Generally, with anything like that, I tell them right off, "What is your budget?" And

Felicity climbs a ladder of swords while Molotov Malcontent looks on.

they say, "Well, we don't have much of a budget." "What do you expect for us to get out of it?" "Oh, well, you get publicity." And I say, "I don't do this for publicity. My people can't eat publicity. And we don't need publicity. We do it for money." And generally, it's the same thing for talk shows on television, especially now when they call me and they want you to bring them some people for nothing. And I say the same thing, "Before we start talking, let me have you understand my position. I am the same as an attorney. I will provide a service for you. You will give me a retainer and then pay me by the hour." And one woman from one of the talk shows said, "Well, what if you don't get these people?" I said, "It's just like the attorney when he takes you into court. If he doesn't win the case, he doesn't give you back the money."

S&A: You've said a number of places, including in your own book, *My Very Unusual Friends*, that the sideshows are nearly gone, that they get harder and harder to book.

WH: It's economics. All economics. First of all, organized carnivals were first started, developed, from the World Columbian Exposition of 1893 in Chicago. At that time there was a carousel and probably a live pony ride. A few years later came the first portable Ferris wheel. So there

The sign says it all.

were no rides at first. But there were all these shows. Museum type shows, girl shows, the Streets of Cairo, the Streets of Paris, so on and so forth. Over the years, even up through the 1930s and '40s, the average large carnival, a big, big carnival, would have about twenty rides and about thirty shows. A medium-size carnival would have twelve

rides and twelve to fifteen shows. A small carnival would have five or six rides and six or eight shows. My research, which is not accurate I know, but the best I can tell, about 1950, along in there, was the apex perhaps of the sideshows, because by then there were so many carnivals. Well every carnival practically and every circus had a sideshow at that time. And there were, I believe, between a 100 and a 110 10-in-1 sideshows in the United States and Canada. At the same time, there were over 400 girl shows. There were over a 1,000 grind shows. Today, there is one sideshow, and you're sitting in it, and really it's not a 10-in-1 sideshow anymore; it's a museum. There is one big illusion show. There are, I think, three motordromes. And there are probably five girl-to-gorilla shows and probably fifty grind shows. In the whole country. And the reason for that is the rides.

Felicity stands on Molotov while he reclines on a bed of nails.

S&A: So what were the mechanics of the change? How and when did it happen?

WH: By 1959, I had a sideshow that had a 200-foot front. I used to get free rent because I had such a big front, because the shows, which they called the back end, created the fence around the rides, which were all down the center. Along about the mid-'50s, carnival owners all of a sudden discovered there was something called Europe. Some of them had been overseas during the war. The European rides were always far more elaborate, far bigger, far better than anything that was produced in the United States. So the owners started importing rides. Prior to that time—you go back in the old *Billboards* and you'll see this—they would advertise, "Want Sideshow; Want Girl Show; Want Minstrel Show; Want Motordrome." The carnival owned the equipment. All the operator had to bring was the attractions. My first carnival experience was in 1948. I was seventeen years old and I went with a carnival out in Kansas. They furnished me with brand new bannerlines, brand new tent; every stick of that show was brand new except the tent stakes were Ford axles. All I had to come in with was sound equipment—which they would have furnished, but I didn't like theirs so I furnished my own—and my acts. And this was the standard deal with every carnival in the United States and every circus. You provided the acts; they provided all the equipment and they transported it. And the carnival received forty percent of the gross. The operator got sixty percent of the gross of the front and all the inside. And in those days, the inside meant the fortune

teller and the tattoo artist and all those things which you don't have now. Railroad shows, which were predominant in the early days, used three wagons for a big sideshow, that's one flat car, and one sleeper for the sideshow personnel. Now they can come along with a big ride. Generally, the ride is on two wagons and maybe twenty-five percent of the sleeping car. So now they can put two rides on the same transportation as one sideshow. The ride can be operated by three people, usually. The sideshow has maybe fifteen to twenty. And the ride works from the time it opens until it closes. And the carnival keeps 100 percent of the ride; they only got forty percent of the show. Now if you want to go to the reviews, the big girl reviews and the big colored reviews, they were even bigger shows as far as transportation and equipment was concerned. The investment in those shows was terrific because they had bigger tents, seats, big stages, scenery, lights, very elaborate

Ward Hall tells one and all about the attractions Alive on the Inside.

fronts, costumes. And they'd have forty to fifty people, some of them. So now these shows would take even more transportation and the carnival generally didn't get anything out of them. In fact, it was the practice, usually, that they would lose $20 to $30 thousand a year with one of those big shows, but it was their big prestige thing. But it's not only that way with carnivals. The 1920s were considered the golden age of circuses. Circus came into town with a 10,000-seat tent, with twenty-five elephants, and every day they gave a magnificent free street parade. Today, I'm going to visit a circus that travels on eight semis, has no street parade, has probably fifteen to sixteen performers, and the music is recorded. And this is typical of today.

It was the end of my day at the York Fair in Pennsylvania, and I was beat, but it was just the beginning of the busiest part of the day for carnival: evening. I was finishing up talking with banner painter/sword swallower/stand-up comic Johnny Meah, just being told how to turn the tip—what crowds looked good, which didn't. Almost in mid-sentence, and maybe to show me how it was done, Johnny stepped up to the inside platform and went into his routine, pitching the blow-off: the World of Wonders freak baby show. Fat Man Bruce "Harold Huge" Snowdon sat waiting to make change, his chair positioned just by the sidewall through which the tip would have to pass. It wasn't much of a crowd, maybe a dozen people, a ma and pa with their baby, a couple of teenaged boys (alternately giggly and smug), some others. Not a soul was doing anything except shuffling in place in response to Johnny's spiel. Finally, playing stick unasked, I cut past the platform to Bruce, gave him a buck and told him to keep the change. Pretty much everybody followed after that.

In the annex which housed the blow-off, a platform stood in a corner, the objects on top covered by an outrageous multicolored day-glo fake fur blanket. Next to it sat a folding metal chair, the kind you might find in a church, school or hospital. On its seat was a black plastic boom box. The crowd fidgeted in place, most everybody giggling nervously now. Outside, Meah was grinding the last couple or two in. And we all stood there. And stood there. Something was amiss. "Ward!" Johnny was calling in a stage whisper. "Ward?" he called again. "They're inside!" At the last moment, Ward bustled through the sidewall, obviously in a slight sweat, popped the flap on the boom box, dropped in the cassette, and hit play, they he threw back the day-glo blanket.

Most of the tip turned and walked out the second that blanket flew from the large jars it covered. On the platform were the World of Wonders bouncers, each floating in its couple gallons of clear fluid. The tape on the boom box, Ward's voice announcing that he was doctor somebody or other, ground out a lecture about, "these replica freak babies," the word "replica" spoken so softly you could hardly hear it spoken, the lecture going on to tell of the horrors of drug abuse. Pretty much, I and those two teenaged boys were the only ones who heard it all the way through. They walked up the minute it was obvious that only Ward and I were left in the blow-off besides them. The expected "Cool!" and "Shit!" could be heard from both of them. They didn't get giggly again until they were almost through the flap, almost back in the sideshow itself, far enough away that the babies couldn't see or hear them.

Ward was having trouble pulling the blanket back down over the bouncers, so I stepped over and gave him a hand. All straightened out, he popped the tape from the tape player and then held the sidewall for both of us to go out behind the show, back to where his trailer sat. Hardly turning to me, he smiled and spoke in a voice softer than I'd have expected. "What a way to make a living." The only way to make a living.

Major LITTLEFINGER & FAMILY ON TOUR with BARNUM 1897

Major Littlefinger and his wife and child, the latter, Little Dottie Littlefinger.

Kobel

Bernard Kobel. The name's as much a siren's call as old Istanbul or Cathay, at least to collectors of the bizarre and unusual in photographs. Until a couple decades ago, and for years prior to that, Kobel ran a service out of Clearwater, Florida, that supplied photos to sideshow operators and anyone else interested in the visually odd. His catalogs included thousands of images ranging from tattooed people ("more than 1,331 photos of highly tattooed men and women of the world, not minor jobs, but in most cases tattooed from head to toe . . ."), to wrestling and boxing women, circus photos, contortionists, women weight lifters, atrocities, odd houses, unusual epitaphs, and animal and vegetable freaks.

And of course there was the human oddities catalog. Numbering close to a thousand pictures in its final form, the catalog offered for sale the greatest visual freak show anywhere. At fifteen cents apiece (ten cents in lots of fifty or more), it was a means to slake the thirst of even the most jaded fan of the shocking, and it was all there at fire sale prices.

"Serpentina" the so-called Serpent Girl. She was born with no bones in her body other than her skull—not even vertebra. She is still alive and apparently in good health and about 40 years old. Born in Oakland, California. Condition is due to arrested ossification.

Though not a collector himself to any great extent, Kobel gathered the images together and put them out there for all to see, at a price not unlike those of the freak shows themselves. And like the surrealistic, homespun poetry of an opening bally, the catalog was filled to overflowing with quirky photo descriptions that are often as precious as the pictures. So precious, in fact, that the catalogs are now collector's items.

These featured photos are accompanied by the descriptions exactly as they appeared in Bernard Kobel's *Human Oddities of Circus Sideshows of Yesterday and Today*. They're reproduced in all their eccentric glory as Kobel wrote then. True to tradition, the text is often filled with spelling and factual errors and grammatical tics. And if that don't make it special, then it just ain't sideshow.

Left: "Tina Brown," the
500-pound fat lady
with an unidentified
but mighty fat midget
man.

Below: Two men, not
identified by name but
billed as the most
homely men in the
world when they were
attractions at Coney
Island during the
season of 1928.

The
WORLD'S
UGGLIEST
—MEN—
CONEY ISLAND
1928

PHOTOGRAPHS

Yours Ben. Corday.

Giant Ben Conway, now dead. Taken with two co-workers when they toured the play Puss in Boots. He later had a tattoo shop in Los Angeles at 100 ½ Main Street.

The bearded lady from Kentucky, Madame Deveere, taken in 1890. Her beard was 14 inches long.

I Dream of Jeanie

I'd been interviewing Jeanie Tomaini in the bait house of her Giant's Campground for nigh onto three hours. About two-thirds of the way through, Jeanie's daughter, Judy, came in and turned the lengthy interview into an even longer exercise in my self-inflicted trial to keep from wetting myself right there in front of them. I didn't want to break the flow (sorry) of their stories, and I felt that any attempt at even slowing them down would be like stuffing a plug into the oracle hole at a showman's version of Delphi.

But finally I couldn't stand it anymore. As I'd tried to do on any number of occasions prior, I told Jeanie and Judy I'd have to stop and make water. It was that or blow up in front of both of them. Judy just laughed. Jeanie wrinkled up a little grin and in her little-girl's voice, the one that always sounds so amazing coming from a lady in her 70s, asked me the question I should've seen coming. "Why don't you just cross your legs?" If it hadn't come from a woman who had been born without any, I suppose it wouldn't have been such an amazingly wry question.

Jeanie Tomaini, you see, once the wife of giant Al Tomaini, was known in her day as the World's Only Living Half Girl. Together, she and Al toured for decades as the World's Strangest Married Couple with circus sideshows and played dime museums in the likes of Atlantic City and Coney Island, as well as owning and running their own sideshows in assorted carnivals. Her parents had her performing in pumpkin fairs (as the small-time, local events would be called) from the time she was an infant. Her parents weren't wealthy, after all, and Bernice Smith—Jeanie's name at birth—meant decent income for all of them, herself included. And she did love to perform. Handstands. Cartwheels. Climbing ladders upside down. Ask Jeanie now what it was like, and she'll tell you without a moment's thought: "I had a ball."

Above: Irene Laswell, Jeanie, and Wild West performers Bob and Betty Sorenson.

Opposite: Jeanie and her dad, Jack Smith, in Denver, Colorado.

Al and Jeanie surrounded by members of the Doll family.

To add fuel to this already politically incorrect fire, you also need to know that when I say Jeanie and Al owned and managed shows, that means they hired and fired other freaks, both born and made, and they had freaks that were out-and-out gaffs. And yes, their blow-offs were the traditional half-and-halfs (usually gaffed but sometimes legit) and/or pickled punks, both powerful draws and, traditionally, powerful attractors of "heat," as legal troubles are called in the business. Jeanie and Al ran a giant turtle show, too. Put the reptiles up in big pits on the campgrounds during the winter season on the banks of the Alafia River, right across from the Cargill fertilizer plant, an old fixture on the river even in the late 1930s when Jeanie and Al bought the property. And when they retired, young by anybody's standards, they adopted kids, ran the campground, set up its restaurant, established the boat yard and bait shop and Al became fire chief and chief of police.

Well, Al's gone now, died relatively young from complications most likely attributable to the glandular anomaly that caused his giantism and made him his fame and fortune. And that fertilizer plant across the river still steams and fumes. One night while I was there staying in one of the cabins, in fact, the plant let out a blast that quickly became a shrill industrial whistle that boded no good if you ask me. I stared transfixed through the shimmering Venetian blinds at the glowing white cloud, lit by the hundreds of arc lights all over the plant that even in less threatening circumstances made it look like the malevolent steel-pipe and electric-light Christmas tree such places resemble after dark. In true unflappable showman fashion, Jeanie didn't even mention the commotion the next day, not until I brought it up. By way of putting the event into perspective, and many more events by implication, she said the plant was a lot better now than it used to be.

Well, nothing's quite like it used to be, especially not in the freak show business. Jeanie's certainly not doing handstands and cartwheels anymore, the feat being pretty tough for ninety-nine percent of the people in their seventies, let alone those born as half girls. But the decline in the business of "presenting human oddities for amusement and profit," as writer Robert Bogdan rather unglamorously put it in the subtitle of his book *Freak Show*, isn't really a factor of the age of the performers. If that were the case, the business would have been over many, many, many hundreds, perhaps thousands, of years ago. Hell, depending on how you look at the "business," it's damn near impossible to date its beginnings. As showmen are all fond of pointing out, if they're exploiting their performers (who are really showmen themselves), it's no worse than the rest of humanity has done to itself since the dawn of time. Think about it the next time you punch in at your nine-to-five.

The long cord between what we term freak shows (the shows whose "demise" so many now lament) and earlier uses of "very special people" is as twisted as any other ancient, much-used piece of twine might be. Midgets, for example, have long been performers in royal courts, have periodically been revered as gods (or at least their images have appeared as such, the Egyptian god Bast, for example), and in more recent times been held up (sorry again) as "the smallest specimen of humanity known." Hermaphrodites have gone from being figures of religious veneration in some cultures to being gaffed in many sideshows because the public demand simply couldn't be filled with the natural-born variety, there being relatively few compared to the rest of us "normals" and fewer still willing to show themselves before the rubes.

Jeanie and another giant admirer, Jack Earle.

Historically, others have not fared as well, perhaps for reasons best known only in the depths of the human psyche. It is, for example, more frequently you find "bad" and "evil" giants in the literature, at least until the more recent days of the shows. And heaven forbid that someone born like Jeanie (or Johnny Eck, inarguably the most famous half-boy of recent history, star as he was of carnival sideshows, magic acts and Tod Browning's film *Freaks*) got any respect until the past couple hundred years.

The freak shows as modern times would have them, though, are not some ancient form of entertainment. The carnival itself, at least in its current, traveling form, with its games and portable rides and its rapidly decreasing number of shows (when any appear at all), is barely a hundred years old. Many date its origins to the Columbia Exposition of 1893 with its Midway Plaisance, a segregated community of ethnic "exotics" (minorities looked upon as freaks) mixed liberally with the other fare of the carnival, including an ostrich farm, Hagenbeck's Animal Show and "Sitting Bull's Log Cabin." Much of it qualified as all carnivals qualify, as a means to a fast buck off the human need to experience something other than the day-to-day. It didn't take a genius to realize that such a show taken on the road, to the deep recesses of the country, could make a fortune. For everybody.

S&A: So when did you get started in the business?

JT: I started when I was three years old.

S&A: Three?!

JT: Three years old. Everybody acts like, "She's crazy!" But I started when I was three years old. I lived in Indiana, that's where I was born, and they had all these pumpkin fairs, y'know, "festival of the crops," one of those things. And somebody told my parents, "People would pay to see your daughter." So they thought, "Well, why not?" We were middle class but more on the poverty side than on the rich side. And a few dollars would help. So we tried it out and it worked out beautifully and people would pay to see me. I think back then it was a dime. We traveled all through Indiana, Ohio and Michigan and all around that territory and any place there was a fair or festival we could book ourselves. I worked all by myself. I was the only one in the show. Well, we were on the road all summer long. When I first became of school age, the first-grade teacher told my mother I couldn't go to school because I was handicapped, so I was a year late in starting at school. And the truant officer was a friend of my mother's and she said that she couldn't keep me out of school. Oh, they made a big production of it. They

got some psychiatrist shrinks to come down and examine me and make sure that I was up to par, and if I was I could go to school. So I was seven at the time and they gave me all these tests. I thought they were a little off their rockers because they sounded so simple to me. Then when they finished, they said, "There's no way you can keep this girl out of first grade. She has the intelligence of a fourteen-year-old." Of course, I've stayed there ever since, but at the time that suited me well. So I started going to public schools, and we'd come in early enough in the fall to go to public school, but even so I skipped a lot of school so I could play these different dates and make a few dollars.

Jeanie surrounded by faces of the famous at Giant's Campground.

S&A: What did you do in those early shows?

JT: Mostly I just exhibited myself as I am, and then I did a little acrobatic routine to show everyone that I was able to move around. I'd walk upside down on my hands, climb a ladder on my hands upside down, somersaulting, one-hand handstands and things like that. Those days are gone.

S&A: You worked with your parents for a lot of years as a single-o. Did your family travel with you?

JT: Yes, well, my mother and my sister and three of my brothers. My father didn't. Actually, he was a house painter, painting was his trade. But you know back in those days you were even lucky to have a job, so he was a taxi driver. He worked as a carpenter, all around handyman.

S&A: When did you get involved with the bigger shows?

JT: I was eleven years old the first time I went with an organized carnival. That was with the Dodson's World Fair Show. They're no longer in existence. We traveled all summer long with them and we wintered in San Antonio, Texas, that year. Well, it was a carnival just like the Padgett Fair here and they had rides and concessions and shows. They had a sideshow, which was what I was part of and the girl show and a minstrel show. Then, all the carnivals were individually owned like the Dodsons, who were two brothers and their last name was Dodson, Mel and Guy Dodson, and they operated the entire show. Of course, they had the lot man to lay out the lots and all that, but under their supervision. I went from there to the Cetlin Wilson show. I was on the Sparks Circus. You ever hear of that? That was awhile back. I was real young then. I was on Ringling Brothers two years.

Jeanie is a little over two giant feet tall.

S&A: You met your husband on one of the shows. What do you remember about the first time you met him?

JT: Well, you know he was a giant. He was quite large.

S&A: They billed him as the American Giant and Johann Petursson as the Icelandic giant, right?

JT: Johann, who used to live here, by the way. He was from Iceland,

and my husband was of Italian descent and people would see them and ask, "Are you brothers?" "Yeah. We're brothers." Well, we were all brothers and sisters, so they didn't lie!

Greeting from Giant's Tourist Camp . . . Wish you were here!

S&A: Everybody assumes you were all related or knew one another, like you and Johnny Eck. You two never knew each other, though you were probably the most famous half people of your day.

JT: No, but everybody told me about Johnny Eck and everybody told Johnny Eck about me. People were always coming up to me, "Have you ever met Johnny Eck? Oh, you really have to meet Johnny Eck." I wasn't looking for a half man. But they say he was really a nice person.

S&A: He became pretty reclusive in his last couple years.

JT: I hope that when I get old I don't become a recluse. You miss out on so much fun, I think. But I guess some people don't consider it fun. They're like, "I spent my years on the road and so I don't want to be bothered by people." Well, I get a kick out of talking about the past. But you were asking what I thought of my husband the first time I saw him. My first impression was that he looked like a very kind person, and I thought he was a very lonely person. I found out later that it was his second year of show business, and he hadn't quite adjusted to all the gaping and staring and so on. The only thing, y'know people say about you being exploited and how terrible it is? I had a ball. I was real tiny when I started in the business, of course, at three, and people would come in and they'd make friends with me and bring me presents. What's to complain about? A lot of people that they call physically handicapped like I am, what else would we do? Go down and apply for a job? "Hey! No legs? Forget it!" But I provide a lot of employment for people now here in the restaurant and so I have not put a burden on society. I have made my way. And I don't have to apologize for anything. While my husband was living he was even more generous than I was.

As police chief, Al stopped a lot of traffic.

He never let any showman come in off the road that was hungry and had no place to stay because by nightfall he had a place to stay and his belly was full. That's the way my husband was. When he was dying in the hospital, they had so many calls coming into the hospital telling me they wouldn't forget the time he did this or that or the other that they just wanted me to know that if I needed their help they were there. They finally had so many calls that they cut them off because they were disturbing me too much. It didn't really disturb me. It made me feel great.

S&A: He was fairly young when he passed away, wasn't he?

JT: Fifty.

S&A: That's not very old.

JT: Not as old as I am.

S&A: So working the shows made you feel in control. I guess you liked that.

JT: I really and truly enjoyed it. I worked a whole circuit with a man that had the world's smallest horse and every night after we closed he'd bring the horse over and let me ride it. It was like a pony, y'know? It made me feel like a big shot.

S&A: You said your husband seemed as though he wasn't adjusting too well when he started out. How old was he when he got involved in the business.

JT: He was twenty-two, twenty-three and he had been taking treatments to prevent any further growth because he was growing so fast they were afraid that he would develop problems. So that had him kind of worried, too. Our stages were side by side and, of course, then we started talking and one thing led to another. We were on Dodson's. I had worked there when I was twelve years old and then I worked there again when I was nineteen. And then this man came, I forget his name, anyway, he came from the Great Lakes Exposition in Ohio looking for acts. He booked me and booked my husband at much more money than we were getting. Still, we were just friends and we wound up at the Great Lakes Exposition in Cleveland and from there we just disappeared one night and got married. Then later on we got married in the church.

S&A: So you ran off to the justice of the peace?

JT: Well, they were bugging us because they thought something was happening, and they were bugging us to get married in front of the world. So I told them, we both told them, "We will do that after we have been legally married in private the way you're supposed to be." And they didn't go for that, so we just took off and got married.

S&A: A lot of people say that working with your spouse can be a real problem because you're always around them twenty-four hours a day. Did you ever find that to be a problem?

JT: No. In that respect we were very lucky. I look at all these marriages

Baby Man, Al, and a lot of ex-residents of Giant's Campground.

now that are on today and off tomorrow, and I think there was a time when we didn't realize how lucky we were. We did everything together, day and night, and never tired of each other. Everybody said, "Oh you're so unusual!" Only our shapes were unusual. Inside we were very compatible. We were married twenty-six years when he died. But he's been gone thirty years.

S&A: How did things change when you went from the small to the big shows?

Newlyweds Al and Jeanie Tomaini on their Niagara Falls honeymoon.

JT: Well, mostly it seemed like I worked harder. On the big fairs it seemed that you were constantly working. An act I worked up in Toronto one time had three emcees working the show and going different ways around, and by the time you sat down it was time to do your acrobatic routine. I stayed pretty slim, though, when I did that. I should have kept it up.

S&A: Climbing a lot of ladders upside down can be rough.

JT: I really enjoyed it. We didn't get to see a lot of the country though. You think. "Whoa, she's been in every state in the union!" Yeah, but I didn't get to see too much of anything! I was working. On the carnivals we'd open late at night unless we did a special matinee and we would open around 6:30 and we would close around 10:30. On the circus we worked all day. On the sideshow you would work until the big top started, and then you would be through until they were ready to let out and then you'd do your evening shows. It's a lot of work. It really is. And then, of course, you had the rain and the mud and the dust and whatever to contend with. But y'know, the one I enjoyed most was Sparks Circus, the motorized show. Nine times out of ten the elephants had to pull us off the lot because we were bogged down in the mud, and we moved every day. We'd come in, set up, do our shows—one in the afternoon, one in the evening—tear down, get ready to move, out early the next morning and head to the next town. I really enjoyed it. We got to travel so much then. We'd see a lot of wildlife early in the morning. We came rolling off the road and everybody said, "Everybody looks like they've been rolling through the knothole backwards, but Jeanie looks like she's been on vacation."

S&A: How long has it been that you've been out of the business?

JT: Oh, a long time. Our last year to go on the road was 1949, and we worked Atlantic City on the Boardwalk. That was kind of boring. It was a little confining. I didn't really care for it as much as I did the open road. But we also worked nightclubs. We worked personal appearances at fairs. We were never completely, what you would say, "out of it."

S&A: What made you and your husband decide to open up a campground after you worked so hard all your life?

JT: Well, we came down here in the winter for a vacation and we stayed across the river in a trailer park, which is now Williams Park. At that time, I don't know who owned the property. It seems that somebody named Mr. Williams donated the property to the county with the understanding that it would always be used for the public, then some enterprising young man started renting out trailer spaces.

S&A: "For the use of the public."

JT: Right, and he did all right and we stayed there several years. It was good fishing, real good fishing, and a lot of our friends came down here and we found out this property was for sale. We thought we had traveled about long enough so we went over to find the man that owned it and wound up buying it. All of our friends that were over there on the other side of the river with us moved over here and they all helped clear the property 'cause it was just a jungle. So we just gradually built it up, and we still went on the road for quite awhile. We'd go on the road and then come back and do a few more improvements and then go back on the road, back and forth. Usually some of our show people who had retired would stay here as caretakers.

S&A: When did you set up the camp?

JT: Well, we've been here fifty-four years. But it was quiet and peaceful back then.

S&A: Not like today, I guess.

JT: No, it was a two-lane highway, mostly gravel, and you never heard a car go by at night or anything. After being on the road all summer, it sounded good to us. There were people living here, of course. It wasn't totally isolated, but it was a deadly quiet town.

S&A: Then the whole idea of the campground was something that predated the retirement. This was where you figured you would be when all the performances were over.

JT: Right, and most of the people were show people. Originally they'd been in our trailer park and they moved out and bought a piece of property here and a piece there and became established on their own.

S&A: How much before you and your husband came down were the showmen first starting to come here?

JT: It must not have been over two or three years. It was like we all started coming down here and found this place. I had a friend who was a circus fat lady, Ruth Pontico. She was one of the best. Well, she lived in Tampa. After my husband and I got married, she asked if we would come down and visit her for awhile. So we came down and stayed at her house, but there didn't seem to be too much room for that, so we soon got an apartment and stayed in Tampa for a while and we'd come out here and go fishing. But none of our acquaintances were out here when we got here.

S&A: So, in a way, maybe you and Al got that ball rolling.

JT: I think that maybe we did.

S&A: The way the business is written about now, by the time you both retired it was the tail end of the sideshows and the midways as they used to be. Did things seem to be changing even then? I know you talk about how things are different now.

JT: In a way they were already starting to change because there were so many do-gooders out there saying, "Don't let these people do that," and "Don't let them be exhibited," and, "That's not right" and so on and so forth, and actually all they were doing was taking a living away from people.

S&A: There was a lot of that around even then?

JT: It had already started, yeah. But, y'know, it's a strange thing. Supposedly, people don't want to see these people and shouldn't show them and all that, but if I get a write-up that big [makes a small gesture] I'll get a half dozen letters. They remember seeing me or my husband and wondered where I had been. They are *very* interested.

S&A: So what was the down side to being in the business?

JT: That's hard to say. I guess we enjoyed everything. I guess I'm glad to be alive or something because nothing seems to get me down. Out of everything, if I could have only had my husband longer I guess that would be the one and only thing. But I was raised in a poor family and

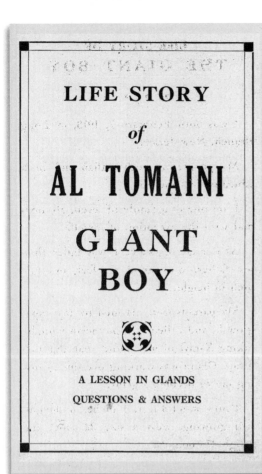

LIFE STORY

of

AL TOMAINI

GIANT BOY

A LESSON IN GLANDS

QUESTIONS & ANSWERS

3. How does it feel to be a giant?

A. It's a living, being like this, but it's a nuisance trying to be comfortable in a world made for smaller individuals.

4. Is your clothing special made?

A. Yes, everything I wear is special made.

5. Do you eat more than a normal person?

A. Yes, for I need more than a normal person to supply my body with enough energy.

• • • • •

A LESSON IN GLANDS

Glands control the height, weight and personality of all people.

The lack of Thyroid Gland causes one to become fat.

An over supply of Thyroid Gland causes one to become thin.

The Thyroid Gland is located in the neck.

Too much Pituitary Gland causes giants.

Not enough Pituitary Gland causes midgets.

The Pituitary Gland is situated at the base of the brain.

I guess I didn't have sense enough to know we were poor because it didn't bother me. I guess I just have an upbeat attitude about everything.

Al's Glands: The book.

S&A: Did your family stay connected to the business when you went with the larger shows?

JT: No. My mother died when I was thirteen, and my father was an alcoholic and he faded into the woodwork somewhere.

S&A: I know you ended up with a "stepmother" after that. Was she a friend of the family?

JT: No, she was a total stranger to me, but she had seen me at one of those pumpkin fairs and she got it in her head that if she had me, she could make a fortune. So she went to the authorities. Back then—this was way back—the orphanages were crowded, and you could get kids for a dime a dozen if you got them out of there. She went to this orphanage when she found out I was there. She told them all her life she had wanted to be a good Samaritan to somebody—tears, crying and the whole bit—and she wanted to take me because she knew nobody else would want to take me and she would give me a good home for the rest of my life. They told her yes and she took me. She had me working in Hubert's Museum in New York City. She had me working there twelve and fifteen hours a day before she had even legally adopted me.

S&A: You were only thirteen?

JT: By then I was fifteen. Having spent some time in the orphanage after my father left and all, she thought she could pressure me to the point where I had no self-confidence. I mean petty little things like, "I can't take you in a restaurant because if people see you they lose their appetite," and, "They don't want to be associated with people like you." And I learned that if I wanted hot chocolate, I ordered coffee and she would immediately change the order—"No, give her hot chocolate." Thinking she had outsmarted me. But I had outsmarted her because I knew what she would do and I got hot chocolate, which is what I wanted in the first place. It's kind of crazy, but that was our life together.

S&A: Life with her as your "mother" must have made it pretty tough to have any friends.

JT: See, she had it in her head that I must not have friends because if I had a girlfriend, well, she was probably queer, and if a couple liked me and wanted to be friends with me they must be planning on stealing me so they could make all of this big money out of me. And if it was a man—oh, not a man! Not a man never! So I was not supposed to have any friends. This one couple came to visit in the winter and you're supposed to open your home to fellow showmen, so she didn't have much choice. She took them in for the night, and they were leaving the next morning. So she shut me in my room. She didn't lock it or anything, but she told me, "You don't leave your room tonight!" During the night it was cold—it was in Indiana—it was bitter cold and snowing and she kept her house upstairs the same temperature as it was outdoors. So I was lying there thinking, "I wonder how I can upset her tonight?" So I got up and I opened my window. She laid down outside my door on the floor with a blanket so nobody could step into my room

The world's most unusual married couple on the bally platform.

and I couldn't get out because they were going to steal me that night. She knew it. So I went over and I opened the window wide open, and the curtains blew. I took a pillow and I put it under the covers and I covered it up nice and neat and then I crawled under the bed. Well, in a few minutes that chill went out to her and she thought she had better check and see what was happening. She came in, "Jeanie! Jeanie! Jeanie!" and she yanked the cover back and there's a pillow. "Where's Jeanie?! Where's Jeanie?!" So she stuck her head out the window screaming, "Jeanie! Jeanie! You'd better answer me! You'd better answer me!" I was very comfortable under the bed, but I thought the old lady may have a heart attack so I thought I'd give up. I came out and I said, "Are you looking for me? I don't know how I wound up under the bed." Another time when she went hunting for me one day—and you know how you set a piece of furniture in the corner and then you've got a baseboard here and a baseboard here—I heard her coming and so I went behind the chair and put one hand on either side and pulled my body up. She went mad looking for me. She looked under the furniture. Nothing. She looked in the bedroom. Nothing. I didn't do it to be mean. I did it to keep my own sanity. Once, up in Canada, they had these fur jackets and they were really pretty and they were so cheap then, like $35 for one. Everybody told her she should buy me one and they made it so heavy on her she felt obligated to. So she asked me what color I wanted. I wanted brown because it was a real rich brown, so she brought me a gray that was the color of a dead rat.

S&A: Where else did she have you work?

JT: Oh, we worked Cincinnati and Coney Island. Ray Marsh Brydon was my boss and he was a character. He had put up tents way off on the side of the park for the people to live in. I loved it, to live in tents outdoors and all. She had gotten a job as a cook and she cooked a long ways from where we lived—all the people on the show would get involved in this so they're as guilty as I am—and she would get busy cooking and they would send word in to her that someone had been in to visit me and that it had been my sister or my brother.

S&A: You didn't see them normally?

JT: No, she didn't let them know where I was for a long time. Not until after I was married did I know where they were. I belonged to her. I was her possession and that was it. Now *that* is exploiting. That really is exploiting. What they talk about exploiting now, that's a joke. Anyhow, we played all kinds of tricks on her. One night, two of the fellas went out behind our sleeping tent and one said to the other, "Now, as soon as they're asleep and that light in there goes out, you reach in and take the kid. I'll take care of the old lady." Well, she got up and I had to sleep in the stupid bus all night because they were going to steal me. But we all had to torture her.

S&A: Well, she deserved it too, I would say. A lot of people make their own hell in this life.

JT: I felt that it was my place to help it along a little. So I did.

S&A: How long did you have to stay with her?

JT: I was with her for five years. We went to the Great Lakes Exposition, and we had an apartment in the building and my husband—this was before we were married, of course, but we worked together—he had a room down the hall from us. She was all for us getting together. She had it in her head that he was a real nice, mild, gentle sort of person, which he was, but he was also Italian. So she went along with the whole thing. She even went with us to get married. We went to Ripley, New York, to get married because I didn't have my father's permission, and I was only twenty. We went and we got married and I moved into his room. And the very next morning, she came down and she said, "Now that you have someone to take care of you, and I know that you're going to be well taken care of, I think I'm going to go on home and you can just send me half of your paycheck every week." And I said "What? I'll tell you what: he's gone out to get some stuff. As soon as he comes back, I'll have him come down and talk to you about it." So I told him about it and he went down and he went into a rage about it immediately, and I said, "Oh, keep calm. Everything will work out. Don't worry about it." He went down there and talked to her. He came back and was practically frothing at the mouth. The next morning she was gone. There was no sign of her anywhere. Much later she came to visit on the circus where we were working, and she sent in word that she had a lot of friends in there she would like to visit but she didn't want to see Jeanie. And I said, "Well good luck! I don't want to see you either!"

S&A: So you never saw her after that?

JT: No, and I never looked for her either.

S&A: You played some pretty big spots in your career. What was it like when you played Madison Square Garden? What's the difference between that kind of show and a tent show?

JT: It's more exciting. The main show was in one part of the building. It's a huge, huge arena, of course, to have all the acts in one building. The sideshow and the menageries were combined. We were in the center of the menagerie and a huge stage with acts along this way and acts along that way and the people would holler, "Doors!" which meant the doors were going to open and you had better be there. People just swarmed in. It was unbelievable how they swarmed in there. When they yelled, "Doors!" you had better be with it. But you see, it was sort of easier at Madison Square Garden because when the big show, when the big top, started they'd announce, "Five minutes to big top!' or ten minutes or whatever. We had nothing to do until the show was over and it lasted a good two hours. Then the crowds came back where we were and they kind of lingered. It was hard to get them out.

S&A: How long would your dates with the carnival and circus be during the season?

JT: Well, the carnival was once a week. Say late April until late October and on the circus it was every day from late April to early October or November. I worked in Canada one time and for the fun of it I counted the number of shows we had in one day and we had eighty-six shows.

S&A: Eighty-six shows?!

JT: Yep, and that one really almost wiped me out. I was turning somersaults and doing handstands all night in my sleep.

S&A: In terms of the ways the performers and the various acts got paid, how did that usually work?

JT: When we had a sideshow, we gave the office, that's the boss, a percentage of our income in order to transport our luggage and everything. And out of our percentage we paid our people their salaries and if they sold pictures or something like that the performers kept that also as part of their income.

Al and daughter Judy offer a $1,000 reward if you fail to see Jeanie!

S&A: Like pitchcards and all of that?

JT: Right. But the office always got their percentage. Most shows always made it a point that payday should be a Saturday, at the end of the week, but we'd make it on a Wednesday so that they all showed up at the next town because carny people have a habit of going the wrong direction. Sometimes during the winter you'd contact different acts to book them for the summer and have to send them money to join and sometimes they'd join and sometimes not. But most of them did.

S&A: When you had the 10-in-1 set up and you were managing your own shows, did you have a blow-off? What would that have been?

JT: We had a half man-half woman and we charged extra to go there.

S&A: Who would be the inside talker for all of that?

JT: My husband, because the outside would stay still while the blow-off was on so the same talker that introduced the acts was in there too.

S&A: So you didn't have anyone separate inside. Who did you have as talkers other than your husband?

JT: Oh, we had a relief talker, but we didn't very often let him work. My husband took so much interest in the job because it was ours. He was so much more in it than someone he hired, he did most of it himself.

S&A: That must have been pretty stunning seeing the American giant as the talker in front of the 10-in-1.

JT: Yeah, it drew a crowd.

S&A: So the business was good to you?

JT: Yep, I really enjoyed it well. I really enjoyed all of my years in show business, but I also enjoy staying here and being quiet.

S&A: You find yourself missing it at all?

JT: Not really because I am surrounded by show people, all that's left of them. And they're in here, in and out and back and forth. I don't really miss

Jeanie's Sweet 16.

it. Of course my husband used to say "You're lucky you can head back to anything!" Whatever I did I adjusted to it and enjoyed it. I enjoyed working down here. I've had a lot of sickness lately, and they're all nagging at me to retire. Yeah, I'll retire when I lay down straight out. Life is a struggle no matter if you're in a mundane business in town or no matter what you are, it's a struggle. I'm happy to say that if I went today or tomorrow I wouldn't regret anything. Just remember to keep laughing and you've got it made. That's important.

I'm the first to admit it: My first day at the Extravaganza, the annual trade fair for the carnival trade held in Gibsonton, Florida, didn't look promising. Were I a weaker-willed man, I'd say it was running dismally. I had no real card of introduction to any show people, and the word I'd gotten from others tangential to the business was that the show people had been screwed over so many times by so many reporters and itinerant scribblers that I'd likely get nothing from any of them.

Well, bring expectations with you, you get back what you expect. At the headquarters of the International Independent Showmen's Association, I'd found that the list of potential contacts—my hoped-for "interviewees"—I'd sent down weeks before had been simply posted on the bulletin board, but no one would actually supply me with any details beyond those I'd gathered myself: no additional phone numbers, no addresses. The privacy of those I'd listed was paramount, they said, and those on the list who wanted to contact me and who saw my posted letter would contact me if they wished. The staff did tell me to check out their association museum, though, and, of course, to check with the curator. Maybe he could be of more help than they could. Maybe I'd get an interview.

But I didn't get an interview. In his flinty way, the curator of the museum's collection refused that option, justifiably perhaps. And he cited the multitude of mis-quoting reporters I expected he would. And he then proceeded to give me a grand tour of the exhibits with elaborate commentary on each, in itself a better education than all I'd read or seen so far. Just as unexpectedly, and best of all, he gave me what his sternness had told me at first I'd never get: contacts.

One of the first of those contacts sent me to a pay phone in Gibtown shopping center, just by the town post office. Completely unexpectedly—I honestly thought I'd have to run some other sort of gauntlet to reach her—Jeanie Tomaini herself answered the phone. And she was sweeter than I had any right to expect. She quickly agreed that the next morning would be fine for an interview, but could I, she asked, make it at either nine or eleven. After a moment's pause at my end, I worked up the gumption to ask why nine or eleven. Well, Jeanie said, CNN would be coming by at ten to do their interview. Laughing out loud, I told her that nine would be just fine. That way, after all, I could watch CNN work and then talk to her about that experience and how all the exposure (my interview included) dovetailed with her entertainment career. Chuckling herself at that idea, she told me that sounded just fine. She told me to come by the bait house at the campground, just across from the restaurant, where she'd be hard at work behind the counter as she had been for years.

So my feeling of being lost there in Showtown was ill founded. And not unlike the sideshows themselves, what I expected was a lot different from what I got. And by way of what I wrongly thought was a run-around, the showmen's association and their museum curator led me to where I should've known I was all along: in the good hands of the World's only Living Half Girl, she and all her friends and kin.

MLLE. GABRIELE.

THE ONLY LIVING HALF LADY IN THE WORLD.

SHOCKED AND AMAZED!

BETTER BY HALF

Above: Legless performer doing a handstand.
Opposite: Top left, Johnny Eck (John Eckert)
posing with his twin brother, Robert.
Top right, Mlle. Gabriele, The Only Living
Half Lady in the World.
Bottom left, A French performer who was
"mutilated as a result of bone disease"
promises "marvelous acrobatics."
Bottom right, Johnny Eck on
the set of Tod Browning's
1932 classic, Freaks.

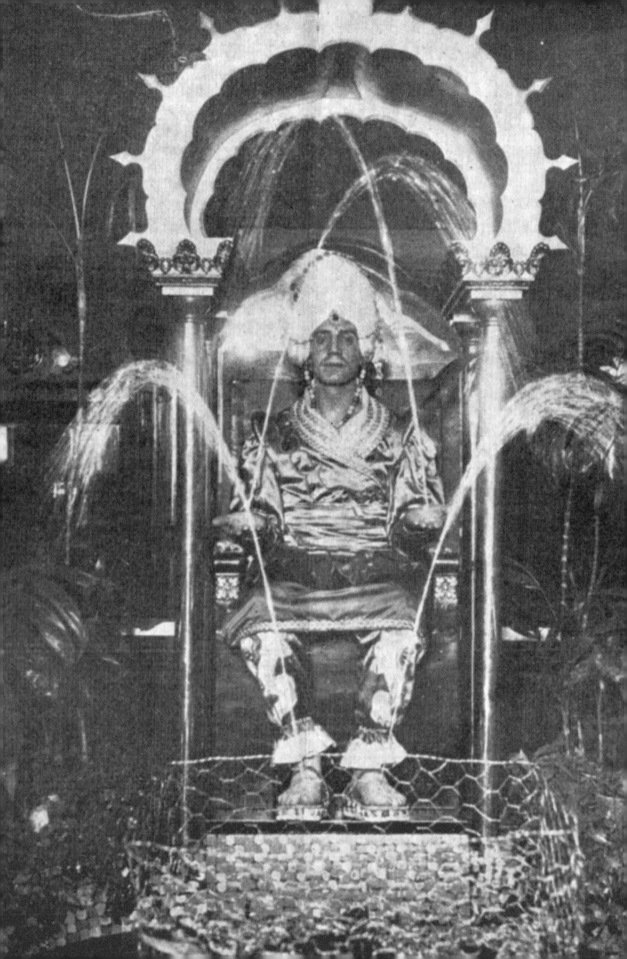

Mortado—
The Human
Fountain

I am a native of Berlin, Germany. At the age of about eighteen, like most youths of that age, I became possessed of the desire to travel, and see the world. Anything that would offer adventure, thrill and excitement. I had already joined the Navy, but as yet had seen no active service, until the first year had passed, on a training ship, and then, at the beginning of the World War, my actual service commenced and there began a series of adventures and incidents that led up to the terrible crisis that shortened my Naval Career, and made me what I am today, "A Human Fountain."

My training, on an old type sailing vessel, made me energetic, and fitted me fully for the after duties. I was then assigned to a cruiser, as ship-boy, and, very shortly started out on the sea of adventure, and this was about the time of the starting of the World War in 1914.

My parents had died when I was quite young and my home was wherever I should rest my head at night. Through influence I was shortly promoted to the rank of a Junior Naval Officer, but my career as such was brief, as the war had started and all the young men of the German Empire were needed the most in the massive army that Von Hindenburg and the Kaiser were rushing through Belgium. I was assigned to special duty in Northern Africa.

While in the Northern part of the Sahara Desert, I became lost from my party. Using my compass I went to the nearest Oasis to await some of my comrades. A band of Riffs, who are a wild tribe of Mohammedans, came riding up to where I was sitting. I knew their hatred toward white Christians and knew not what my fate would be. However, I had not long to wait. They robbed me and disrobed me of

Opposite:
Mortado—Aqua-awe!

49

A BRIEF SKETCH OF
MORTADO--- *The Human Fountain*
INITIAL APPEARANCE IN AMERICA, APRIL 27th, 1930
At Dreamland Circus Side Show, Coney Island, N. Y.

Mortado when an OFFICER in the
German Navy, 1914.

My address in the U. S. A. will be:
"Dreamland Circus Side Show," Coney Island, N. Y.
For the summer, and my permanent address:
Berlin, N. O. 55, Ryke Strasse, 51, Germany.

Thanking you,

MORTADO, the Human Fountain.

all my clothing and carried me to a large wooden water wheel, which was used for drawing water.

They gave me what the Americans call the 'spread eagle,' driving large wire nails through my hands and feet through the soft or fleshy parts, and crucifying me, so to say, to the wheel, and abandoned me to my fate. I must have been there for hours unconscious and fortunately was discovered by some white men who released me, carried me to civilization, and notified my commanding officer of my condition. In a few hours an ambulance came and conveyed me to a base hospital, and for many days I suffered intense agony. My condition was such that I was returned to Berlin and there I was under treatment in the army hospital for over two years. Incapacitated and unable to do any manual labor, and at a loss what to do, a friend who was a showman and had made several trips to America with novel attractions, suggested to me to build some kind of an exhibition whereby I could exploit myself and my experiences, and then the idea of the Human Fountain came to me and I planned and constructed the act that I am now presenting to the public.

I first presented the exhibition in Berlin, in January, 1929, and it met with instant favor from both press and public. A New York booking agent, learning of my success, sent a representative to interview me with the result that I signed a contract to appear at Dreamland Circus Side Show, Coney Island, New York, for the summer season of 1930.

If my offering has pleased you and you have found it "just as represented," kindly tell your friends to come and see me. I will be pleased to give any information desired at any time.

Opposite: Mortado explains it
all for you in this pitchbook.

Mortado——The Human Fountain

Daisy and Violet
TEXAS SIAMESE TWINS

The Intimate Lives and Loves of the Hilton Sisters

By Daisy and Violet Hilton

You won't find it mentioned anywhere in the unabridged version of Violet and Daisy Hilton's "autobiography," but they were featured in perhaps the greatest cult horror film ever made, *Freaks*, along with Johnny Eck, the world's only Living Half Boy, and Prince Randian, the living torso, and other famous sideshow freaks of their day. Then again, one could argue that there's much in the autobiography that hints of embroidery or outright omission. But we marks expect nothing less.

Milwaukee gallery owner, Dean Jensen told me that, essentially, the big picture of their autobiography is accurate, but the details, well, the details leave a lot to be desired. Jensen should know. He's hard at work on the definitive biography of the famous "Texas Twins," born, of course, in Brighton, England. The Twins, not actually the daughters of a military man. The Twins, whose natural mother probably didn't even know who the father was, or didn't want to reveal him, as no name appears on the birth registration. Whose trail of woe from one showman to another (principally from Ike Rose of Rose's Midgets to Myer Myers, their last "Sir") sounds almost crueler than that depicted by them. Jensen also told me that, as wild as this abridged autobiography is, it isn't half as wild as the true tales of Violet and Daisy. Heaven knows, their story here is as exotic (and erotic) as purple prose can be.

Above: Lobby card from the cult classic, Freaks.

Opposite: Daisy and Violet Hilton: Texas Siamese Twins from England.

Now, without further ado, the Hiltons . . .

The eyes of a curious world have been focused on us almost from the moment of our birth. You are undoubtedly wondering many things about our union as you read this, the story we never intended to tell. We have not told it before, so perhaps you, too, have imagined that, joined together as we are, there could be no such thing for either of us as a private life. So much wonderment has centered around us, especially how two human beings can endure constant, continuous living together harmoniously. Yet, we two, without parents, without one intimate friend until we were twenty-four years old, have found a fascinating and interesting life.

Joined in the fashion called Siamese because the first known twins with a similar indivisible bodily bridge were born in Siam, we are believed to share identical thrills, pains and even diseases. The truth is that we are as different in our reactions as day and night. I, Violet, often weep over something which makes my sister chuckle. I had whooping cough a year and a half before Daisy. We did not even catch measles from each other! Yet every breath, every second of the day and night, we are never parted. We will never be, in life, although the scientists often tried to persuade us to allow them to experiment in cutting us apart.

Scene from the critically unacclaimed Chained for Life.

Because of our bond we register moods and movements of each other. We sense thoughts, feel currents and vibrations, but then, two good friends may have such experiences. Sleeping, eating, walking, bathing and dressing, drinking and making love, we share our lives, just as amiably as we shared our childhood toys, without quarreling.

We have known the full-scale emotions, even those that burn and bless and mature the hearts of women. Yet, we have never been jealous of each other. We never consult or advise. We simply tell each other our wishes. For instance, I, Daisy, may want to go shopping when my sister, Violet, has a headache. I, Violet, tell Daisy that at a certain time the following day I'll go shopping with her. Having once given her my word, nothing will stop me, at least, nothing ever has. We never coddle, pet or obviously humor each other. Our companionship would be endangered and neither of us wants to become a martyr.

Double your pleasure with the Hilton sisters.

We have loved, hated, dreamed and hoped and wept. We have been engaged secretly to prominent, handsome men other women admired. We have both been married. Our marriages were headlined throughout the nation. Listen—I, Violet, will tell you the weird story of heartbreak which lay hidden behind the bold-faced type as it printed the sensational news that twenty-one states had refused to issue a marriage license to dark-haired Maurice Lambert, the popular band-leader, and me. I have a right to love and marriage, just as my sister has. We have always longed to have homes and husbands and simple lives others experience. When James Walker Moore, my six-foot-two dancing partner, and I said our vows, more than 100,000 persons attended the wedding. I looked out over the crowd and pulled my wedding veil over my face to hide my excited tears, but Daisy was convulsed with mirth. It was six years later when I, Daisy, married the wavy-haired, blue-eyed dancer, Harold Estep, son of a well-known Philadelphia family. Surely no girl was ever more serious and in love, but my sister, Violet, who of course was with me through it all, was analytical, friendly but unusually quiet.

Yet we never quarreled through these emotional trials. It is as though some power, greater and stronger than ourselves, has given us this inner harmony to compensate for our being forced to live constantly as an entity. And that harmony has been with us through the years—a harmony that has amazed many who have known us.

Here we are carefully, factually setting down the tangibles and intangibles we have learned about human relationships. About each other, too. Loving each other, bound by physical and spiritual ties, we spare each other nothing, except advice and domination. And we do not magnify or minimize our weaknesses and strengths. No facets of our characters are hidden, or can be, from each other. And yet we have worked out successfully a way to live our separate and very private lives.

"Do you really like—or hate—each other through your inescapable moments of intimate knowledge?" many have asked us. "Who makes the decisions? Who determines your joint activities?" And a million other questions, equally poignant. In almost all human relationships, friendship, love, marriage, even business, one person rules. In our relations, neither dominates. While you expect us to have similar tastes, it may surprise you to learn that we even have different circles of friends. Even our thoughts are bent on foreign tracks. They are as different as the types of our blood, which the Red Cross in Pittsburgh recently discovered when we became donors to the bank, are unlike and run in separate streams.

> **I, Daisy, am blond and green-eyed. I weigh ninety-three pounds, wear size eleven dresses and one-and-a-half shoe. I'm five feet tall. . .**

I, Daisy, am blond and green-eyed. I weigh ninety-three pounds, wear size eleven dresses and one-and-a-half shoe. I'm five feet tall. I like show business. I live in my mind. I am impulsive and talkative and quick-motioned. I, Violet, have dark hair and hazel eyes, I've never weighed more than eighty-nine pounds. My shoes are size one. I'm four feet, eleven inches tall. I've always longed to become a nurse. I live in my heart. I'm not a talker, and I seldom do anything on impulse.

> **I, Violet, have dark hair and hazel eyes, I've never weighed more than eighty-nine pounds. My shoes are size one. I'm four feet, eleven inches tall. . .**

You can see that together we have contrast and balance. It may seem odd, but we can remember when we were so very young. Even back in the days when we were turned loose on the floor to crawl. We seemed to move without much effort, because we propelled each other. There seemed only a short time until we gained speed and direction.

Walking came easy. We balanced each other. We learned to listen early. We learned to say a little, although we talked before other children our age.

There was a speech repeated to us daily, over and over again like a phonograph record. It was spoken by a big, curly-haired woman

Private Life of the SIAMESE TWINS

who bathed, dressed and fed us. She never petted or kissed us, or even smiled. She just talked: "Your mother gave you to me. You are not my children. Your mother gave you to me." The speech grew longer as we grew older: "I'm not your mother. Your mother was afraid when you were born and gave you to me when you were two weeks old. You must always do just as I say."

This woman was Mrs. Mary Williams, the midwife who attended our coming into the world. She kept us clean and fed and taught us to rely on each other. We were taught to call her Auntie and each of her five husbands was Sir.

Auntie had a daughter, a big girl, named Edith, but we were unable ever to learn from them much about our parents. Mother, they said, was named Kate. She was young and pretty and she married a Captain Hilton. He married Mother in Texas. She ran away from him after we were born. We were unable even to learn our father's first name. Auntie and Edith couldn't remember. However, Auntie remem-

The Intimate Lives and Loves of the Hilton Sisters

bered to tell us later that our father had died in action during World War I.

Auntie was a tall woman with a pretty, oval face framed with well-tended hair. About her waist was always a wide leather belt, fastened with a large metal buckle. And it took only a little jerk to release the buckle. Her temper was something that her daughter or husbands could not control, and when we displeased her she whipped our backs and shoulders with the buckle end of that same wide belt.

"She'll never hit your faces, girls," Auntie's third husband, Sir Green, whispered to us one day. "The public will not be so glad to pay to look at little Siamese twins with scarred faces."

Our awareness became accentuated. We were very knowing and we developed opinions although we were treated like animals, living in a cage. We were kept in one room, regularly whipped, scolded and trained. We were never permitted to play with other children, and when we looked over the sill of our window and saw little girls walking alone we felt quite sorry for them because they were not as we were.

We were always being looked at—on stages, in large and small theatres. It was a frequent occurrence to awaken and find a row of doctors and scientists surrounding our bed. How we loathed the sight

Daisy and Violet at 13.

of a hospital and the very bedside tone of a medical man's voice! We were punched and pinched and probed until we were almost crazy, and we always screamed and scratched and kicked. When the doctors and scientists left, Auntie would often whip us with the belt and call us ungrateful brats.

Then one morning, as we pretended to be sleeping, we overheard Auntie talking with a doctor. "The cartilage, muscle and bone could be severed," he said. "It will be a worthwhile and interesting experiment to separate the nerves of the spinal column. You see, there has never been a set of Siamese twins operated on while they were living and science is deeply interested in making the experiment."

We lay there listening, straining to hear what Auntie would reply—and our hearts turned over. "Siamese Twins" . . . "cut apart" . . . "doctor" are the first words we seemed to remember. They stood for fear and created our longing to remain joined by our birth-bond of flesh and bone. Our earliest memories center about a doctor pleading with Auntie to permit him to cut us apart. His voice was a cold, sharp blade through our hearts. To this day it symbolizes the aggregate of doctors' voices, begging to experiment with us.

"Doctor, the girls belong to me," was Auntie's frequent remark. "I'm going to keep them the way they are!"

Auntie was too eager for profit to let us become the object of experiments. So she set about making us "the smartest Siamese twins alive!"

At an early age, we were taught to recite, read and sing. We spoke plainly, perhaps because we got so much practice from talking to each other and because we were never permitted to be with other children. We copied the speech of grownups. However, today we probably talk to each other less than ordinary twins living in the same house. We have been forced to do this because we would destroy each other's privacy. As strongly as we have fought against being separated, we have determined to live harmoniously in our bond and yet be able to have our private lives. In order to do this, there are many rules we are forced to follow. Among them is not to seek advice from each other, not to advise, ever, and not to speak aloud our thoughts.

These rules were really our early habits. They began so soon we were unaware of their formation. Yet, it seems oddly pathetic to us that so many persons, when there are five or six in the family, fret against having to adjust to one another! You see, we have learned by experience that there is no adjustment in human relations that cannot be made, and made happily.

Our earliest lessons in getting along were taught to us in the tiny cabin of a ship, where Auntie, her daughter, Edith, and Auntie's husband crowded in with us. In the close quarters Auntie and Sir (Auntie's husband) quarreled frequently. He wanted us to be taken into the air. He thought we should go to religious services. She argued that people would not pay to look at us if they could see us for nothing. Auntie won.

Our early thought development was remarkably adult. Our voices strong; I, Violet, liked low tones; I, Daisy, chose a higher pitch. We harmonized in many ways which made living together more satisfactory.

We liked the vibration of the violin as it traveled over our connecting bridge. The piano was too detached. However, I, Violet, studied hard to accompany Daisy's violin.

When Auntie discovered that we could stand in a chair, rock until it turned over and flip in the air without falling, she added dancing lessons to our long days of study. We had new dancing partners and Violet's was a youngster who'd taught us the Black Bottom. Today the world knows him as Bob Hope.

It was amazing how much training was crammed into our early lives. In preparation for our debut in Berlin, our first appearance in a theatre, we had endurance tests. I, Violet, played the princess waltz two and a half hours without a mistake. I, Daisy, played my violin and directed an orchestra of fourteen.

The theatre thundered with applause on our opening night and as we came off the stage Auntie and Edith rushed us into the dressing room in the midst of the cheering. They refused to open the door to the knocks from backstage folks.

"Won't you let the girls come out to a little supper with us?" Vivian Duncan asked one night. Vivian succeeded in coming to our room for a few minutes, and Sophie Tucker and Harry Houdini were among the few who seemed to sense our need for friends.

"Read all the newspapers you can," Harry Houdini whispered to me, Daisy, one night as he passed me in the wings, as if he knew that we had never been permitted to have a newspaper. After that we hoarded every news sheet we could. We read the sensational trials and began to look forward to the day when we'd become eighteen and could get legal aid to straighten out our affairs.

Our lives were spent in study and practice. Years went by, somehow. Then we were in the United States, in San Antonio, Texas, making our debut in the Temple Theatre. We had become strangely wise and filled with unvoiced thoughts. I, Violet, had a quarter hidden in my shoe. A stagehand had slipped it to me in St. Louis. I, Daisy, had fifty cents. And for seven years these were our only pieces of money, yet we were making thousands.

We were not allowed to have friends, but Edith, Auntie's daughter, received her beau in our crowded room while we were appearing with a circus in Australia. He was the balloon man, and sold candy, too, on the grounds. We thought that even when he begged Auntie to let him marry Edith his eyes were cruel. "We need a man to travel with us. Will you give up your balloon concession?" Auntie, who was nearing fifty and had lost her fifth husband, asked.

Edith and this new Sir (as we called him) were married, and when

Auntie developed an infected leg, Sir helped with our bookings and travel. He told us how a brute had raised him in Perth and whipped him when he did not obey. We took this to mean that he approved of Auntie's thrashing us with her belt buckle.

In Birmingham, Alabama, Auntie died, and as we looked at her, our first corpse, and you might say, our first friend, the cunning and shrewdness seemed out of her face. I, Daisy, did not care that she was dead.

"Why cry?" I asked Violet. "We have hated her forever!"

"I'm afraid without her," I, Violet, answered. "Now Sir will boss us."

"Let's run away!" we whispered. We had gone to the funeral parlor with the quarter and half-dollar in our shoes.

"We'll never have a chance like this again!" Violet urged.

Edith was crying beside her mother's casket.

"Let's run!" I, Daisy, said. Naturally, Violet came with me. But I had gone only a few steps when Violet lagged. I felt a sudden alarm tremble through her. Sir clutched my hand and we stopped.

"Don't touch me," I, Violet, cried. He clamped his fingers around our arms, and without a word he led us back to our seats.

The funeral services were over and after a while we were back in our room, with Edith and Sir. The tension was electric as we sat waiting for them to speak. I, Violet, cried. I, Daisy, laughed in their sullen, suspicious faces. Our emotional reactions are not usually the same. Perhaps laughter and tears both serve to release tension. I, Daisy, felt equal to any ordeal. I, Violet, felt that I could not compete with the possessiveness I read in the faces opposite us.

"Tell them, Sir!" Edith said after what seemed hours.

"You girls belong to us now! You'll do just as we say. See here— Auntie left you to us. You and her jewelry and furniture are ours! Do you understand?" He waved a paper in our faces.

V OLET a d DA SY
Eng sh S an ese Tw ns

f we have nterested you k nd y te your fr ends to v st us

The Hilton sisters want you to tell your friends about them!

The Intimate Lives and Loves of the Hilton Sisters

Willed as an old ring or chair! It couldn't be! While I, Daisy, protested, I, Violet, kept crying. It couldn't be . . . yet, it was. We had to work as hard, and the only privacy we were to have was in our minds. Our new owners slept in the same room with us. We were never out of their sight.

Theatrical lights over the world soon blazed with our names. Our work as musicians, dancers and singers stood out. But at eighteen, stage fame did not answer the wish in our hearts. I, Daisy, was in love. I wanted to get married. I, Violet, wanted to become a nurse. I was in love, too, but the man of my dreams was married. But at eighteen and with the world at our feet, we had never had a date, never held hands with a man or been kissed!

The Hilton sisters stick together during the filming of Freaks.

"Why can't we go out and have some fun? Other girls our age do. We've never smoked a cigarette, tasted a cocktail, had our hair cut. We . . . "

"You are not other girls! You are Siamese twins!" was always the answer from both Edith and Sir.

In the wings of the theatres, across footlights, men looked at us, not as unusual performers, but in the way they look at girls they long to know. Romantic interest had overcome the scientific lure. Charm was in the air. We sensed it, and naturally we fretted because our guardians herded us into the dressing rooms and back to our hotel.

Our need to let down and get our minds off work was met with inevitable cups of hot chocolate each night. We had no haven of refuge and we had to do as Harry Houdini once said to us: "Live in your minds, girls." He told us that as we stood beside him in the wings one night in a Detroit theatre. "It is your only hope for private lives. Just recognize no handicap!"

During the ten years following the death of Auntie, the midwife to whom our mother had given us, our hearts were scarred. But our minds grew strong and our Siamese bond of flesh and bone became one of real understanding between us. Our desire to harmonize with each other was, indeed, our real salvation.

So much happened during those sad years when the audiences of the world believed us cheerful and carefree. We had learned, you see, to put our worries aside and in no way ever inflict them on each other. Therefore, as we danced, played and sang, only pleasure and the feeling of well-being ever was projected by us over the footlights of theatres. It wasn't easy to laugh while our hearts ached and yearned for freedom and love. Notes, gifts, love letters were sent to us in the most sophisticated cities, in little towns. Under the management of Edith and Sir we played India, Egypt, the great cities of Europe and every theatre of any size in the United States and throughout Central America.

"Big-time!" Sir would say. "You should be grateful and willing to do as I tell you!"

Big-time. The largest booking agencies handled our act. The social and handsome William Oliver, of Kansas city, traveled three weeks ahead of us as advance man, having our pictures on billboards and stories about us in all the newspapers when we reached the cities in which we played.

"Bill," as we called him, was one of the few men Sir ever allowed in our presence, and then we saw him only seldom and briefly. He was in love with his wife. He called her Mildred and showed us pictures of her. "I often tell her about you," Bill would say. "Autograph a picture for me to send her." If we could only have foreseen what the autographed picture was going to bring about in our lives! But we were too unsuspecting and not even Edith and Sir seemed to think anything about the sentence which I, Daisy, penned, and both of us signed: "To our pal, Bill, with love and best wishes from your pal Daisy and Violet Hilton." With love didn't mean that we loved Bill Oliver. It was just the way we had observed other showfolk autograph pictures. We soon forgot about Bill and never once saw or met his wife.

We were big-time: forty-six weeks on the Marcus Loew circuit at $2,500 a week. Our salary jumped then to $3,000. Then followed forty-four weeks on the Orpheum circuit at $3,850 a week! We signed contracts which Sir never read to us. All our activities were in his hands . . . and we learned that he had himself named our legal guardian. What's more, we understood that if we ever ran out on him, if we ever refused to perform at his command, we would be put in an institution. We lived constantly in fear, and at eighteen we still were forced to share the same bedroom with our managers, so that at no time could we run away or plot together.

As we waited in the wings of Loew's State in Newark, New Jersey, one night for our turn, Don Galvan, the headlined guitarist, looked at me while he played, and every word of his song seemed meant for me. Now my heart hammered the way Violet's did the night the famous bandleader, Blue Steel, dedicated his song, *Darling*, to her. Don Galvan bowed off the stage and stood beside me. Our hands clasped for a throbbing second, and I heard my sister gasp for me. The surge of emotion swept through both of us as Edith elbowed Don away from me.

Sir kicked the bunch of yellow roses which Don left at our dressing room door. He would not permit us to pick them up. At the hotel that night I recalled Auntie's punishments. Visions of the leather strap came to me as Sir came over to us. Remembering the clasp of Don's hand, hearing his song in my heart, for the first time I was not afraid. I turned my back to Sir. Auntie had always strapped our backs, never once hit our faces.

"Go on!" I said. "You won't kill us. You wouldn't destroy your meal tickets!'

His black eyes turned to flames. We had never talked back to Auntie. We had been too frightened of her heavy strap. Her whippings had come to be a part of our lives. We had accepted them along with our daily irritations, struggles and monotonies for love of each other. We tried, within our minds, to turn each quarrel and bickering and nagging incident into some kind of lesson for our own harmony. Now, a new fight had begun in our souls.

"We've made thousands for you, but we never received a dollar of our earnings! You still keep us caged up like animals in a circus! But tonight is different. Listen Sir, we are eighteen years old. Don't you strike either of us or we'll yell like wildcats! And get us a separate room. We're grown ladies, and you should be ashamed to force us to share your and Edith's room!" So that night Sir's bluff did not work. Edith passed the cups of hot chocolate without a word. This firm stand and the reaction to it gave us some spiritual courage. After all, they depended on our well-being more than we did on theirs.

Then we were in San Antonio, Texas, living in a $75,000 home, a showplace on Jackson-Vance road. The furnishings and grounds were ornate. Stained glass windows. Tile roof. A swimming pool, greenhouse. Frank Lloyd Wright, the architect who designed the famous Tokyo hotel, had drawn the plans. And while the five acres of surrounding gardens were landscaped and strewn with lights so that a night lawn party could be given, we were never permitted even to entertain any of our friends there. We could never enjoy the magnificent and splendid estate, let alone call it our own home. During our rest periods, the servants were fired and we did the cleaning . . . "You need exercise" we were told coldly.

We had made only one demand of Sir: "Buy us diamond bracelets. Not with small stones. Big ones." It was the plea we made in the presence of the beloved Daddy Morris, of the William Morris Agency, our bookers, before Bill Oliver and before any friend of Sir. Other stage stars had jewels, and this seemed reasonable for us because in that way we could really get possession of something we could use for money. He never had given us cash.

We got the bracelets. We sneaked newspapers. We had a room and bath to ourselves. But now we were twenty-three years old and we had never had a date. I, Daisy, was in love with Don. We had appeared on several bills with him, and although Edith and Sir guarded us too closely for conversation, I always thought Don told me with his songs and his brown eyes that he loved me.

Blue Steel had worked on the bill with us several times. He would arrange for his band to play either before or following our act, so that he could play *Darling*. "Dedicated to a darling Violet Hilton," he would announce. Then he would play *You Can Take My Heart*.

Just then there seemed only one person in all Texas we wanted to see. In a copy of *Variety* we read that Don was booked there and was stopping at the St. Anthony Hotel. We were reading the sneaked paper in the greenroom when Sir burst in. He was excited; Edith was calming him.

"Just look at this!" Sir flung a newspaper down on the table in front of us. "What have you done? Bill Oliver's wife has named you in her divorce suit. You've alienated her husband's affections and she wants a quarter of a million dollars!"

"We don't love Bill Oliver! You know that!" I, Daisy, cried.

"Why did you write 'love' on that picture you autographed for him to send his wife?"

We were too stunned to reply.

Sir put us in the car and drove to the office of a lawyer, Martin J. Arnold, who kept his eyes squinted in the bright Texas sunshine all the while Sir was telling him why we had come to engage his services. "The girls have got to fight this," Sir kept saying. We were told what the complaint charged; that Bill was reported to have admitted friendship with us and that we both loved him. It was even claimed that we were jealous of each other, that despite our physical condition we would go for weeks without speaking a word to each other.

We tried to speak. Again and again we tried. Then, I, Daisy, pulled up from my chair and Violet balanced me, giving me all her

> "Just look at this!" Sir flung a newspaper down on the table in front of us. "What have you done? Bill Oliver's wife has named you in her divorce suit. You've alienated her husband's affections and she wants a quarter of a million dollars!"

Daisy gets a kiss while Violet longs for love. A scene from Chained for Life.

strength, it seemed, as I raised my voice so all could hear. "There is something very wrong! My sister and I have had only business relations with Bill Oliver, never have been with him or anyone else alone. We've never been alone in our twenty-three years!"

For the first time the lawyer spoke. He looked at Sir but his words were to us: "A woman who has never seen the twins dares to say they have compromised her husband?"

"Read her complaint!" Sir said.

"Leave us alone," Mr. Arnold said in his deep drawl. "Close the door as you go into the other room. I want to ask the girls about this without your being present!"

"You can't send me out. I'm their guardian!"

"They are over twenty-one, aren't they? They don't need a guardian. Now, will you leave us?"

Reluctantly, Sir closed the door behind him. We sensed that we had reached a momentous period in our life. We were confused, of course, by the unwarranted charges made against us. But I, Daisy, seemed to have found courage in the kindly appearance and soft voice of the Texas lawyer who, I felt, would give us protection.

"Is there any truth in what Mrs. Oliver claims?" the lawyer asked in his kindly drawl.

"Not a word!" we cried together.

"You are two frightened girls. Isn't something else wrong? Do you want to tell me?"

"We're practically slaves!"

"Slavery hasn't been practiced in this country since the War between the States."

"Then help us get free." We produced the pathetic pieces of silver from our shoes. In our great moment of opportunity we had left our bracelets at home. "Please, Mr. Arnold, please help us. We're afraid!"

◆ ◆ ◆ ◆ ◆

One of us is usually cautious, the other impulsive. We seldom wish to talk about the same subject at the same time, but if this happens, one always gives the other the floor. That day in the law office of Martin J. Arnold in San Antonio, Texas, we both were talkative.

"No one will believe our story," I, Violet, usually the cautious one, ventured to say.

"We've been lonely, rich girls who were really paupers living in practical slavery. The public doesn't know all this, and if we tell a judge he might send us to an institution."

"I'm all for the trial," I, Daisy, declared.

"Just talk to me," said the lawyer in his easy drawl. "Walk up and down the floor if that will help."

"We're Siamese twins who want to live and die joined just as we were born. Neither is a parasite on the body or mind of the other. We want to live as other human beings live, when they're over twenty-one, to work and earn, yet Edith and Sir completely dominate us. We've done nothing but work during all our lives."

For forty-five minutes we talked out our hearts, while outside Sir waited. Lawyer Arnold had asked him to leave us; for us to explain why Mildred Oliver, in her divorce suit against our former advance man, William, had claimed we were in love with her husband and asked that we pay her $250,000 for alleged alienation of his affections. Sir left us reluctantly and it took only a second for the attorney to toss aside Mrs. Oliver's absurd claim. Then we told him about ourselves, sketching in our story from birth, as best we could.

"What became of all the money you've earned? What about the beautiful home you have on Vance-Jackson Road?" the lawyer asked. We told him. And as we talked a sudden sob broke through the tension. It came from behind a screen where the attorney's secretary, Lucille Stotzer, a pretty, brown-haired woman, had been taking down every word we said.

Mr. Arnold asked her to come out and meet us, and it was a strange experience for us to see a stranger crying over our predicament, something we had never done ourselves. We have never known self-pity.

"We have no money now, Mr. Arnold, but we need help."

"I'll help you. From now on you're my clients. You don't have to go home with this man."

We were supposed to go to a music lesson directly from his office, so we made a plan which would throw Sir off our trail. As soon as he left us at the music teacher's door and drove the car around the corner, we phoned Mr. Arnold's secretary. Sir was to call for us in an hour, he had said. Could she pick us up and take us to a hotel before that time? A taxi soon pulled up to the curb. Lucille Stotzer was in it, beckoning for us to come out. We stood in the door a moment, looking in both directions, making sure that Sir was not watching. Then we kissed the teacher and ran out, to begin what was indeed to become a new life for us!

In the suite at the St. Anthony Hotel we found flowers, candy, a radio, magazines and newspapers already provided for us. "Girls, you're Mr. Arnold's guests. Order anything you like," said Lucille. "Telephone your friends. See if you can't enjoy yourselves."

> ... For the first time we could order something on a menu which we wanted. We had dresses sent up, and selected no two alike, and all the silly hats we wanted. ...We got permanents and pinned up our hair. I, Violet, had always wanted to drink a cocktail. I, Daisy, wanted to smoke a cigarette. We did.

It was like a dream during the next few days while we waited for our trial to begin. For the first time we could order something on a menu which we wanted. We had dresses sent up, and selected no two alike, and all the silly hats we wanted. We could dress and act our age, and no longer be made up as children with bows in our hair. We got permanents and pinned up our hair. I, Violet, had always wanted to drink a cocktail. I, Daisy, wanted to smoke a cigarette. We did.

We actually seemed to grow in stature during our frequent interviews with our lawyer. And between interviews we added daydreams to the other pleasant indulgences. What a unique sensation it was to telephone a man! I, Violet, long-distanced Blue Steel, whose band, I learned from *Variety*, was playing the Peabody Hotel in Memphis, Tennessee. Then, I, Daisy, telephoned Don Galvan.

"I'm here alone," I said, and told him the hotel room number. It was perhaps the first time I ever spoke of being "alone." Of course a Siamese twin could never be alone. However, it did not seem strange to Don.

"Daisy! I've hoped so long that you would break away from Sir," he said. "I knew you'd call me if you ever had the chance!" A little later Don was at our door. We went to let him in and a thrill ran through us. This was our first date. Then Don stood there looking at me, Daisy, and forgetting that Violet was with us, too. He was even better looking than I had remembered. His dark eyes glistened and his teeth flashed white against his Spanish complexion.

I, Violet, could not will myself to be immune to my sister's emotion, then, although we both soon acquired the ability to blank out the other in romantic moments. This was, however, our first reality of romance and it intoxicated both of us. I was as anxious for my sister to experience her first kiss as she could be.

There seemed no words adequate to span the years that Don, I thought, had looked at us and sent thought messages to us across stages and from the wings of the theatres in which we had played. We, always guarded from men, had no way of learning to say certain little niceties expected at sentimental moments. Till now, you might say our private lives had been barren of adventures which might have profited us now.

There was a nervous ecstasy about Don's wordlessness. Then he held out his arms, "Daisy." We were never to forget that Don's lips then pressed against Daisy's forehead! My first kiss, but it was as real as it was disappointing. I was to learn that it held all the romance I wanted it to hold, but that Don was old-world and did not believe that a man should kiss his lady love otherwise before they were engaged. I, Violet, used to say: "Gee, Daisy, I'm tired of waiting for Don to kiss you!"

"Siamese twin-slaves! Poor little rich girls without spending money! No friends! Twenty-three years old and never a beau! Earned thousands and never collected a dollar . . ." so went the story unfolded in the San Antonio court. And every day we sat there, with Judge W. W. McCrory listening and shaking his gray head as if in disbelief and with Edith crying. Her husband, Sir, glared at us like a hypnotist.

When Edith's mother died she willed us to Edith and her husband, and now in court we learned that our own mother, a frightened young girl in Brighton, England, gave us to the midwife soon after our birth. Edith told how she, as a girl, had helped her mother care for us. She told how it hurt us when we learned that our mother had signed our lives away, and then how we had been willed to Edith and her husband, along with other possessions. We wanted freedom, an accounting of our money and a receiver appointed to manage our property. We wanted the contracts broken which we had been induced to sign, making Sir our manager, compelling us to work for him for $500 a week, which we had never collected. Most of all we wanted an injunction preventing Sir and Edith from ever interfering in our lives again!

Judge McCrory listened to first one of us, then the other. All this time Martin J. Arnold, our lawyer and friend, seemed to be our shield, protecting us from the influence of Sir, who sat there gripping the arms of his chair. Mr. Arnold knew our whole story by heart. He knew, too, that the only happiness we had ever known was during the few days we had been his guests while he was preparing the case for our trial. He had given us courage to run away and fight for our freedom.

What had Sir done with our money? We calculated that we had earned more than $2,000,000. When asked, he looked at Attorney Arnold and said he had banked it. "It was being kept in the family," he declared.

"In other words, you made it a family affair?"

"Yes, it was a family affair until you stepped in and corrupted it!" Sir retorted. The courtroom was filled with hisses.

Questioned about his conduct toward us, Sir straightened in his chair. Why, he had always treated us in a gentlemanly manner, he said. "Once I raised my hand as if to hit Daisy, but my wife interceded. The girls had rushed at me and had torn the shirt off my back, beating me about the body before my wife could stop them." The crowd applauded and cheered and ignored for whole minutes the hammering of Judge McCrory's gavel.

Wasn't it generous of our manager to give us those diamond bracelets? Was it! Our attorney showed that while Sir claimed to have paid $7,000 of our money for them, actually only $4,000 had been paid. This was brought out in testimony. Where was our fortune? What had really become of it?

"What bank do you do business with?"

"I don't know," Sir answered flatly. The packed courtroom resounded with boos.

But Attorney Arnold tracked down a receipt for $36,000 which we had been induced to sign when guardianship proceedings were completed. It was said to have been paid us, but we had never received even a dollar of that sum from him for spending money.

"Isn't it a fact that the twins signed the receipt but never received the money?" Arnold asked.

"I don't know. They were paid through my bookkeeper in New York."

"Don't you know where that $36,000 went?" Arnold pressed.

"I offered it to them and they refused to take it from me. I wouldn't throw it into the gutter. I kept it," he said.

Contracts were produced which called for forty weeks of appearances at $3,000 a week. So many weeks of appearances. We signed our names on so many dotted lines. During my (Violet's) time on the witness stand I looked at Sir and said; "The contracts we signed were always covered, except for the dotted line. When we hesitated to sign, Sir would rave and ask us if we thought he was a thief and if we didn't trust him, and if we were afraid, so we always signed."

No one could forget Edith as she had sat in the witness chair choking and crying so she could barely talk. Looking at the judge she said through sobs, "The girls don't seem to be making any allowance for the time I have spent with them, constantly caring for them and attending to their wants. I have spent the best part of my life in their interest—and now they ignore me. Why, they didn't even send me a card while they've been away from us!"

When I, Violet, was asked by Judge McCrory about our earnings, I recalled that until 1925 we did not attempt to keep track, but from that period until the time we had run away to start court proceedings [Dec. 1930], we had made $52,500 to $53,000 a week. In 1929 we became legally of age. We asked Sir then where he had placed our earnings. He said he had invested them in a trust. I testified how from the time we had reached our majority, we were kept under even a stricter guard, as if we might in some way learn of our legal right to liberty.

Violet and Daisy get ready for bed in Chained for Life.

No, we knew nothing about guardianship proceedings in 1927. Then Attorney Arnold said: "I'm going to file proceedings to have the final report of guardianship proceedings set aside on grounds of absolute fraud!"

As I, Violet, did most of the talking, I was stimulated and strengthened by my twin's concentration. My answers came clearly and quickly. When I hesitated only slightly, Daisy would prompt me by the movement

of her arm against mine, or shrug her shoulder. There are, you see, many times when being a Siamese twin has its peculiar advantages.

I said we were never paid the $36,000 which Sir said a bookkeeper paid us. I told how we longed to run away but were afraid because we had so often been threatened with being deported to England or put in an institution if we did.

Photographers and newsreel men and reporters

Violet and Daisy behind the scenes during the filming of Chained for Life.

crowded around us, and there were hundreds of well-wishers when the testimony finished. They followed us to our hotel and crowded outside our room, so we asked our attorney if we could not move into a small apartment somewhere until a decision had been reached.

The night when Lucille Stotzer, Mr. Arnold's secretary, went with us to the little apartment she had selected for us, we found that the electricity had not been turned on, although Lucille had arranged everything before our arrival.

"Wait, I'll find a match," I, Daisy, cried. Having learned to smoke, I had them in my handbag.

Before I could strike the match, Lucille cried: "Don't! I smell gas. The place is filled with gas. We might all be killed!" We ran out into the hall and she called the superintendent. He came with a flashlight, and then we learned that the jets of the kitchen stove were turned on full force. The discovery was very upsetting to both of us.

By the time we reached the hotel again, the crowd seemed off our trails—that is, the actual crowd was off, but there was a reporter waiting in the lobby who ran up to us as soon as we entered. "I've been trying to find you," he said breathlessly. "I've just got word from my office that your lives are in danger. A tip came to the city editor. Someone called and said, "The Siamese twins may be killed tonight."

This information scared us no little and set us thinking. But we were sure that no matter how many enemies we might have made, none of them would want to go to the extreme of killing us. Finally we dismissed the reporter's story from our minds. We ascribed it to someone's fertile imagination. Attorney Arnold arrived shortly afterward, and with him were five plainclothesmen who kept constant guard of our suite until Judge McCrory's decision came through.

One day in court Sir was ordered to produce bonds and books about which we had testified. Joe Freeman, one of the leading businessmen in Texas, who formerly had a seat on the New York Stock Exchange, was named as our receiver.

Judge McCrory looked at us, then out over the waiting crowd and said something we were never to forget: "Jack Dempsey was nothing but a ham-and-egger until Jack Kearns took hold of him and developed him into a world champion. The Hilton twins would not be where they are today had this defendant not managed their affairs and proved a good promoter."

But we had never longed for fame. We did not want promotion and management. We only wanted liberty, freedom to live as we wanted to live, to live as other girls our age lived.

The Judge ordered Sir never to interfere with our lives again. We were given $67,000 in bonds, $12,000 in cash and $20,000 in personal effects. Sir was no longer our guardian and manager. All contracts existing between him and us were dissolved! Of all this our freedom was the most important and that part of the court decision which gave that freedom rang loudest in our hearts.

We did not care that the palatial home and grounds in San Antonio was given to Edith and Sir. Perhaps they had earned them.

We cried and laughed. So many persons rushed up to shake our hands and cry "Bless you!" that court attendants had to hold them away. It was a dramatic climax to the unusual life we had lived for so many years.

Our new life began almost immediately. We went to shows, night clubs, dinner parties. Attorney and Mrs. Arnold threw open their beautiful home in our honor, invited our show business friends to a dinner and musical. Don Galvan brought his celebrated guitar. He won everybody with his singing. We drank wine and smoked. Two young men begged us to dance. The "don'ts" of our childhood were all "dos" now, and we revelled in it. It seemed as though we had been transported into another world. We looked forward to a future promising real happiness.

It was not long before Don asked me, Daisy, to marry him, but even as he asked me he took the cigarette from my hand, pushed my wine glass aside. Even he would suppress me! "Marry me, Daisy, and forget about show business. Come to Mexico and live with my family."

Give up my little pet habits! Give up show business . . . Wherever I went, Violet, my twin, must go. She must share my life. Should she be subjected to such restraint? After all, we had just succeeded in getting freedom. Why should I submit both of us to another life of censorship in which we couldn't be ourselves? I asked for a little more time to think.

Just before the trial was over, Don called one night and there was a new seriousness about him. "You'll soon be free of Sir," he said, "then can we be married?"

We stepped back a little. I, Daisy, felt my sister start. But I thought that he couldn't very well ask her to consent to marry me. Yet, I wondered if she should not be consulted, since she would share every moment of my life with my husband. Actually being confronted with this odd situation was very different from what I had imagined. Could either of us marry? Could any man adjust himself to our lives? Don had conducted himself well, but now there were lights of unrest in his dark eyes.

"Don, have you thought this out? Violet, my twin, will be with us every minute."

"I've thought it out, Daisy," Don said. "I'm sure I can make allowances for Violet." His voice was confident.

"How?" we both asked.

"This way: You will be my wife for six months of the year. Then, for the other six months you may go wherever Violet wants to go. And if she should get married then, naturally, you must spend six months with her and her husband."

We were not prepared for such an arrangement and for a few minutes we were silent.

Then, I, Daisy, spoke: "Don, I know now that I would not like a separation from the man I married. And I would never want to be separated from my twin. I couldn't bear to be separated from either of you."

Suddenly we all began to laugh. This was what it felt like to be happy. And for the next few hours we three began making all kinds of plans, in all of which Violet shared enthusiastically.

Yet in this, my most gleeful moment, I, Daisy, realized that my sister loved in a different way from me. She loved Blue Steel, who belonged to someone else. Yet, she seemed happy to go on being content just to hear his voice over the phone and over the radio. Love was nothing that belonged to her, not something or someone she needed with her, as I did. To her, love meant letting go. And here is a true-love code, perhaps, though one which never could be mine. Marriage, with its legendary love and romance, became our most serious thought.

Despite the fact that we are Siamese twins, we seemed to attract many admirers. It gave us grave moments and much wonderment when our suitors were embarrassed by the inevitable presence of a third person. However, few were discouraged in their ardor. Some schemed ways to talk to one of us alone over the telephone. The shyer men wrote and wired.

I, Daisy, worried because Violet still carried a torch for Blue Steel, the musician, and listened nightly to his broadcast. I, Violet, knew Daisy was worrying about me. I felt hopeless about Blue. So I tried to forget him. And, to my great relief and Daisy's, I got a crush on Harry Mason, handsome English welterweight champion. Harry dimmed my torch for Blue, although he did not quite put it out. He had no objections to my being a Siamese twin. In fact, he liked Daisy. But she was interested in Don Galvan, the guitarist.

Yes, I, Daisy, liked Don very well. The trouble was, he said, that, if we married, we'd all have to live with his family in Mexico. I used to go on dates with Violet and Harry and never hear a word they said. Then suddenly I decided I'd have to give Don up. At that time, Violet planned to marry Harry, who wanted her to travel with him in England. How could we both be happy?

But I wasn't the extra girl on Violet's and Harry's dates very long. Jack Lewis, the dark-haired band leader, entered my life, and I almost forgot Don. Also, he brought brown-eyed Maurice Lambert, another band leader, to meet Violet. We had a gay foursome, and it wasn't long before Violet broke her engagement with the ring champ and began wearing Maurice's diamond. However, after a while, I realized that too many of my conversations with Jack took place over the phone. And when he asked me over the wire to marry him, I knew that his shyness made him unsuitable for the husband of a Siamese twin.

And when I did break my engagement to Jack, Maurice became upset. Fearful that Violet would throw him over, he raced to City Hall, New York, to get a marriage license.

I, Daisy, worried because Violet still carried a torch for Blue Steel, the musician, and listened nightly to his broadcast. I, Violet, knew Daisy was worrying about me. I felt hopeless about Blue. So I tried to forget him. And, to my great relief and Daisy's, I got a crush on Harry Mason, handsome English welterweight champion.

You're one of us.
We accept you.

"What? You want to marry a Siamese twin?" the clerk asked. "That's impossible! You'll be marrying two girls instead of one! That's bigamy!"

Maurice was not to be discouraged. He applied for a marriage license in 21 states—all of which refused him for the same reason: "Contrary to public policy on the grounds of morality and decency." Poor Violet!

Indeed, I, Violet, felt deserving of sympathy. "Is it fair?" I asked court clerks. "Just because an accident of birth made me a Siamese twin, is that any reason why I should be prohibited marriage, the natural desire of every woman?" But no matter what pleas and arguments were offered, marriage was not for us. Or so it seemed at that time.

Thus, the tempo of our life changed. We went to cities and towns where there was excitement in fashionable seasons. We leased a swank apartment overlooking New York's Central Park, and entertained. We had a continuous round of beaux. Some were rich, some poor. We saw many men of various types. We talked them over, trying to weigh the question: "Can we be happy with them?" There was no adequate, satisfying answer.

One day after a late supper party we awakened in our canopied bed. Central Park was sunny and green, and the futility of our years of play swept through us. "Let's go back to work!" we said.

We organized a troupe and fashioned a revue to our own liking. We played violin, piano, saxophone, did ballet and adagio dancing and took part in sketches. Again we toured Europe and the United States. We eventually were able to immerse ourselves in our work.

Terry Turner, our ace press agent, a jovial, handsome Irishman, came to us with a gleam in his blue eyes, announcing, "A wedding of one of you girls would be the greatest publicity stunt ever pulled off since September Morn!"

"That can't be, Terry," I, Violet, said. "Maurice Lambert tried to get a marriage license to marry me in twenty-one states, and he couldn't."

"That's right! But if I get a license, will you go through with the ceremony?" Terry challenged.

"I'll be the goat, if you can manage," I replied.

Terry's eyes fastened intently on my dancing partner, James Walker Moore.

"Jim's it. He'll mean more publicity for the act. Are you game, Jim?" asked Terry.

Jim smiled good-naturedly and shrugged his willingness.

Not one of us had any idea that Terry could ever make his big idea come alive, and no more was said about it for several days. Then, things began to happen. They began with a page one announcement that I, Violet, would become the bride of Jim at Texas Centennial. Terry had secured the license for us! Texas was, it so happened, one of the states that Maurice had missed.

The ceremony was to take place right in the great Cotton Bowl, on the fifty-yard line. Daisy was to be my maid of honor. And Joe Rogers, famous Broadway character and a close friend of Terry, was to give the bride away.

The wedding day arrived. We were all ready when Joe Rogers began to shake. He needed a drink, he said. About twenty minutes later, he returned. He no longer shook, but his dress suit was ripped and dirty. His eye was blackened and his nose was a red smudge.

"I can't go through with it!" Joe cried humbly. "I got in an argument with the bartender. I guess you'll just have to give the bride away yourself, Terry."

Terry moaned. But not for long. His eyes lit on a tall, good-looking young guy, leaning on a broom. He was a janitor of the Cotton Bowl. Terry went over to him. "Rent a dress suit and be back here in thirty minutes!" he commanded. "You're going to be in a wedding!"

The janitor appeared shortly afterwards, as smart-appearing as a movie star. The ceremony began. Cameras clicked. It was as Terry had said, a great publicity stunt. Reporters rushed up to interview us, especially Daisy, "the extra girl on the honeymoon."

A crowd pursued us to the very door of our wedding suite, where Terry Turner and Jim's sweetheart and other members of our troupe were waiting, to join us in a laugh and a supper in celebration of a publicity stunt which won space on front pages from Texas to Maine.

We have never gone through the formalities of a divorce, but Jim, in the service now, knows that when he wants the ties, made only in the name of publicity, broken he will have our full cooperation. As Terry figured, the stunt paid off. We went to Hollywood and made several films.

Life marched on swiftly then for us for about five years, until I, Daisy, fell in love with the singing, dancing master-of-ceremonies of our act. His name was Harold Estep, known professionally as Buddy Sawyer. He was eight years younger than I. "I'm going to marry Buddy Sawyer," I told my sister when I had made up my mind. I sensed, when she said nothing, that she was a little startled.

Yes, I, Violet, was startled. But I did not argue with my sister about her choice. We had never argued. I felt then that her marriage with Buddy would not be right. I thought she had not weighed the idea well. Buddy was pleasant to me, and he was most friendly when we all sat down to talk over our future life together.

The marriage took place a few days later on Sept. 1, 1941, in Elmira, N.Y. A crowd gathered despite our efforts to avoid publicity. And all that night and through every night and day for the following ten days we were pursued. Then, one morning when we looked across at the twin bed where Buddy had been when we drowsed between the incessant phone calls from reporters, Buddy had disappeared. I, the bride, who had not yet known a honeymoon, tried to believe that Buddy would come back. For a while I waited for him, although I knew he would not return. When I began divorce proceedings some time later, I read in a newspaper his reason for leaving me: "Daisy is a lovely girl," he was quoted as saying. "But I guess I am not the type of fellow that should marry a Siamese twin. As a matter of fact, I am not even what you would call really gregarious. In the show business there are times when you get tired of seeing anybody, let alone twin brides."

The sad thing about love is, you get over it. However, it took long, weary months before I faced the fact that this was true and that both our marriages were without anchorage. We had to turn our thoughts again from emotion and think of the only thing we ever really were masters of: work. We had lived a variety of lives, virtually as prisoners and as rich playgirls. We both had been married, unsuccessfully. So, romance had palled. We had known freedom, had celebrated it, and then had failed to enjoy it. Work alone never had failed us. And it isn't strange that we again longed to return to it.

It was at this time that out of the blue a wire reached us from Pittsburgh. It was sent by Don D'Carlo, whom we knew as one of the best-liked theatrical agents and head of the D'Carlo Entertainment Service. His wire was like a beckoning hand of welcome from an intuitive and understanding friend. It read: "Will you accept headline booking at Don Metz Casino?" We knew it would be fun to sing with the tuneful orchestra where the guests laughed and drank. We wasted no time in answering Don D'Carlo's wire.

It was wonderful to be part of a new world, the night club world. We had friends in and outside the theatrical profession and now we were to enter the night club sphere. And from our opening night till now, we have enjoyed our pleasantest years. Yet we still long to find real romance and love equal to our own tolerance and forgiveness. We dream of having homes and families. (Doctors tell us there is no reason why we can't have children.)

Perhaps you have seen through this story that life has given us plenty of problems and that we have adjusted ourselves to most of them. And somewhere still, we believe and hope we will find the right mates, to whose understanding and love we can entrust our private lives.

U P D A T E

Sideshow, *a musical about the Hilton sisiters opened on Broadway in October 1997.*

Not every story has a happy ending. Unfortunately for Violet and Daisy, the success they had with their nightclub dates and after was mixed. Though they made a rather successful appearance in Tod Browning's Freaks, their film Chained for Life is considered by many to be one of the worst films ever made. Well, it does have an awful charm. Violet and Daisy are both obviously beyond their prime as entertainers in the film, and its value as filmic autobiography is a leap in the dark, at best.

In the sad years that followed its release, the Hiltons were to slide through a number of failed business ventures, each leaving them with less and less to fall back on. They'd taken to touring a series of revivals of Chained for Life at assorted drive-ins, trying to make a living off a movie that just couldn't generate the cash. When its last spot failed, it left them stranded and virtually penniless. Their income at the end came from their job in a small-town grocery store in Charlotte, NC, where they worked as a "double produce weigher." In 1969, when they failed to show for work for a few days, they were checked on at their home where they were both found dead, apparently of the Hong Kong flu. I don't think I've ever read whether it was Violet or Daisy who passed away first.

The Intimate Lives and Loves of the Hilton Sisters

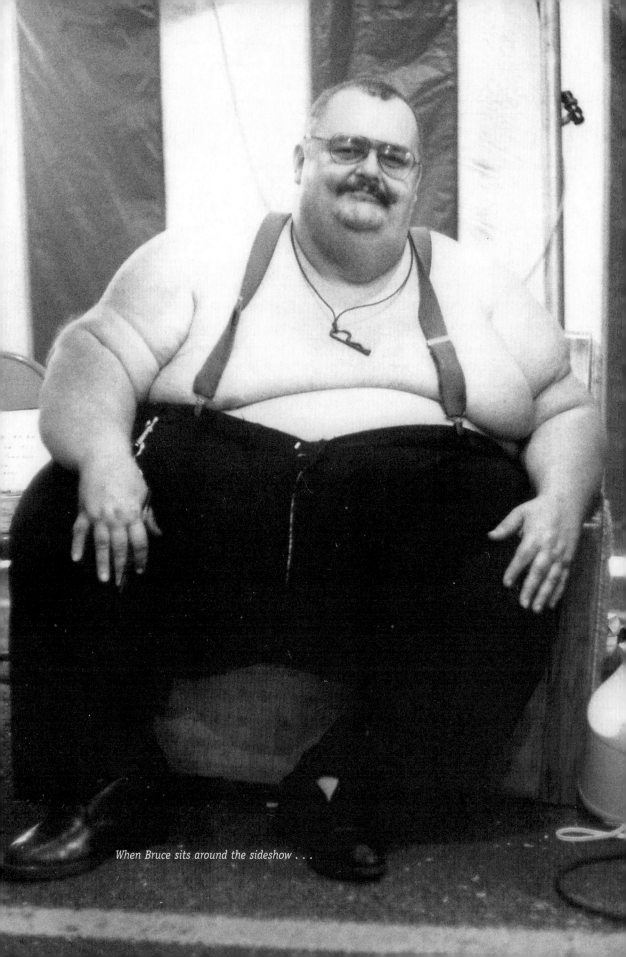

When Bruce sits around the sideshow . . .

SIX GALS TO HUG HIM AND A BOXCAR TO LUG HIM

here's a seminal moment in the BBC production *The Last American Freak Show* in which Bruce Snowdon, aka Harold Huge, Big Bruno, Howard Huge, etc., is just up and outside in the early a.m., before the show starts at the Ward Hall/Chris Christ World of Wonders. Even there in Perry, Georgia, it's not exactly 100 degrees in the shade, not this autumn morning. And Bruce stands in all his voluminous glory, buck naked, getting ready to bathe the only way perhaps this last remaining fat man on any midway can when he's on the carnival lot: with 50' of green garden hose.

There in the early sun, the chiaroscuro behind the shows and the showmen's trailers, Snowdon is transformed into the fattest man on earth. It suddenly doesn't matter whether he weighs the full 712 pounds the banner claims out front. For all you care, he weighs a ton, and you're some mere bug about to watch a true sideshow wonder revealed: how the fats keep clean. The minute the night-cold water hits him, you find out: with great difficulty and no small amount of adventure. "I usually like to let the sun impart a little solar energy to the hose before I do this," he says, by way of explaining to the cameraman the obvious shiver when the water first hits him.

Well, I suppose BBC got what it wanted. And through the rest of that documentary, Bruce does his lines with the dutiful attention of the real trouper. Not a character you'd recognize when comparing him to the Bruce Snowdon you'll meet when you visit the real show, but a character fit for the documentary anyway. In the flesh (and lots of it too, make no mistake), he's infinitely less stiff, less formal, but no less knowledgeable. About a lot of things. Paleontology. Medicine. New York City history. Illegal fireworks for Chrissake. You name it, Bruce has read it. The primary occupation-

al hazard for the sideshow performer, especially the freak performer, is boredom. Doing the same act over and over. Day after
day. Show after show. One tip after the other. And when you're the
fat man, especially in a museum show like that run now by Hall and
Chris, there's precious little to do if you've got no inner resources.

Bruce has inner resources. Either that, to paraphrase the "Billy Reed—Horrors of Drug Abuse Show" Bruce mentions during his interview, either that or he's a damn good actor. Nah. He really knows all this stuff. And loves to philosophize on it. And he's very much the fin de siecle philosopher. Blasé and cynical at times, priding himself on being a keen observer of the human condition. That, of course, is what Bruce Snowdon has all the time in the world to do. Read and enjoy the view.

Seventy-some years ago, the view from the platform (and from the tip too, for that matter) was significantly different. In those days, between the world wars, you wouldn't just go to see a lone fat in a sideshow. You'd go to see a fat review. A

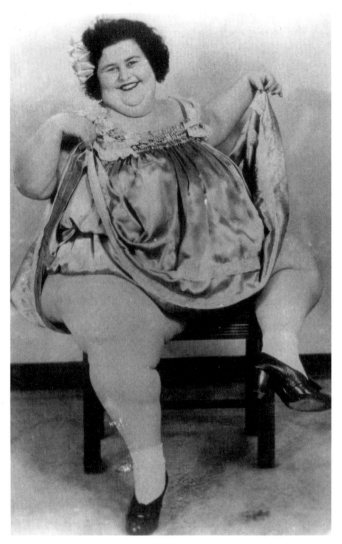

Bruce wasn't the first or the fattest. Celesta "Dolly Dimples" Geyer smiles prettily in a pitchcard.

Congress of Fat People. Fat families. Tons of fun. Acres of human flesh. How fat were they? They were really fat.

But of course the crowd would have been only marginally different, in spirit anyway. Go read Celesta Geyer's ("Dolly Dimples") book, *Diet or Die*. When she met her mentor, "Jolly Pearl" Stanley, the advice Celesta got could've been pure 1990s: "You know, honey, everyone laughs at you now. Don't you think it would be a good idea to make them pay for their fun?" It didn't take Celesta long to pick up on that advice. Within weeks she was on the show with Jolly Pearl, polishing her act. And before it was over, she'd become the "It Girl of Fat Girls" (so dubbed by Clara Bow, "The It Girl" herself), and she'd learned the two most vital lessons for any sideshow performer: " . . . when you enjoy doing this work, your audiences reflect that enjoyment" and the ever-important advice about pitch-cards (or any pitch item for that matter), that "There's real money in these pictures." Now there's the sideshow equation at its best.

Bruce learned that equation pretty early on as well, and he may yet be the last fat to employ the knowledge on the midway. That knowledge was much in evidence when I interviewed him in the Hall & Christ World of Wonders show at Winter Haven, FL, the roar of the midway outside, Bruce holding forth inside with his gravelly voice on subjects many and varied.

S&A: You've been with Ward Hall's shows a lot of years haven't you?

BS: I've done a number of things. For a number of years I was an illegal M-80 bootlegger. We used them to settle our "backwoods firearms interactions."

S&A: When you were a kid?

BS: No, I wasn't a kid.

S&A: I guess it's dangerous regardless when you make them.

BS: It's very easy to explode right in your face if the mixture isn't right. It can tear you apart if it detonates.

S&A: I know you got busted for making them. What's the story with that?

BS: It didn't come to trial for a year. I was willing to plead guilty since I was just going to get tossed on probation. I go to see the probation officer. "How are you?" "I'm still making M-80's." "Oh. Okay. See you." This guy, this probation officer, he's got 800 coke freaks, a thousand junkies, one M-80 bootlegger. Needless to say the M-80 bootlegger got, "Oh? Don't do it again." When it was over I got a note saying, "Congratulations, you have successfully completed probation."

S&A: Meanwhile, you hadn't seen the guy but a couple of times in months.

BS: Yeah.

S&A: When did you hit the road for the first time?

BS: I went out the first time in '77. This is a freaky story about how this happened. I had put on a lot of weight between the time I was twenty and twenty-five. I was up to about 450 in those days. I went to the local library, and I was poking through some old circus books and

I see this one picture about a sideshow, maybe circa 1905, and I'm looking at this fat man and I'm saying to myself, "He can't weigh more than 350 pounds." Now, I ask myself, how the hell would I go about getting into a sideshow? I'd never even seen a sideshow in my lifetime. In the late '70s the industry was a very pale ghost of its former self. Instead of thousands, there were maybe dozens left then. So I figured, logically, there's got to be some sort of trade journal for the carnival industry. It's *Amusement Business*. And I'm looking through the *AB*. Taking a lucky stab, I wrote the editor, Tom Powell. And Tom Powell happens to be a very good friend of Ward Hall. Bingo. I had the job.

S&A: What does your family think about you in the business?

BS: My mother's met Ward Hall. She knows I like it. I think now she considers me less unfortunate than she did. I think she wanted me to be a lawyer or something like that. The way things are going now, she's really glad I can feed myself on the job. That's the thing about lawyers: About three-quarters of them are incompetent; three-quarters of them end up starving to death. You've got some guy, his grandfather was a junkman. His father tried to make it as a lawyer, but Junior had a real straight head. He kept his grandfather's junkyard. Running a junkyard these days is very, very respectable. You're a recycler. "Recycling modules," not junkyards!

S&A: So what kind of things have you done in your act?

BS: [grins and rocks back and forth, sloshing his belly like a waterbed.] I have a routine about how I eat 50,000 calories worth of food at a time. I probably only eat about twice as much again as you do. You might be able to eat one TV dinner with dessert. Instead, I'll eat two TV dinners. But I don't eat 25 chickens and a barrel of beer, thirty pancakes, two dozen eggs, sixteen pounds of bacon. That could kill a sperm whale, never mind a human being. Two things: Yes, I do like to eat too much and I'm not very active. I also have a tendency, of course, to "be heavy." I probably am the heaviest man who ever lived in my family, but not by more than a century. My father used to bounce up and down from 250 to 350 and back again. And when he was on the way down, life in that family was hell. He was one of those people that, if he was miserable, he wanted everybody else to be miserable. If there's a bitchy type of human being, it's somebody on a diet. You're driving down the street and you cut somebody off, you just drive in front of them, they might snarl at you. But every now and then, it's a lot worse. They're the ones on the diets.

S&A: How does your season go? What is your business year like?

BS: Most generally we go out in May and stay out until about the end of October, the first part of November, then call it quits. You're on the road for almost nine months out of the year and you're pretty doggoned tired and you want to get back home, kick back and relax. Until recently, I went to Maine, but uuggh! You get cold. I can't hack those Maine winters. As far as I'm concerned, they can keep their snow and their pine trees and all the rest of it. I want sun and palm trees around me. If I never see the place again it'll be too damn soon. When you're my age, the cold hits you two ways: one, it's arthritis; two, it gave me a case of the flu. Or it could be a fungal infection from the moldy old house. You know, it becomes bone dry in the wintertime. It could be the heater misbehaving. You get headaches and chest congestion. You could end up with carbon monoxide poisoning. All sorts of lovely things it could be. When I got sick up north, somebody said to me, "Maybe you should go to a hospital." I said, "What I got is a bad case of Maine." Another thing that was bothering me then was my prostitis. But I take this antibiotic that's strong enough to wake the dead. I know this stuff will cure anything. About half a dozen pills will cure anything. I think northern winters just don't agree with me anymore.

S&A: So is it pretty tough staying healthy on the road?

BS: Out on the road you have to be careful. My way of handling it is TV dinners and throwaway silverware. If silverware's the tiniest bit dirty, you're going to get bacteria, then you're going to get diarrhea. This is not a good place to have diarrhea. Plus I take vitamins. But this summer I think it's been lovely. You get into some of these tents with the sun hitting on you it can be sixty degrees outside and inside the tent it's in the upper 90s. And you sit in here for eleven or twelve hours. Summers, legitimately, I'll go through a case of pop a day when it's in

Bruce Snowdon and boss canvasman Jimmy Long, left, prepare backstage at the World of Wonders.

FARMAR'S FAT FAMILY.   TOTAL WEIGHT - 3773 LBS.

It's all in the family: Farmar's Fat Family pitchcard.

the 90s. Open a can and pour it down your throat and whoosh it's gone. It's out your skin like a bad habit. But the rain is worse. Especially on a dirt lot. On this one it's nice because they have sand down on the ground. Some places it's a mixture of dirt and clay. Two inches of dirt turns into six inches of mud when it rains.

S&A: I heard you had a rain storm your first day here.

BS: Yeah. Thank God I drove down here. I would have hated to get off the bus in that. The temperature was in the forties, there was thirty to forty mile per hour winds. The rain was streaming into the truck. Thank God I had about four sleeping bags on.

S&A: How do you find dealing with the crowds?

BS: There are some fairs that are known for their obnoxiousness. Like Brockton is the fair from hell. Brockton, Massachusetts. Until recently, they used to sell beer for about a buck for a twelve-ounce cup. And the selling criteria was, "Old enough to reach up with your money, pick up your cup of beer and toddle off with it, you're old enough to drink." So every kid, every fourteen-fifteen year old weenie that lived within fifty miles, would drive to Brockton to get drunk at their fairgrounds. There are few things more objectionable than about ten sixteen to seventeen year old teenage boys with their bellies full of beer. They all think they're the wittiest things on the face of the earth. Fortunately, you can take them apart easily. They all invariably say, "How big's your penis?" The first way you can rip their heads off is to ask them, "Do you always go around asking strange men how big their penises are?" The kid will half the time turn about the same shade of red as that snake box. It really terrifies the average American eighteen-year-old boy to think that his friends will think he's a homosexual.

S&A: You were with Ward's shows back when he had the big 10-in-1, back when he had more acts. The acts here are pretty much just you and the pincushion. What's that act like?

BS: There are a series of acts that are generically called "Torture Acts." Sword swallowing, human blockhead, another one called iron tongue, fire eating and pincushion. Pincushion is the one that really involves physical discomfort. You take a hat pin and WHAM! That one will guarantee that people will talk about it. But Ward even has a hard time with it. You know it's real sideshow if Ward Hall can't stand it—he goes "Eeeww!" When we had the 10-in-1, the guy who did the pincushion, he got up to do the ding. Prayer pennies and miniature bibles, all sorts of junk. He walked up there to peddle them and you'd look down and you'd see the drops of blood.

S&A: That's pretty spooky. Right up there with the geek acts. I guess you don't see much of that anymore either.

BS: There's this guy out on the road called "Billy Reed." He's in a wheelchair and there's this python and the schtick is he thinks this python's his best friend and he sticks its head in his mouth.

S&A: Ward was saying that you really packed them in here last night.

BS: Last night . . . last night was really rocking. It was one of the biggest spots we've drawn. I had a wad of one dollar bills like this, maybe seventy-two, and about fifty five dollar bills and a twenty. When you get money in here like that, you are really in a poor area. Up north you're going to have maybe one five dollar bill and a ten and you're going to have a shortage of one dollar bills. There's more money up there.

S&A: In the acts you have seen in the past, what are some of the best ones you've seen, ones that stick in your mind and make you say, "I'm really glad to be on the platform with them"? I know you were on the shows with Otis Jordan, the Human Cigarette Factory.

BS: He worked pretty hard. You know what those Thalidomide babies look like? He had German Measles and they did the same thing. His arms were little bitty stubs, his legs were little bitty legs. He'd take a rolling paper and he'd hold the paper with his tongue, put the tobacco in it and put the business into his mouth and what would come out would be a finished cigarette. He'd tuck the cigarette in one side of his mouth, pick up a kitchen match in his lips, strike the kitchen match and light the cigarette. He'd cook his own food too. This college professor, a writer, came to the show a few years ago. He was very much upset by this old black guy.

S&A: Otis?

BS: Yeah. It was very obvious. People think there's so much discomfort. I mean, we like it out here. It's something we like to do. But I could no more get that through his head than I could push my finger through that center pole.

S&A: I suppose it's good that professor's not the only one writing about the shows.

BS: Have you read any of Joe McKennon's books? He's got an encyclopedia now. In totally exhausting detail he posits that the industry—the modern carnival industry as we know it today—started in 1893. Chicago World's Fair. My suspicion is that it goes back much further than that. Probably the real organized carnival is less than 100 years old. Prior to that it would have been a sideshow for the circuses. You'd have a big name circus show and off to the side you'd have a sideshow. For circus people, it's rough. The hours aren't the best in the world. I mean it's a vacation on the Riveria for carnies compared to the circus. A circus jump, you set up one day. You set it up in the morning, tear it down tonight and then go to bed. Jump to the next spot. If you're lucky you get some sleep there. A lot of carnies aren't moving that much.

S&A: The prejudice against carnivals in general goes back a long way. The games maybe more than the shows.

BS: They've been writing articles—like Walter Gibson wrote articles in the 1920s and this gets repeated—an expose of carnival midway games. It's an on-going process, something that gets repeated every couple of years: "Oh, we're going to expose the games." That and the cops will make a big whoopee by raiding them. No way are you going to change them. There are always going to be ways to make it harder to win. But most of these games are on the up-and-up. They depend on the fact that your average American citizen has the athletic ability of me. I have a hard time throwing a baseball into a barrel sitting from where I am. The average American could do no better. Anyone who drops 100 bucks in one of those goddamn joints—to me that's stupid. Some guy will go in these joints for a teddy bear, and he'll blow a week's pay trying to get it when he can go to the Toys-R-Us and buy one for $50 that's four feet tall and much better construction.

They're so desperate some of these people. They'll spend all their money. You'll say to one of these guys, "Well—the boss isn't around. You give me $50 for this toy, I'll sell it to you." And they'll do it! There's the basis for the television show *The Price is Right*. Most people don't know the value of things. They'll have an advertisement for washing machines—I bought one a couple of years ago for between $450 and $500—and you'll get people off the street, average citizens, and they'll be saying things like, "$1,600, uh, $200." The closest call will be $900.

S&A: I guess, "That's entertainment." How do you think the shows will be remembered?

BS: In '76, the Smithsonian Institution created a full-size carnival for one night. It made you wonder.

I'll be watching some television special and you'll see those grainy old movies, the 1890s. It's weird. You just don't get that strange feeling when you read text about the Victorian days. Five hundred years from now, what will people be able to do, just by pressing on some buttons or working from a keyboard? They'll be able to access the [Ward] Hall and [Chris] Christ tapes and look at them just like they're alive. I think about this: You get this feeling you're being watched by the next ten generations.

S&A: How do you think they're going to perceive your act?

BS: It's hard to tell. They are going to wonder why anybody could be this fat now!

I've talked with Bruce any number of times since this interview was conducted. During one of our meetings—always in the show, him as big as a tool shed, sitting in a chair that's just wide enough to hold him squeezed in—he told me he wondered about all the future generations and what they'll think "looking down the well of history" at all of us here at the bottom. Of course he was talking directly about the sideshow biz of today, but if there's a bigger question for everybody, I don't' know what that question could be.

Bruce still appears in Hall & Christ's World of Wonders.

He's too sexy for his shirt. Bruce strikes a pose at Winter Quarters in Gibsonton, Florida.

THE STRAND
The Fabulous Creation

By William G. FitzGerald

You're not hearing it here first, but I'll say it anyway: The sideshow was invented in America. Well, we know that, literally, that's a pile of elephant squat; what people mean when they say "invented," though, is pretty much irrefutable: Sideshow has come into its own here like nowhere else, to the point where countries and cultures that could clearly contest the statement act as though sideshow were invented here.

England, for example. Home of the Elephant Man, Joseph Merrick. Scene of some of the greatest triumphs of P.T. Barnum and Tom Thumb (who, though tried and true Yankees both, were treated more regally there—by Queen Victoria herself— than they ever could've been here). Birthplace of the Bartholomew Fair, the granddaddy of all modern fairs, complete with its own retinue of freak shows and outlandish performances mingled with the livestock and veg-

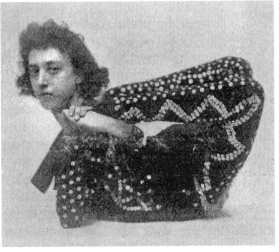

Leonora posing as a human boat.

etables. And on and on. None of that seemed to matter to William FitzGerald when writing on the subject for London's venerable *Strand* magazine. Perhaps he was coming to the subject anew; perhaps, though, it was just the old sideshow formula: If it's foreign, it's exotic. And America has always been a lot of things, but not the least of them was exotic.

Special train belonging to Coupe's traveling show.

They are of very ancient date. It has been stated that the various colossal skeletons that come to light from time to time are merely the remains of prehistoric sideshow giants, in fact, that were in former times exhibited at one stone axe per "time." However this may be, sideshows have long flourished, and, doubtless, will continue to flourish so long as inquisitiveness remains a part of our nature.

Shows of all sorts thrive exceedingly on American soil—and coin. Barnum was a millionaire several times over during his wonderful career; and Adam Forepaugh had more money than he knew what to do with. Traveling shows in the United States are conducted on a tremendous scale. The staff may number hundreds, and then there are the human freaks (ever jealously guarded from the non-paying eye), the huge menagerie, and hundreds of horses of all kinds, from the *haute-école* Arab right down to bony "Jimmy," who drags a van.

No wonder they require special trains! The photo reproduced here shows the passenger part of one of these. The center panel of the great Pullman car is adorned with a modest portrait of the proprietor of the show—or "director-general," as he loves to be styled. He probably owns the whole train, as well as the show, by the way. Advertisement being the very breath of the showman's nostrils, you will also notice lurid lithographs on the side of the car, so that the whole makes a stirring ensemble as the train enters a great terminus, with perhaps the bearded lady as engine-driver, and the pig-faced gentleman astride one of the buffers.

The born showman is so earnest in manner and gesticulation, so leathern of lung, and so profuse—not to say incoherent—in opulent adjectives before potential patrons, that he at length believes implicitly in every statement he himself makes. Such a one was Coxswain Terry, shrewdest of sailors, who owns the show next depicted. It was announced as "A 'air—raisin' piffomance"; and certainly it was a little uncanny, though not exactly up to the standard of the pictures hung outside. These depicted a gigantic individual, apparently in the last throes of death beneath a tropical sea, and surrounded by every conceivable (and inconceivable) denizen of the deep. Sword-fish and shark, whale and octopus—all were attacking him with staggering unanimity.

Visitors to this side-show see a tank containing 500 gallons of water—positively guaranteed not to burst and nearly drown the spectators, as similar tanks have often done. The water is heated by gas overnight to a temperature of about ninety degrees, and into it are thrown six or seven good-sized pythons or rock snakes (some over twelve feet long), who protest fiercely against the whole thing. They would leave the water forth-with, were it not for the strong wire-netting on top of the tank.

Presently a man, young and scantily clad, appears at the back. He removes half the wire-netting and drops into the water among the snakes. They instantly twine themselves about his legs, his waist, his arms, and his neck; but some, more knowing than the rest, neglect him altogether, and endeavor to hurry out of the hated element.

A confederate mingles with the crowd in order to warn the submerged performer when one of the reptiles is half-way out; to help him when he is severely bitten (as he frequently is); and to render assistance when he is in danger of being strangled by a python about his throat.

The performance is one wild, whirling struggle with the writhing reptiles—sinking to the bottom from time to time with an armful of them, merely to drag them hither and thither to keep up on the excitement and give patrons value for their money. About once a fortnight, each snake takes a rest and a meal, the latter consisting of live rabbits, birds, and rats.

The baby, Thomas Sabin, whose portrait next appears, was a great blessing to his parents, who were people of no great weight, either in

Top: Underwater among the snakes.
Bottom: The biggest baby in the world.

the literal or social acceptance of the term. For years he brought them ten pounds a week, his weight increasing, but his age almost standing still. He has a nice face, but few would care to dandle him on their knee. As we see him in the photo, this phenomenal baby is just turned two years of age, and weighs nearly eight stone. The child was born in Banbury, and was in no way remarkable for some considerable time. At length, however, little Tommy began to put on flesh so rapidly, that his parents, alarmed, sent for the local doctor, who in turn summoned a specialist from London. All this, of course, created some sensation, and in due time the inevitable showman came along with tempting offers.

It is more or less well known that vigilant agents are forever scouring the universe, from Whitechapel to Central Africa, for freaks of Nature—"refined freaks," as one professional paper-tearer remarked, whatever he meant by that. The famous "dime museum" is the habitat of human freaks; and America is the home of the dime museum. You will find one or more of these interesting institutions in every considerable town from Maine to California.

The proprietor takes an empty shop or store in the principal street, rigs up a circular platform, and seats the freaks thereupon. Some waxworks or a cage of monkeys or lions are provided by way of adventitious free attractions; and perhaps there will be a "bijou theatre" at one side, in which fifteen minutes' performance is given at intervals; this latter, however, is an extra. But the freaks are the mainstay of the show. There they sit all day, beaming sympathetically on the inquisitive crowds who surge around them. There are fat ladies, Siamese twins, and skeleton men, bearded ladies and elastic-skinned people; giants and dwarfs; armless artists, and cave dwelling pigmies; girls with hair of phenomenal length; people half black and half white; and countless other monstrosities whom to see is a nightmare.

Every half-hour the official lecturer clears his raucous throat and proceeds to deliver the history of each freak, with many an impressive flourish, whilst the freak himself (or herself) glares down with conscious pride on his throng of admirers. Such is the typical dime museum.

The skeleton man, next seen, has been the round of innumerable shows in the Old and New Worlds. His wife and son are photographed with him, and are in no wise abnormal. On the other hand, freaks—particularly midgets—often marry among themselves, mainly for business reasons.

The etiquette of the side-show holds a super-abundance of clothing highly improper. Freaks must exhibit a good deal of their person *in puris*

But the freaks are the mainstay of the show. There they sit all day, beaming sympathetically on the inquisitive crowds who surge around them.

naturalibus, so as to do away with any suspicion of humbug. For the side-show cannot exist in an atmosphere of scorn and doubt; enthusiasm, energy, earnestness—these are the notes that herald success and fortune.

By no means the least curious of the American side-shows is the kiosk of the professional paper tearer, which is seen in the next illustration. The entire façade of this elaborate little structure is made wholly of paper torn into shape by the Professor himself, who boasts of using no other implements whatever than his own ten fingers. This is certainly very wonderful when one looks closely into the photograph and studies the delicate lace-work, the arch and columns and ornaments, and the flowerpots and birds within—all made of paper torn with the fingers.

But this unique artist had a somewhat ignoble end in view; as a fact, he sold a patent blacking, using his stall and his handiwork as a lure for the unwary, who were ultimately almost forced to buy.

"Miraklus Cont'nental Sensation. The Mawvel o'the Age. A wild, fiery Hafrican Elephant walkin' on the tightrope, an, a dawncin' on a row o' bottles." Thus overwhelmingly was our next sideshow announced to the expectant crowd. What the wild, fiery one did do is seen in the photograph; and it certainly is an interesting spectacle to see the enormous brute picking its way with patient care along the "bottles," which, as one may judge, are massive blocks of wood mounted on substantial planks. There is a platform at either end, and on to this the elephant steps with an unmistakable air of relief, after having accomplished the perilous passage.

There is still a mint of money in the side-show business. Tom Thumb received £150 a week, yet his presence (scarcely "services,"

Top: The Skeleton with his wife and son. Bottom: Kiosk of the Professional Paper-Tearer.

since he did nothing but strut about the platform) was worth double that sum to his proprietor.

It was the famous freak-hunter, Farini, who introduced to the London public Zazel—"a beautiful lady shot from a monstrous cannon." Zazel was paid £100 a week at the Royal Aquarium. The cannon itself, I gather, was a French patent concern; it was made of wood, printed to resemble steel. Inside there was an ingenious arrangement of powerful India-rubber springs, which acted upon the plate on which Zazel herself stood. The lady got right into the cannon and lay upon her back, her feet resting upon the plate that was to propel her. The whole thing was made wonderfully impressive. The showman called for perfect silence at so serious a moment, and the band stopped playing. A flaming torch was applied to a fuse and there was a terrific explosion—outside the cannon. Simultaneously "the beautiful woman" flew out from the muzzle, some thirty-five feet, and ultimately dropped into the net below.

There is one peculiarity common to all freaks and human curiosities. Directly they enter the show business, they assume another name—a name more or less appropriate or descriptive. Thus, midgets will be "billed" as Princess Topaz, or Little Dot, or Captain Tiny; and fat ladies as Madame Tunwate, or some inelegant but suggestive cognomen.

Top: An elephant walking on bottles. Bottom: A beautiful lady shot from a cannon.

"Knotella" the contortionist is a case in point. His real name—like the birth of Jeames—is "wropt up in a mistry." However, his photograph proves that the man can throw himself into most amazingly bizarre postures. It is an interesting fact, by the way, that photography plays a very important part in the lives of professionals of this sort. Suppose they live

in Vienna and want an engagement in London. They give their best possible show in a photographer's studio, and then send a complete set of photos to the London agents, supplementing this photographic record of their entertainment with a full written description. The agents, in turn, place the photos before the managers of the variety theatres; and thus an engagement may be definitely fixed without the performer leaving his home in a distant part of Europe.

It is difficult to say whether male or female contortionists ("benders," as they call themselves) are the more successful in assuming strange and fearful attitudes; certain it is that Knotella is run pretty close by a charming young lady whose professional name is Leonora. Clad in snaky, scaly tights, Leonora throws herself into postures that simply baffle description.

In the first photo the lady is seen in an attitude of quiet contemplation, her body hidden altogether. In the next she has formed herself into a kind of ship, with a decidedly prepossessing figurehead. This contortionist tells me she practices incessantly, and is forever trying to devise some new and startling posture which, without being in any way repulsive to an audience, will yet demonstrate the marvelous pliability of the human frame.

The pony, lamb, and dog seen in the accompanying photograph are a diminutive trio, and they go through their performance without extraneous assistance of any sort. A

Top: Knotella doing his wonderful backward bend.
Bottom: Three performers who give a show on their own account.

Top: Mr. Chambers, The Armless wonder, shaving himself with his foot. Bottom: A quiet musical evening.

highly ornamental kind of stall is provided for the pony, and, standing in this, he faces the audience. On a plush-covered canopy over his back stands the lamb, whilst the dog sits on a sort of third story above. Presently, out trots the pony for a gallop round, and as he passes the tier of canopies for the third time, the lamb skillfully leaps down on to his broad back. Then comes another round or two of this jockeying, and when the little dog thinks the public are in need of a new sensation, down he jumps on to the lamb's back, and round they all go, looking as if they really enjoyed it. In turn the riders watch their opportunity and regain their platforms, and at length the pony backs into the lower stall, to receive his share of well-merited applause.

Mr. John Chambers, the "Armless Wonder," when not sideshowing, keeps a comfortable little shop at 697A, Old Kent Road. The famous Indian Armless Boy, who created such a sensation in America, didn't have to shave, or travel on the railway by himself, or use a latch-key, or put on boots, or read the daily papers, or write letters or make himself useful in the house as becomes the father of grown-up girls. Mr. Chambers does all these things, and more.

Never shall I forget his performance before a railway booking-office. He asked for the ticket, and while the clerk was getting it, the right laceless shoe was off, followed by the stocking, revealing a wondrously white, sensitive foot, with a wedding ring on the second toe. Like lightning this foot was lifted and dipped into the low inside pocket of an Inverness cape, and next moment, simultaneously, with the production of the ticket, the exact fare was "planked" smartly down on the ledge.

There is hardly a single thing which ordinary men do with their hands that Mr. Chambers cannot do with his feet. He owes the inception of his invaluable training to his mother, who, as she saw her baby kicking on the hearth-rug—as babies will—conceived the idea of teaching him to use his feet as other children do their hands.

The result of lifelong practice in this direction is perfectly astounding. Look at Mr. Chambers shaving himself, in the first photograph. The plentiful lathering, the sure touch and sweep of the keen razor over throat and face—these must be seen to be realized. I have hinted that Mr. Chambers is useful in the house. He uses with his feet mallet and chisel, saw and hammer, as well as any expert carpenter and he points with justifiable pride to floor-cloths laid, and meat-safes, writing-desks, and other domestic articles manufactured entirely by himself.

Chambers is one of a family of six boys, and all his brothers are perfectly formed. The second photograph shows this wonderful armless man having a little musical evening at home. He is playing the cornet, whilst his eldest daughter presides at the piano. I repeat, there is virtually nothing that Mr. Chambers cannot do with his feet. Mr. Chambers also conducts his own correspondence, business and private. That he writes a very creditable "hand" will be evident from the following specimen, which he was good enough to write specially for this article.

Kert Louw, the Bushman Chief, is the next sideshow to figure in our gallery. Here is his story in brief. A great showman, who must be nameless, chanced to be exhibiting a Zulu troupe in London, when he was approached by a certain South African millionaire, financially interested in side-shows: "Why don't you bring over some pigmy earth men?" suggested the millionaire and the suggestion found favour in the sight of the showman. He dispatched an expedition, whose leader was

Written with the foot. for the Strand Magazine by John Chambers 12th Jan 1897.

Top: Specimen of Mr. Chambers's writing with his foot.
Bottom: Kert Louw— the Bushman Chief.

instructed to proceed to Cape Town, and work northwards from there in search of the pigmy races. The expedition was assisted by the Cape Government officials. Said one of these latter: "Apply to Kert Louw, the Bushman Chief of the Kalahari Desert; he will get a whole tribe for you, if you like." But Kert Louw was not in favour at the time, and so was not easy to find. As a fact, a price of £100 was put on his head by the Cape Government, to whom he was something of a scourge by reason of mail robberies and murders on a huge scale.

But promises and guarantees at length brought the chief from his hiding-place, and he agreed to produce so many "earthmen" in return for a stated number of sheep and goats, and a quantity of tobacco, powder, and Cape "smoke," or vile brandy.

Thus the expedition was successful. In fact, it not only carried off the so-called earthmen, but it also managed to smuggle out of the country Kert Louw himself; and the Bushman Chief's photo is here reproduced. Clad in unaccustomed garb, he became part of the show; and he only secured his release and return to his native wilds by a ruse quite in keeping with the cunning indicated in his villainous countenance. Having noticed that the showman-in-chief was passionately fond of diamonds, Kert Louw took him aside one day and assured him by all his gods that the knew of a diamond mine that would utterly efface the fame of Kimberly.

The showman subsequently announced to his subordinates that he was about to revisit Africa, accompanied by the Bushman, on another freak hunt. So Kert Louw was taken out to the Cape in the gorgeous state-room of a union liner, and conveyed up country in grand style— only to disappear from the showman's side and be lost in the wilderness. It was not a freak hunt nor even a mine hunt—merely a wild-goose chase.

The three photographs next reproduced of Sadi Alfarabi, and his striking "business," give an excellent notion of what the great professional equilibrists of the world can accomplish. Sadi is a Russian by birth, and every single member of his family was an acrobat, each vying with the other in devising startling feats where-with to take Europe by storm.

In the first photo, we see Sadi standing on his hands on the summit of a miniature Eiffel tower thirty feet high. A shaded oil-lamp is balanced on the back of his head; and as the point that supports him is movable, he revolves slowly on his perilous eminence. The second photo shows the equilibrist performing a peculiarly difficult feat— walking on his hands on four billiard cues, his legs perfectly perpendicular in the air. He tells me that this hurts his hands exceedingly, and is likewise a severe strain on the muscles of the back. The third feat of

the Russian performer shown here is considered the most difficult ever attempted by an equilibrist. It is really a very miracle of balancing. The chairs are in no sense trick chairs. They are not particularly light or frail, but solidity and weight are absolutely necessary to the accomplishment of such a feat. This photograph, as well as others, gives one an idea of the trouble which foreign specialty artistes take to insure that their photographs shall do them justice. There is the labour of dressing; the conveyance to the studio of all the necessary "properties"; and last, but by no means least, the actual successful accomplishment of the feat, which must be sustained until after the crucial moment of uncovering the lens. And after all this the photos may be utter failures! While I am on this subject, I may mention that on one occasion, in Buda Presth, Sadi Alfarabi, whilst posing for the chair feat, incontinently collapsed in the photographer's studio. A fresh camera was afterwards necessary, likewise a fresh photographer.

Sadi Alfarabi: A marvelous balancing act.

The Strand: The Fabulous Creation

The next "artiste" on my list had a line peculiarly his own. He was a fine, jovial fellow from one of the Southern States, and, chancing to notice at an early age that his mouth was of unusual capacity, and he smartly came to see a fortune in it. He began to practice, and was always more or less in form. He supplemented his more natural endeavors by a gutta-percha ball, which was made to expand by a screw arrangement. The result is, I submit, perfectly apparent from the photographs reproduced on this page. First the merry fellow is seen displaying his extraordinary ability in what I might term an "assisted yawn." In the next illustration he has inserted a hand, comparable only to a small leg of mutton; and in the third he has gravely placed in situ a good-sized plate. He would remain like this for hours if necessary. Observe his aspect of strenuous eagerness in the first two portraits, and contrast this with the expression of mild complacency—even benignity and broad philanthropy—in the third. He is a thorough good fellow, is that guy—good-natured, good-tempered, hilarious, making heaps of money and spending it recklessly. What a unique advertisement he would be for somebody's tooth-powder, with his expansive smile and superb set of "ivories"! These photos were forwarded to the well-known showman, Mr. E. H. Bostock, of Elgin House, Norwich, by his brother, Mr. F.C. Bostock of Boston, U.S.A., with a suggestion that possibly the "Man with the Largest Mouth in America" might prove to be a great draw in Great Britain.

A decidedly novel show is that provided by the Nahl and Bradley troupe of Living Bronze Statues. As may be judged from the heroic group reproduced, these entertainers are men of splendid physique; indeed, they have in former, and less successful, days sat as models to painters and sculptors. The show is at once simple, yet striking and unique. Messrs. Nahl and Bradley wear bronze tights, stand upon circular slabs (such as one may see in the British Museum), and then assume attitudes similar to those of the antique sculptures. Their hands and faces, even, are bronzed with a special powder. So closely do these artistes imitate their famous inanimate models, that in photographs, at any rate, it is almost impossible to distinguish between the living and the real subjects. The set of a single muscle is studied with scrupulous care; and drawings and photographs of statues to be copied are made for the guidance of these professional poseurs.

The photo reproduced here is a gladiatorial subject; and I am told that the work of posing in this way is surprisingly tiring. I can well believe it; and this probably accounts for the curious phenomenon I witnessed at the refreshment-bar of a certain variety theatre, where Achilles and a brother hero were imbibing Scotch Whisky, in a distinctly unclassical manner.

The cycling feat of Messers. Hacker and Lester, which is seen in the next illustration, is considered by competent critics to be the most difficult of its kind ever attempted; yet, the very fact of its being photographed proves that it is accomplished with comparative ease. These well-known cyclist-acrobats go through a performance which would be thought sufficiently amazing were it conducted on terra-firma instead of on a bicycle. And observe, neither acrobat wears upon his head any sort of protection.

A whole library of entertaining facts might be written about the romance of freak-hunting and curiosity-finding for the side-shows of the world. Miss Virginie Brisou, who, in place of hands and feet, had powerful lobster's claws ten inches long, was actually kidnapped by an eminent French anatomist, who only yielded up this unique "case" when the law was set in force against him. The story of Farini's costly expedition to Northern Siam in search of "Krao the Missing Link," reads like one of Jules Verne's wildest flights; the "Esau Girl" of Virginia was stolen, as a valuable piece of property, by

Right: Living bronze statues.
Below: A wonderful balancing feat.

a traveling phrenologist, who made a small fortune out of the girl before falling in an ambush prepared by her relatives.

There was once shown in New York a stalwart individual garbed as a sailor, who was billed as having "crossed the Atlantic in an open boat." He had never gone beyond the Bowery, but what matter? What distinctive mark could there possibly be about the real article? On the other hand, I have known cases in which "heroes" of this sort—genuine heroes, who may have walked across America on all fours—have been really on show one night and have left a deputy the next. This deputy takes all the vicarious glory with surprising gravity, and narrates his supposed adventures with a great show of feeling. Remember, I am speaking of America—the land of real humour, of ingenuity, of resource. When some important political or other events agitates that great country, topical sideshows spring up with amazing promptness. They may be genuine sideshows or they may not. Certainly it is far easier and cheaper to engage and "fit up" as the "Cuban Wonder" an astute individual from the New York slums, than to send costly missions to the Pearl of the Antilles in search of human curiosities.

> There was once shown in New York a stalwart individual garbed as a sailor, who was billed as having "crossed the Atlantic in an open boat." He had never gone beyond the Bowery, but what matter?

The funniest bogus side-show that ever came under my notice was the "Iron-Skulled Prince," who was on view at a small museum in St. Louis. He was just an ordinary fellow, with a preternaturally serious face. Of course, he was rigged up with feathers and blankets and things, and by his side lay a seven-pound hammer. This hammer would be taken outside at intervals by the showman and handed round for inspection among the crowd. By the way, the posters showed this "novelty" putting his head under Nasmythe hammers and hydraulic presses. "A sevin-pound 'ammer," cried the showman shrilly (he was Cockney). "E 'as bin known to 'it 'imself on the 'ead with it. Come an' see the iron-skulled man pufform 'is wunnerful feats." People came in and talked to the bogus wonder, who told a wonderful tale of imaginary adventures in Hawaii, then the topic of the day. When any of those nasty, truculent people came in who want value for their money, they generally took the "sevin-pound 'ammer" in hand with a business-like air, whereupon the showman anxiously confronted them with this placard: "All experiments and demonstrations must be conducted at the patron's own risk. The management takes no responsibility for what may happen." Could anything be funnier?

A vastly different show is that given by Miss Jeannette Desborough, who in the photographs, is seen floating angel-fashion apparently over a distant city. This lady gives a beautiful, graceful, and refined entertainment in mid-air, swinging on invisible piano wires. Sometimes she poses as the Angel of Death, chanting a dirge of a doomed city as she sweeps downwards, the rustle of her wings sounding above the sweet note of her lyre. The general effect is altogether extraordinary.

The next side-show is the tiny Strong Lady, or, to give her proper title, "The most diminutive Lady Samson in the world." This is Madame Rice, a lady from Birmingham, who, aspiring to rise from the ruck of midgets, went into the "strong" business with such success, that we see her in the photograph lifting a 56lb bar-bell at arm's length above her head with one hand. Her husband, the major, is 1 ¼ in. less in height than Tom Thumb; and this tiny pair ride about in a miniature brougham drawn by a pair of Shetland ponies. Madame Rice, I should add, was discovered and trained by the well-known showman, Mr. J. Ball.

Many of the freaks, especially in England, have a wretched time of it, receiving probably just as many shillings a week as they are "billed" (and earn their proprietor) in pounds. They live in a deplorable manner, and are regarded precisely as valuable cattle would be by a speculative farmer. Their proprietor is occasionally a "melancholy humbug," mostly to be seen in drink, and an imitation fur coat.

Among the most extraordinary side-shows imaginable are the performances of armless men. The Indian boy, Warrimeh Boseth, whose portrait is here shown, was discovered in Vancouver by the ubiquitous freak-finder. Possibly Warrimeh might not shine at a Bisley meeting, but it is no exaggeration to say that he was a wonderful shot with the bow

Top: An angel o'er a distant city.

Bottom: A tiny strong lady.

and arrow. He used to lie on his back in the forest, and send pioneer shafts here and there into spots where he knew game lurked; and as the bird or animal tried to escape from that dangerous vicinity, a second unerring arrow from the "hand-footed hunter" would bring it to the ground. Of these feats the boy thought nothing. Though unprovided by Nature with the slightest suggestion of hand or arm, hunting came as natural to him as breathing. But one day the showman appeared on the scene. The showman saw, and conquered (or rather, his presents to the aged chief did); and the Indian boy left the solitudes and came into great cities.

Top: The "hand-footed" hunter.
Bottom: Mr. Western writing his name in shots.

I saw Warrimeh in a New Orleans "museum" during the Mardi Gras Carnival. He half sat, half reclined on a couch and fixed his fine eyes on a pigeon-trap, such as they use at the Monte Carlo shooting matches. No sooner had the bird risen ten feet than Warrimeh fell back; his supple toes twanged on the bow string, and the pigeon fell heavily on to the platform amidst thunders of applause.

Frank Western, the well-known shot, is next depicted in one of his fascinating exhibitions with the repeating rifle. You will observe that Mr. Western is literally writing his name with his gun, the letters being first traced, either in tiny lighted tapers, or else in clay pipes. The expert is seated on an armoured tricycle, and it is a very pretty sight to watch him glide rapidly here and there, firing incessantly and with perfectly marvelous aim, until the last pipe-bowl, or light in the "n" is demolished or extinguished. I remember seeing Mr. Western go up into the gallery of a large London theatre, and actually shoot a clay pipe from the head of his assistant on the stage. I believe a Lee-Metford rifle and cordite ammunition were used; but so risky was the

"William Tell" feat considered that before long the management vetoed it, in spite of the famous crack shot's earnest protests.

"Unzie the Hirsute Wonder"—"Unzie, the Aboriginal Beauty from Australia" next makes his bow. He is something of a *litterateur* and minor poet. He wrote his own biography. Now, I should mention that in pretty well every side-show and dime museum there are printed biographies of the freaks to be had. These fetch from 1d. to 6d. each, and such "takings" form one of the freak's own perquisites (presents from the public are another), in addition to the standing salary. And many of these "Lives" are monumental efforts of unconscious humour.

Unzie commences his autobiography with these lofty lines, which are meant to convey a sense of profound mysticism:

> How Nature's field of knowledge doth expand,
> Yeah! Far beyond her continents of land [sic]
> Beyond the mighty ocean and the sea,
> Beyond Man's comprehensibility.
>
> *—Unzie*

Unzie, The Hirsute Wonder.

Yea, we say. Yea. It is to be feared that Unzie knows no more about metre than a gas inspector; but, after all, the sentiment's the thing. Notice the poet's name at the foot of the verse—as it might be "Milton" or "Tennyson." Unzie was born in 1869, at Tarrabandra, New South Wales. His parents were swarthy Australian aborigines, yet the prodigy himself at birth, has snow-white hair, skin like alabaster, and a few front teeth. There was consternation among the Minjery people, among whom Unzie's father Boco (!) was a powerful chief. The natives regarded the little snow-white stranger as a harbinger of evil; but local popular opinion presently veered round, and the child became an object of worship. Years passed away, and one day the phenomenon was kidnapped by an adventurous showman and was taken to Melbourne, where he commenced his public career. The great mass of snow-white hair that stands out all round the Albino's head like an open umbrella measures 6ft. in circumference. It is so fine in texture that when Unzie walks abroad he can tuck the whole "bush" into an ordinary silk hat. It is, however, impossible to run a comb through the hair, so brushes are instead used. It is trimmed every six weeks. Unzie's eyes are likewise wonderful—bluish-grey in a subdued light and purple after sunset. He can see well in the dark and enjoys perfect health.

A novel acrobatic entertainment is the next to be dealt with. Acrobats and gymnasts know full well that unless they can devise some-

Above: Mr. E. F. Harris, the American Wire King, and his wife.
Right: Portrait of Mr. Gladstone, with inscription in gold wire.
Far right: Portrait of the Queen, with inscription in gold wire.

thing startling or strikingly original, they will draw more yawns than applause from their audience. A trapeze or parallel-bar act has to be supremely excellent to pass muster in these critical days. The performers seen in the photograph, however, are both clever acrobats and expert skaters. The photo shows one of the men carrying his colleague on his back. The two will be skating furiously to and fro, in and out, on the stage, when suddenly one picks up the other in this way and skates swiftly along with him. The thing is done so quickly that, for some moments, the skate-wheels of the acrobat on top revolve noisily in the air by reason of the impetus they received but a second before.

Among the skilled craftsmen who are also side-shows, Mr. E. F. Harris, the "American Wire King," must take a high place. The first photo shows Mr. Harris's stall. All over his person and that of his wife are fastened specimens of his work—namely brooches and bangles chiefly. Two coils of the gold wire and a tray of rings are seen in the center. You walk up to the stall, write the name of your wife or sweetheart on a scrap of paper, and hand this to Mr. Harris with a request for a brooch of that particular name. The "Wire King" takes a pair of pliers and length of wire, and in a few minutes he hands you an elegant name brooch, pin and all for a shilling or two.

It is not too much to say that Mr. Harris can do in wire what others do in ink or pencil. Look at the two portraits on this page—one of Her Majesty the Queen and the other of Mr. Gladstone. These the wire-worker was good enough to prepare specially for this article. The inscription is, of course, also in gold wire, and gives an idea of what the name-brooches look like. In 1887, Mr. Harris was apprenticed to a jeweler in Providence, Rhode Island, and his particular work was the making of circular earrings of gold wire. In his spare time he took to twisting the wire into various shapes; and one day he got the idea of making a brooch in his mother's name. Friends saw this and wanted similar brooches. The young man soon threw up his situation and became what I might call a "working side-show," at the Mechanics' Fair in Boston. At this time, Mr. Harris completed (it took him three months) a beautiful model of the Brooklyn Bridge, all in gold wire; it was 4ft. long, and designed for an advertisement. Great is the ingenuity of the American people. The "Wire King" next "wrote" a letter of congratulations to Mrs. Cleveland on the election of her husband as president. This beautiful and unique epistle was, of course, wrought in gold wire, and mounted on a blue velvet cushion. It brought a graceful reply from the White House. Another of the wire-worker's ingenious advertisements was a model of the terrestrial globe, with several strands of wire twisted around it. This was to show at a glance how many thousands of miles of wire Mr. Harris had worked up with his busy pliers in brooches, rings, and bangles.

It is funny to see the "Great Human Ostrich," billed under the name of Monsieur Antoine Menier—which, however, is his real name. When I saw him he was without the warpaint—a modest Frenchman; but doubtless his business manager thought that no one with Antoine's ability should pose before the public as a civilized white man; hence

the spots, quills, and the nose-ring. But why not give the poor young man another name? Let me suggest "The Coke-Eating Yahoo."

But there can be no doubt as to Menier's right to the designation of "human ostrich." At Fell's Waxworks in Glasgow he drew crowded houses ten times a day for six weeks. Without going exhaustively into this wonderful man's history, I may mention that his daily "food" in public—the menu is usually hung outside—consists of coal—"common house coal"—candles, soot, broken glass, brass, dust saturated with paraffin, needles, wood, paper, and bricks; a choice assortment of these appalling comestibles being washed down with a measure of train-oil, ink, and methylated spirit. Periodically, the unfortunate "ostrich" has to retire from business for weeks, presumably to give his poor outraged stomach a rest. Lest anyone would doubt the genuineness of the performance, atrocious though it may be, I hasten to say that I witnessed it myself several times, and assisted in the weighing of the coke and other dainties.

There are an extraordinary number of animal monstrosities scattered among the side-shows of the world—the double-mouthed calf, the elephant-skinned horse, the three-legged cow, and such like. There is, however, something more or less repellent about these, and so they have not found a place in these articles. But the long-maned and tailed horse, whose photo is here reproduced, is in no way disagreeable. The animal was shown at Fell's Waxworks, Trongatte, Glasgow. The length of the mane is nine feet nine inches; foretop, eight feet, nine inches, and the tail twelve feet eight. It was bred at Marion, Oregon, and was owned by Messers. C.H. and H.W. Eaton. This horse recalls Farmer Broadhurst, who was born at Congleton, near Macclesfield, and had a beard seven feet long. When the worthy farmer took his walks abroad, the beard was packed away beneath his waistcoat.

One man will try for years to devise new dances—on his legs. Another suddenly conceives of the idea of making a pair of boots for his hands and dancing on them. The accompanying photograph shows Cinatus, the upside-down dancer, whose performance is the queerest imaginable. The

Top: Menier, the Human Ostrich.
Middle: A champion mane and tale.
Bottom: An upside-down dance.

power of his arms must be great, for his upside-down "step" is astonishingly light and nimble. There is nothing like a jig by Cenatus to "bring down the house," in managerial phrase. The applause, as the dancer bangs his booted hand on the boards for the last triumphant "step," is both spontaneous, vigorous, and sustained.

The next photograph was kindly sent to me from Hamburg by Carl Hagenbeck, the renowned wild-beast importer, whose stock is somewhat bigger than our own zoo. It will be noticed, by the way, that the whole world has been searched for these photographs of these articles.

The snake-charmer depicted is an Indian girl—Saidor A. Isoha; curious that nine snake charmers out of ten should be women. At one time, Saidor used to have a lot of cobras, but she gave up this species on seeing a man die a horrible death after a cobra-bite. She used to catch her own cobras, teasing them with a bit of cloth until they bit savagely at it, and then snatching it away, breaking the reptiles' teeth. The lady did big business by organizing public battles between a cobra and a mongoose. This was a little costly, however, for the cobra was always killed.

Saidor now has six Indian pythons, three boa-constrictors, and three African pythons, all between eight feet and twelve feet long. She has a real affection for her snakes, and they for her. One large python will form himself into a living turban about her head.

The entertainer that figures in the next illustration is one of the Phoite Pinaud Troupe of eccentric performers. This kind of show is mostly given by Continental artistes who rely mainly on the outlandishness of their attire and "properties." The entertainment usually consists of music, singing, and perhaps dancing, all of which must be wildly fantastic. Notice the colossal instrument of the player, in the photo. It probably has the strident note of a penny tin-whistle, alterable at will to that of a funereal bassoon.

Top: Saidor, Indian Snake Charmer.
Bottom: A tender air on the big bassoon.

Nobel, the ventriloquist and his lay figures.

The accompanying reproduction shows M. Nobel, the ventriloquist, in his highly diverting and original performance. M. Nobel has so ingeniously arranged the dummy figures that the old woman appears to be supporting him, as well as a comic French man of the criminal-beggar type. The illusion is marvelously complete. The old woman hobbles laboriously about the stage, beneath her heavy burden, singing a plaintive song in a harsh, cracked, and quavering voice. Next, M. Nobel himself sings in his natural voice, whilst the Frenchman on his back leers and nods approvingly.

To all intents and purposes there are here distinct persons present, and their voices, motions, and gestures are wholly dissimilar. M. Nobel tells me that he was formerly a telegraph clerk in the employ of the Danish Government in Copenhagen. He is very proud of having invented the whole of his performance, and having made the figures and their mechanism.

Now and again one comes across a freak in a side-show who aspires to rise above the ruck of his or her fellows and strike out a new line. Such a one is the astute fat lady seen in the next photo. She lays in a little piece of her own composition called "The Old Maid and the Baby," and the accompanying photograph is designed to recall the title of that little farce. Certainly the idea is vastly funny. The little old maid is primly got up in poke bonnet and shawl, disdainful of mien and sour in expression; while the ponderous "baby" (thirty-seven and one-half stone) cleverly assumes a certain infantile insouciance and a ridiculous toy horse. The dialogue may not scintillate with epigram and wit, but no one can deny the humor of the "situations."

(My grateful acknowledgements are due to the following well-known entertainment caterers, who have kindly lent photographs and other material; Messrs. E. H. and F. Bostock; Mr. Chas. Reynolds of Liverpool; Mr. C. C. Fell, of Trongate, Glasgow; Mr. H. Crouch, of Argyle Street, Glasgow; and Mr. J. Ball, of the Agricultural Hall.)

The old maid and the baby.

Delicious Delilah.

Eye Candy

"I may not know art, but I know what I like," wasn't inspired by the girl shows, but I can only think of them when I hear the line, that and the universal admiration of the female form. Now, for those of you who think you know from girl shows because you've been to a strip joint, time to get with the program. On the midways there were motordromes and then there were motordromes. There were girl shows and then there were girl shows. And just because you were female didn't mean you could make the cut in them all. There were revues (where burlesque met Broadway under canvas for the likes of rubes like you and me) and there were kootch shows (where taking your clothes off would be the first part of the act); there were Sunday school spots (where a revue might be the only girl show you got) and there were spots that were wide open (where if the kootch shows didn't "serve lunch," then it wasn't hardly a show).

Sylvia Cassidy, a.k.a. Delilah, the Girl from the Pearl, came into the high end of the business—the revues—honestly, via her parents who ran some fair-sized (no pun intended) shows in their day. And Cassidy was a feature attraction, a headliner, a fact she's as no-nonsense about as she is about the business itself.

The business, depending on how you choose to view its various forms, can be seen to be as old as history itself or simply as old as traveling amusements, at least the carnival end of it. Most historians wouldn't kick, though, if you traced its carnival incarnation to the World's Fair of 1893, the Columbian Exposition, its "White City" (as they called its gleaming palaces of plaster, straw and horsehair or "staff"), and, more importantly, its Midway Plaisance. On that midway were the infant incarnations of all that became true carnival: the rides of course, some games, but especially the shows. And those shows

Femme fatale with feathery fans.

115

represented the archetypes of all that followed: the menageries, the thrills, the exotics.

The exotics. Now that's how to make the female display educational. Tricked out in the theatrical garb of assorted nations, the Streets of Cairo, the Streets of Paris, the Streets of Any Damn Exotic Place You'd Care to Name (as long as it wasn't your home town) became the showmen's way to insinuate onto the midway every form of belly dancing and disrobement ever imagined by the likes of humanity. In 1893, it imagined Little Egypt who, perhaps, was not even Egyptian. Like it mattered. She was, after all, bumping and grinding in the name of Egyptological education, or some such foolishness.

Education, of course, is simply the satisfaction of curiosity. And satisfaction of curiosity (however lurid, however innocent) has always been the stock in trade of the girl shows. And if the entertainment quotient is a bit heavier in the equation than some of the more prudish rubes would like, you know you can't please everybody. Besides, if you didn't want the education, you didn't have to part with your money.

S&A: Tell me something about your mother and father and their origins with the business. I know that's how you got your start on the shows.

SC: My mother, Roxanne, was a supervisor for twenty-one schools in music and English in West Virginia, and she answered an ad during the summer to travel with an all-girl band. She was twenty-eight, not much

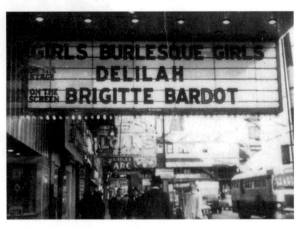

What a lip-licking lineup!

older. She and a girlfriend that played saxophone answered the ad, which turned out to be a carnival—which was pretty upsetting to them—but she went ahead and stayed. Later, she met my father and they got married.

S&A: You used to hear a lot about people in the show business answering ads that they thought were going to be something other than what they turned out to be.

SC: In those days I think it was more prevalent.

S&A: Did your mother meet your father on the shows?

SC: Ron Mason she met in a nightclub; he was my stepfather. She met my real father on the carnival talking the front of the girl show she was working. They split up when I was five. Years later, she met my stepfather. I was nine when she met him.

S&A: You worked the big revues in the carnivals. Can you talk about the different types of shows that would have been classified as girl shows?

SC: Well, they had a black show—years ago they used to call them jig shows—of course, we don't do that anymore. We call them black shows or black revues. Essentially, they were all revue-type shows with singers and dancers on them. Then there were revues like my mother and father ran. Then there were kootch shows, which had just strip acts. There was something called a "single-o" which had one girl working it and, of course, she took everything off.

S&A: You don't normally hear much about single-o girl shows.

SC: Well, naturally, they didn't go over as well. But there were some spots where they had them.

S&A: What would a typical revue look like? How would it be framed?

SC: On a semi trailer. There would be steps leading up onto a platform where wings would fold out to make a front. Then a huge tent set up in the back with seating for a couple hundred and then a stage set up in the back. There was walk-over fronts and then there was walk-around fronts.

Saddle up, cowpoke— it's going to be a bumpy ride.

Eye Candy

S&A: "Walk-around?"

SC: Those you never came over the bally or over the front of the semi. You just walked around the side. It depended on whether you had a revue or a kootch show. Revues were more designed for families. Women attended them more. They were always, always walk over because they didn't mind people seeing them walk over into the door. They would be on display because they were at a height. Kootch shows, you usually went around the side because they were designated for men so they could kind of sneak in.

S&A: What was your average night like on the show?

SC: It depends on what spot you were playing. It could be anywhere from five to six shows a day to twenty shows a day. I once did twenty-two shows in a day. The fair would start at 9 o'clock sometimes and go 'til like 1 o'clock in the morning. And they would cut the shows to make them shorter.

S&A: Were they running them back to back?

SC: Yeah.

S&A: How would they gather a tip? In a 10-in-1 they would bally.

SC: They also did. They had bally girls; that's all they did. They just worked the bally. Then the chorus line ballied also and sometimes your principals ballied. But that depended on the show operator also. For example, on Royal American, I never ballied. But on my mother's show I did. It was like the finale of the bally when they turned the tip. "There's a ticket box there, there's a ticket box here. Showtime in five minutes. If you're ready to go, we're ready to show." Then music and we kind of hoogy-boogied it off.

S&A: Could you describe an average day?

SC: We would get up whatever time they gave the call. That could be at 10 or 9. You had to be ready forty-five minutes to an hour ahead of time. You'd put your makeup on in the dressing rooms made up of smaller semi trailers. On one wall would be a folding shelf where you would set up your cosmetics.

S&A: I suppose it was segregated, men and women.

SC: Yeah. On Royal [American] they had one strictly for the chorus line. Then the principals would have another. If there were male acts, they were in with the producer. So sometimes there were actually three. The male acts were singers, a comedian. There were bands. The bands would be two or three people. Organ, drums and usually a horn.

S&A: How would the typical show run?

SC: There are usually three chorus numbers—one at the beginning, one at the middle and one at the end. And usually they introduced a particular solo act, whether that be a comedian or a singer. A comedian would come later in the show. If there was a singer, they would come first or a magic act.

S&A: Was there an emcee introducing the acts?

SC: All along. My father did it. My dad didn't do the front. My mom did; she was quite good at it.

S&A: Isn't it unusual for a lady to be talking the front of the show?

SC: Yeah, though there has been others. Normally it would be male. My mom was very good, like I said.

S&A: You were the principal in a number of shows. One of them was a wedding show, wasn't it?

SC: Well, the whole show was themed around brides, with the music and the costumes and all. But the shows would change every year. The year following it was the Jesse James Show, a western show. Those were the two I'm familiar with because those are the ones that I worked. The choreography was done for that show and it stayed the same for the whole year. We'd have a week's rehearsal before the show ever opened in St. Louis. We would start early in the morning and work until late at night. Each show would run about a half-hour.

Delilah emerges from her clam.

S&A: What were the differences between your parents' show and the ones on Royal American?

SC: Royal carried a larger crew of people. They carried more chorus line, where principals would double in my mom's show. Like I, for example, also worked the chorus line and I was a principal act. The band stayed the same, two to three pieces. The stage crew of seven people was down to like two people.

S&A: What were some of the show themes your parents had?

SC: They weren't as thematic as Royal was. They would change the acts.

It wasn't a basic theme per se. Royal was the only one that ever focused itself around a particular theme. My parents had more of a variety show.

S&A: What were you doing when you first started in the shows?

SC: I was a bally girl. I wasn't in the show. They said I was in the show, but I was a bally girl. Me and a girlfriend of mine on Olson Shows, we were bally girls for Lash LaRue. It wasn't a girl show; it was a western.

S&A: So you were just the draw?

SC: Yeah. We wore short skirts with fringe on it and a white blouse with fringe on it.

S&A: What would you do on stage?

SC: Nothing. We stood there. They'd put on a little music and I would shimmy a little bit. Not a lot of work. So I did bally with this other girl for him for a season. That was my first job. I was also a bally girl for my mom and then I broke into the chorus line. Then I became a principal.

S&A: How old were you when you started as a principal?

SC: You mean when I started dancing? Stripping? Sixteen.

S&A: That seems pretty young.

SC: Well, yeah. It was normally later. [Most girls] weren't raised in that atmosphere.

Birds of a feather flock together.

S&A: When you first became a principal, what was your show? I know you were billed as Delilah during most of your career in the shows. Were you billed as Delilah then?

SC: Yes. That was the original stage name I got. Actually, I really started with "Mary Krismas," but that didn't last too long. I think the first act was the oyster shell.

S&A: How was that act choreographed?

SC: Well, it was a prop; they call anything like that a prop. My stepfather had built it. It was a very large oyster shell and I lay down in it and there was a smoke machine and a bubble machine that came out with it. When the spotlight hit it, the music started and the shell would open, and I would put a hand out and kind of move it around, hopefully pretty gracefully. I had wonderful hand movements. And then a leg would come out and then another leg, and then I would get out. Then I would dance, not really too much of an act. But then at the end I went back into my shell and closed it. They had a girl in a champagne glass and she worked out of a Plexiglas champagne class. She took a bath in it. I was around then.

S&A: Did you start working the burlesque clubs as soon as you became a principal?

SC: No, I was eighteen when I started working in the clubs. Before that, I was still in school.

S&A: How long were you with your parents' show?

SC: With the exception of three years, I was always with their shows. They were with a carnival that is no longer in existence, Century 21. They were with them a long time. I spent two years with Royal and one year with James E. Strates. Leon Miller was the producer of the show on Royal American and a fella named Jack Norman and his wife Betty on Strates. It was called "Broadway to Hollywood," the revue show on Strates. That show was more like my mom's, but I think that my mom's was nicer. The same deal. Royal, the route they played were huge spots, so their grosses, of course, were huger and their crew was larger.

S&A: On Royal and Strates, you were the principal. Was that all you did?

SC: Yeah, that was it. I was the star. That was my job.

S&A: I guess it was tougher and more intense working with Mom and Dad.

SC: No. They had me doing other stuff, but I did it willingly. In those other shows, no. That's all I did.

S&A: How long did your parents stay with the girl shows after you left?

SC: Oh, jeez. A lot of years. They did girl shows and they bought a couple of grind shows like a Spidora show.

S&A: So you started working the clubs when you were eighteen. What was the biggest difference between working those shows and working the carnival?

SC: Three shows a night as opposed to ten, twelve, or fifteen, and the clubs normally were one strip after another. So it wasn't like revues where you had chorus lines, etc., except when we traveled with Mamie VanDoren in "This Was Burlesque," and she was the star of the show. She was doing a semi-strip. It was over in New York in a theatre called the Hillside Theatre. Then we went into a club called the Venus in Baltimore. Then we played another one in Columbus, Ohio. I forget the name of it. That was the only spots we played with that particular revue. It wasn't a theme show; there was a belly dancer in the show and I had a girlfriend that did a strip. There was a burlesque comedian and a straight man. A comedy act (they do skits). There was a singer in the show and there was me. I was doing the fans.

S&A: Is that the act you were doing at a lot of the clubs that you played?

SC: Yeah. That or the oyster shell.

S&A: What were the other acts you were doing other than the oyster shell and the fans when you were on the road?

SC: When I was on Royal, they choreographed what I did to fit the theme of the show. It would be a basic strip; the moves and all were choreographed by the producer who was Leon Miller.

S&A: A basic strip as opposed to . . .

SC: One with a prop.

S&A: Getting back to your mother, she worked up a half man/half woman act on which I've seen others do a variation. Was that an act she had from her earliest days?

SC: As far as I know, yes. She always had it. There would be a park bench and a street light. It would start off on a park bench, and they would appear as though they were smooching, kissing and rubbing shoulders and they would get up and dance. Then they would sit back down on the park bench and he would proceed to make strong advances to the female side and she finally surrendered. Then black out.

S&A: I know you did some shows overseas.

SC: I was twenty-two and I went to Puerto Rico and Dutch Guyana-Surinam. That was contracted through an AGVA (American Guild of Variety Artists) agent, which I was a member of for I don't know how long. I was over there for two weeks, but I ended up staying eight. I

DELILAH
In "The Birth Of A Pearl"

A gem of a show.

was doing fans. That show was a dinner theatre, technically.

S&A: How long were you in the business before you quit doing the shows?

SC: It didn't quite happen that way. I got married to a fella that had carnival games and he really didn't want me in that business. He wanted me in his business. I was twenty-five at the time.

S&A: And now you're operating guessers. That seems like it's a pretty far cry from the girl shows, even if it is on the midway.

SC: It's still the same thing.

S&A: How so?

SC: You're still entertaining.

When my associate editor, Kathleen, and I caught up to Cassidy at her guesser concession at the York Fair, she was calling to the crowd over her headset, looking for all the world like a savvy phone operator on her day out. More marks walked by, of course, than stopped, but more than enough stopped to keep her busy cracking wise about this old bird and that fat guy. Always she soft-peddled her jibes to keep it friendly. "Take your glasses off," she told every one of them who tried to beat her behind their Foster Grants and Ray Bans. After she'd eye each one like a guy would eye up a dame on the runway, she'd scribble on a tiny pad whatever they picked as their poison: their age or their weight. She'd hold the pad up, her handwritten guess turned to someone else in the crowd, and ask the mark to call out the gross tonnage or the antiquity, whichever had been chosen. She'd ask for the figure to be confirmed by a stranger, and it had to be close, close enough to ensure she'd won the duel. When once Cassidy had been too far off on a man's age, the mark looking at the number on the pad called out to the winner, "You don't want to know what she wrote, man!" For the life of me, I couldn't tell from the look on Cassidy's face at that moment whether she'd truly misjudged or if this was just more entertaining.

The many moods of LuVerne.

SOMETHING
For Everyone

So you're living in the latter half of the 19th century, maybe the first half of the 20th, and the show comes to town. And there you are in the freak show, and the lecturer starts up with what all your friends and neighbors have already primed you to expect. "Now, ladies and gentlemen, this next act is not advertised on the front of the show. We charge an extra admission to see this amazing attraction and we make no apologies for that. We think you'll agree that it's worth every penny once you're on the inside."

Or so it might have gone for any blow-off attraction from a pickled punk to a human pincushion. The real draw, though, was always a half-and-half, what your more erudite fairgoer would term a hermaphrodite, and what your average showman would consider the biggest drawing gaff attraction to ever work a midway. The vast majority of the half-and-halfs, you see, were down-home American males. The only thing female about them was their presentation . . . well, half their presentation. There's really no way except by gaff to account for the variety of half-and-halfs: one side female, the other male; top half female, bottom half male; top half female, both sexes down below. Mother nature, of course, can play many tricks, but most of the wild male-female combos billed as half-and-halfs were simply fairy tales at the biological level. There might have been some true hermaphrodites—where the male and female sex organs were both present below the waist—but all the other sexual deviations pitched to the rubes, though, were phony as $3 bills.

Sexual bizarrity is always one of the biggest draws. More than one showman has told me that a good half-and-half could

Swarzette was also known as James Muldoon.

125

carry an entire show, earning in excess of what was taken in on the front. What's amazing then, I suppose, is not that they were so wildly fascinating to the midway crowds but that even doctors who inspected them came away fooled. (More than one showman also has told me about actual inspections—without other witnesses of course—of half-and-halfs by trained medical professionals who came away attesting to the biological reality of at least some of the purported hermaphrodites.) I guess we really were a more naive people in the bad old days. And I guess we'd be too sophisticated to be fooled, shocked or amazed by such a show now. And I guess water runs uphill and pigs fly south for the winter.

JULEE—JULIANE
Nature's Phenomena

The Classical Greek mind had a particular interest in speculating about it, traces of it are found in Chinese mythology and it has been stated that primitive man was a man-woman.

Since I have been on exhibition, appearing before the leading medical universities in the Country and abroad, as well as appearing before the public, there has been one question that seems to be in the minds of everyone: whether or not I am a Hermaphrodite.

The male portion of my body, my double voice, and the beard, are all birthmarks and I do not possess hermaphrodite characteristics.

The most feminine of women have a growth of colorless hair corresponding to the male beard, and in some cases very pronounced.

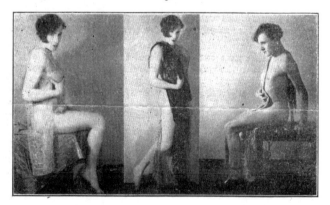

JULEE -- JULIANE

NATURES PHENOMENA

Julee—Juliane has all the bases covered.

To begin my story, dear friends, we must go back to the first inhabitants of this world, and they were the protozoa. Zoa is the Greek word for animals, and protos means first.

All subsequent creatures developed from these ancestors of animal life on this globe. Every animal goes through a series of changes of process of evolution before arriving at maturity. Regardless of whether it is Animal or Man, it always begins as a one-celled animal. We all go back to the beginning of life.

Hermaphrodite Characteristics are common in plant and animal life. We take another step up the evolutionary ladder and find the earthworm. Each worm has the organs of the two sexes properly developed. In this instance we have true hermaphroditism.

There are some human beings who possess hermaphrodite characteristics; this is no new discovery, in fact, very ancient.

Women with a more or less definite masculine cast of figure, manner or voice are commonplace, as is the opposite phenomenon.

In regards to the other so-called Half man-Half woman, as there are several others on exhibition, it is a known fact that I have been proclaimed nature's nearest complete union of male and female in one body.

LU VERNE
Not a Deformity, but Purely an Entertainment Feature

Dear Friend:

Now that you have witnessed the performance of my unusual act, I am sure that you will have many questions in mind. The photographs will answer many of them as well as giving you the opportunity of studying this presentation more intimately. I am now twenty-four years of age and have been on exhibition almost continuously for the past six years. In private life my interests are almost exclusively literary and I spend much of my time reading. My preference being for

Lu Verne

Not a Deformity, but Purely an Entertainment Feature.

biographies and autobiographies. I am often asked if I am married. The answer to which is that I am not, and never expect to be; although I have many good friends and well-wishers among both sexes. May I number you among them?

Most Sincerely,
LU VERNE.

Purely entertaining indeed.

Bill Durks: Here's looking at you, kid.

In the Kingdom of the Blind

I'd like to say that I interviewed him, the king of the three-eyed men, arguably one of the most amazing sideshow performers of this century. Of course, I couldn't: Bill Durks passed away years ago. Never one willing to let a subject die (sorry), I was delighted when a showman tipped me off to Durks's surviving stepdaughter and her husband, Dorothy and Joe Hershey. In fact, they're a pretty amazing pair themselves: They once raised rats as pets and for snake food, Joe's been in circus most of his life (at least until the past few years), and did I tell you he's completely blind? Not just legally, mind you. Stone blind. Can't-see-your-hand-in-front-of-his-face blind. But you couldn't tell that. In fact, in order to show you what he can do, he only need show you the pictures of him helping the guy he'd hired to erect the 100+ foot short-wave antennae in the back yard. The tower erector was afraid to climb to the top to finish the job, so Joe went up and did it himself. "I figured," he told me, "it wasn't any different from putting up a circus tent."

Others, of course, knew Bill Durks too. In his days with the shows, most notably with Strates, probably no one knew Durks better than Melvin Burkhart, anatomical wonder and inventor of the Human Blockhead act. (See Melvin Burkhart's interview on page 144.) Their friendship was well known in the business and is even chronicled in Arthur Lewis's Carnival. (Lewis's stories of the pair are pure humbug, unfortunately; he has the actual number of eyes all wrong for Durks, and he has Burkhart spelling out his name by curling the shape of each letter with his tongue, an impossibility Burkhart readily admits. It's as though Durks and Burkhart weren't amazing and entertaining enough as they really were.) And then there's Ward Hall,

Bill Durks, Santa, and Sealo make like the three Wise Men.

grand old showman himself, who tried for years to lure Durks from the Strates sideshow, only to succeed for a mere season.

So let's reminisce with Hall, Burkhart, and the Hersheys, as close as you'll get to one of yesteryear's greatest midway attractions: The Man With Three Eyes.

Ward Hall

S&A: You knew Bill Durks for a long time, but I believe he only worked for you and your partner, Chris Christ, for one season.

WH: That's right. One season. I think he may have worked with us once or twice in the winter at the Florida State Fair. He and Melvin Burkhart worked for us when they were in their off-season. That would have been back in the days when Royal American still had the fair but after they had lost the downtown fairgrounds. He worked for us, I think, possibly one or two other times, but we were only able to lure him away for one whole season, a feat I never was able to accomplish with Melvin. Melvin was with (Slim) Kelly-(Whitey) Sutton for thirty-one years, and he worked for us numerous times but only when that show was closed. And I think Durks was there most of his career, too. I believe he came from a farm near Jasper, Alabama, and attended the county fair and they—it seems to me like a woman and a man—they had him in a sideshow after that.

S&A: He just came onto the midway and they picked him up from there?

WH: Yeah. He came on the midway, they saw him and put him on the show. I have done the same thing. They will come and see the show and you will get some of the other attractions to start talking to them and find out if they are interested.

Bill Durks and a man's best friend.

S&A: How did you manage to lure him away from Kelly and Sutton?

WH: Oh, I think I paid him more money. Well, I wasn't the first to do that sort of thing. Harry Lewiston and Ray Marsh Brydon, for example, were arch enemies and competitors and they used to do that. Sometimes an act would change shows two, three times in a season because the competitor would offer more money. From Ray over to Harry and pretty soon some emissary from Brydon would come over and lure them back over and they tell me this used to happen with regularity in Coney Island between Rosen and

Sindel who had the sideshows directly across the street from one another. They were brothers-in-law and they hated each other and were famous for doing those things. Bobby Reynolds is famous for telling those stories. "How much you getting kid?" "He's paying me forty cents an hour." "I'll pay you fifty cents an hour." A dime at a time!

S&A: So you lured him away. Was he married at this point?

WH: No, she had died already. I think that was one reason he might have been willing to leave the other show, too, because it wasn't that long after and everywhere he looked, it reminded him of her. So anyway, we made the jump upcountry from Gibsonton, Florida, that year. I would think it was with the Million Dollar Midway. I expect we opened in Pennsylvania, and Bill came over from where he was living at this time. When we got in we spotted things, and all of a sudden,

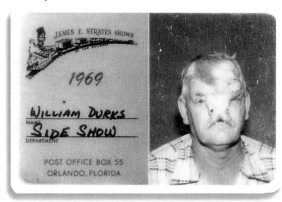

Chris notes that Bill is out there helping put up. So he went out and he called him to one side and he said, "Bill, you know you don't have to help set up and tear down. That's not a part of the deal. After all, you're the star of the show." Bill said, "Oh, Chris, I love to work and I've worked hard all my life and I like to do it." Chris said, "Well if you want to do it, we could certainly use the help. I'll pay you extra." So we had a pickled punk show, and he became the man in charge of putting up and taking down the pickled punk show, in charge of that crew, and did a wonderful job, so he got another pay for that. It was good for him and it was good for us. I think, in my opinion, that Bill would have stayed with us, but he didn't have the sociability around us that he had on Kelly's show. That was true not only of Bill Durks but at another time with Sealo. Sealo was only with me for another year. I don't remember if Bill played cards, but Sealo was an avid card player and around Pete Kortez's show there was always a card game going on, and around our show I don't guess anyone played cards. And with Bill, on the days when the show wasn't open, he and Melvin Burkhart used to go places and do things. That was missing with us because everybody had their own thing to do. But when Bill was with us, he wasn't having as much fun as he used to have and I understand that. Most fairs close on Sunday and open again on Friday, so you have one day to make the jump and three days that they really didn't have much to do.

S&A: What was his act like? Did he lecture at all or was there someone else lecturing on him?

In the Kingdom of the Blind

WH: Oh yeah, he would lecture on himself and he had some makeup and an eye pencil and some rouge and he would make up that indentation to make the third eye. "The man with two noses and three Eyes." In those days we tried to keep it at an hour. We didn't use but one act at a time. That meant Bill would be on stage maybe five minutes out of an hour. Of course we had others on the show too. We would have had Patricia Zurm—"Lady Patricia"—swallowing swords. I think when he was there it might have been the year we had the Reed Sisters—Doreen and Sandy.

S&A: I guess Sandy wasn't swallowing swords if you had Lady Patricia.

WH: No, she wasn't doing that then. I think she learned on the Sutton show. I wouldn't swear on that. We would have had Bill Cole, the quarter man, Emmett the Turtle Man would have been there. I think Bill Fich was doing pincushion and probably Altoria the tattooed lady. Our fat man very likely would have been Paul Fish; it was before Bruce Snowdon but it was after Tiny Hicks. We may have had, I think, Cliff and Mamie King, the two dwarves, Freddy Lulling doing blockhead and eating fire, Bobo, for the rubber man; if I was on the show, I was probably doing magic and juggling.

S&A: The picture I'm getting is a pretty lonely guy after his wife died.

WH: Well, he just didn't have anybody to run around with there. He didn't have a companion. He made friends with everybody on the show. He just didn't have somebody to hang out with, like I mentioned Sealo, too. There was little for those guys to do in their off time. There was always conversations and things, but that wasn't the point; it was the activity that he missed.

Melvin Burkhart

S&A: What was Bill Durks like when you met him?

MB: He was very shy and disturbed. When I say disturbed, I mean he would easily get upset by people because he wasn't used to being around people. He was put into shows and exploited, but there was nobody to take care of him and make a friend of him. He was so wild-looking that most people would just shy away from him. When he came over to our show on Strates, he was very shy, and they asked me would I let him ride over with me when they closed the show down and go to the next town. I was a good friend of the bosses on the show. I was a mediator, you might say, between the acts and the office.

S&A: How many years had Bill been in the business when you met him?

MB: Not very long. He didn't know how to do an act or anything. I taught him how to get up there. First of all, he would just get up there and look around and you would have to talk on him: "Ladies and gentlemen, this is William Durks, born in the backwoods of Alabama . . ." and make up a story on him.

S&A: Do you know who discovered Bill Durks? And how old was he when he got into the business?

MB: He came from a backwoods family and they were ashamed of him. They were from Mississippi or Alabama, some place like that. You could never get it out of him real well. When company would come they would put him back in a closet and he would have to stay right there. They wouldn't allow him to come out when company was there. They wouldn't take him anywhere—to church, the stores, or anything. They were ignorant people, and they were ashamed of the way he looked and his effect on other people. Somebody told them it was a sin they were being punished for by having a child who looked like that. I guess they wanted to hide him. So some guy came along one day and offered them money to take him along with him and put him on a show. And he sent money back to them and then his parents died or something. I think he was only about 37 when I met him. He didn't know hardly anything about show business. I got him to the point where he would do a spiel about his cards. I'd introduce him and tell them about him. I told Bill he could sell more cards if he said something about himself too. I used to help him sell the cards at first. Soon he got to be pretty good when he saw all of that money come in.

Bill and Mildred Durks.

S&A: Did he ever talk about what he had done before he got into the business?

MB: He was a handyman on a farm, and they kept hiding him too! I think they were scared he would scare the livestock or something. He did a lot of handyman kind of stuff. I never met any of his folks. We had one guy come in one day who said he was his brother-in-law, but

I never had a chance to meet him. No one else ever came up to see him. He was a lost soul, but one of the nicest guys you would want to meet. He didn't have any airs about him. He would say, "I know I'm ignorant," but he wasn't stupid. He could handle his money.

S&A: I suppose he was pretty shy about a lot of things.

MB: Oh yeah. He didn't go into restaurants, you see, so he would want me to go in and get him a sandwich. On many occasions, we couldn't get the show up in time, so we'd go to the motel and I'd get him a room there. Then he would ask me to bring him something to eat. Finally I

They're magic men.

said, "Look you've got to get out of that. Go right in there with me. You're going to walk in there and sit down and pay your money and if anybody does anything and makes a face, you make a face right back at them." He said, "Oh, I wouldn't do that." (He was very slow in his speech.) But pretty soon he got to the point where people would smile at him and he would smile back. Many of them, of course, would be shocked. I told him, "People are going to look at you. You're making your living that way. Understand that. Learn to live with it and don't pay any attention to it. If you see something funny and you look at it, you're not going to worry about it are you?" "No." I said, "If anybody sees you and thinks you look different, they're going to look at you." In about two or three months' time, I had him going into restaurants with me and going into hotels and theaters and so forth. It worked out fine. In fact, I kind of looked after him up until the time he died.

S&A: Do you remember when Bill started lecturing on himself in his act?

MB: I don't remember the first time, but I do remember telling him, "Bill, we are selling very few pictures. If you could just go out there and pass out a few of them, you could sell at this end and I could sell at that end." I got him to push a few then. People would come from my end to go and buy pictures from him!

S&A: As shy as he was, it seems odd he would have pitchcards. Was that his idea?

MB: No, it was the bosses'. He had worked before at this one place that had taken all of the money he had made. The bosses at Strates were doing a lot for him that they wouldn't do ordinarily for other acts, like arranging for everything for him, things he didn't know about or couldn't understand. I took over after we became friends.

S&A: I suppose you were pretty friendly with his wife, Mildred, too. How did they meet?

MB: That came about when we played a trick on him. We had Mildred, an alligator-skinned girl, on the show and they had taken an instant dislike to each other for some reason or the other. Finally I said to her, "Funny thing of it is, Mildred, you and Bill are always spiking each other and he really likes you." "Well he don't act like it." "Well," I said, "He's a little shy and backward with the way he looks, kind of like the way you are because of your skin. You keep it all covered up." Then I went down to him and I said, "You know the alligator-skin girl thought since you were a little shy

Alligator Skin Girl, Mildred Durks.

around her and didn't speak to her, that you didn't like her." "Oh, I didn't say that I didn't like her." Pretty soon they got to sitting down and eating together, and I would take them with me on the runs from one town to the other. One day they said, "We're thinking of getting married." Well, it wasn't anything I hadn't suggested, you know, the World's Strangest Married Couple: the two-faced man and the alligator-skinned woman. So then they got married. I still kind of took care of them by getting them through the runs.

S&A: So you were there when she died, weren't you?

MB: Yeah. She had asthma one night—she was very bad—and she said, "I think I have to go over to the hospital and get a shot." I ran her over to the hospital and took her to the emergency room. She was wheezing and they took her into a little cubicle and laid her down. They said they couldn't get to her right away because they had some emergency. So Bill and I went to sit down, and pretty soon we saw a doctor walk out into the cubicle where she was at. And he came out with a strange look on his face. I thought he was surprised to see the alliga-

In the Kingdom of the Blind

tor skin. And he started talking to the nurse who pointed to us. He came over and said, "I'm afraid I have bad news for you. She's passed away." At first I thought he had said "passed out." And I said, "Can't you bring her to?" He said, "I'm afraid not. It would be a miracle if we could. She's dead." He said that she had a heart attack. She died right there in the hospital. When Mildred died, he didn't have one suit to his name. He only had jackets and shirts and things like that. We went down to the Salvation Army and for $15 we got a nice serge blue suit and I had to cut off the sleeves and sew the hem for him. He had that suit until he died.

S&A: I heard he took Mildred's death pretty hard.

MB: Yes, he did. She was the only person who had ever been really nice with him. He went to live with her daughter after Mildred died.

S&A: There's a story about Bill Durks where, supposedly, some guy comes up to Durks in a grocery store and gives Durks a hard time about him having his hat pulled down over his face. Is there any truth to that story?

MB: It happened a couple of times. A woman came up to him one time and he had his coat collar turned up and his hat down. This is in New Jersey. She came up to him and she said, "What's the matter with you? Don't you know that somebody might think you are trying to rob the place?" And he turned around and looked at her and she gasped, "I'm sorry! I'm sorry!" and she ran down the aisle. I know that happened. He was very shy about his appearance. He knew he had a shock on people. It was something he couldn't control. I heard that a fellow came up to him one time and was pulling his coattail and Durks was turned away from him. The fellow said something to him. When Durks turned around to face him, the guy did fall down and he ran away and got the manager, "Did you see what is over there?" I wasn't there for that one, but they told me about it later.

S&A: In one version I've heard of that story, the guy fell over, hit his head, and died!

MB: The guy didn't die or anything. Bill was bound to run into crazy people though. You never know when you'll run into a "normal" person who has crazy ways.

S&A: Did Bill have to put up with much of a hard time working the shows?

MB: They didn't try to give him too much of a hard time. A lot of people were afraid of him; they didn't know what kind of reaction he would have. I spread the rumor around that he had nearly killed some guy in a fight back in his hometown because they had made fun of him. I spread that around to some of the working men that liked to play cruel jokes and wouldn't be careful of what they would say in front of him. I said, "I don't know if he's still on parole or not, but he nearly killed a guy back where he came from. I wouldn't mess with him myself." I had

Bill going along with this so he would get the respect he wouldn't have otherwise. It helped keep people from trying to make a fool of him. Which they thought they could because he was very slow in his speech and there wasn't anything very sophisticated about him. He enjoyed a joke, but he wasn't sharp at it. If you pulled a pun on him, he probably wouldn't understand it until you explained it to him. He couldn't stand to read the funny papers, because he couldn't understand them. He couldn't read in between the lines.

S&A: So what kind of jokes did he like?

MB: One of the jokes I pulled on him, he got the biggest laugh. You get your hand wet by dipping it in water and then you get up behind somebody and turn your head and sneeze and cough and shake your hand and water sprays all over them. "You furnish towels with those baths?" That was one that I made up years and years ago. He saw me doing it and he wanted to do it. You can imagine doing that to someone and having them turn around . . .

Melvin Burkhart, Sandra Reed, and Bill Durks.

S&A: And there's Bill Durks! That's classic. What did Bill like to do after the shows were over?

MB: I used to take him to the drive-ins with me and he liked to go to the motels so he could have TV and he liked to go to restaurants and

Banner for the World's
Strangest Married Couple.

eat. At first he was a little shy, but I told him, "Look, as long as you go in there and pay your money, we'll go in there where people won't see you so easily. You can sit with your back to them." And pretty soon it got to the point where it was all right.

S&A: Other than you, who were Bill's friends on the shows?

MB: Really everybody. Everybody was friendly with him. He was kind of a lonesome, shy guy and he was kind of like a puppy dog: If you made friends he was glad to be friends with you. He didn't seek friendship in the strict sense of the word, but if you wanted to be friends with him he was glad to be friends with you. And he was a very even-tempered guy unless you did something really bad and then he'd fly off, boy. He had been in a couple of bad fights where he was from, but I don't know that he'd ever killed a guy. He was strong as an ox, too. Evidently he did hard work where he had lived. You take a person like that and take them into a strange circumstance and they're bound to be bewildered until somebody straightens them around. It seemed that no one there was willing to accept that except me.

Dorothy & Joe Hershey

S&A: How long had Bill Durks been working in the shows when he met your mother, Mildred?

DH: Since he was fourteen. He'd been in the sideshows for most of his life. He worked for Gooding's Million Dollar Midway. The circus. He was on Strates. Mother was always on Strates, too, but he was in lots of them.

S&A: So a lot of shows featured "The Three-Eyed Man"?

DH: Daddy only had one eye.

S&A: He only had one?!

DH: Yeah. He only had one. Daddy always wore a hat over his one eye because you could tell he only had one. They would paint one eye in the middle, and then he had a dead socket. His aunt was there when he was born and the eye came out onto a little thing—it was stuck out and nobody knew what it was. They thought he was dead, and they wrapped him in a little rug and put him underneath the woodstove until the doctor came. And he still wasn't dead when the doctor came, but that eye was ruined. They just wrapped him up and stuck him under that wood fire until the man could get there and that was the next day.

S&A: He wasn't crying or screaming?

JH: No. Then when the doctor come, he said, "This child is still alive!" So they naturally got him back to breathing real good and that's what happened. Bill Durks had a story behind him before he ever entered show business. He had a heck of a time getting into this world.

S&A: Your mother was in the business some time before she met Durks. How did she get into the business?

DH: She was in Coney Island first of all. I had met Bill Parnell—he was like my mother, born with alligator skin—when he was up in Flemington, New Jersey. We were all standing up in the audience looking up at him and this guy next to me says, "Oh yeah, well that was put on with wax or something." And I said, "Oh no. Don't tell me that's not for real, because my mother was born that way." He said, "What? We were told it was put on with wax." I said, "Well, it's not." Afterwards Bill Parnell came down and said, "Is your mother really like this?" I said, "Yes. How would I know if she wasn't?" He said, "Bring your mother up here." I told him I couldn't right then because she had asthma. When we went to see him, we went to Coney Island because that's where he was. He said he would be there for two weeks, and the minute my mother walked in they hired her. Jewish people ran the show. I went every week to see if my mother was all right because Bill drank. He was a lovely man and he was lovely to her, but he drank. At Coney someone bet Bill Parnell that he couldn't drink a pint of wine without stopping, and he drank the pint of wine right there. When he did my mother called me and told me that Bill had collapsed and they'd taken him to the hospital at Coney Island and he died. After that, the show went to Pensie and that's where Daddy came on the show. He was getting $25 to $30 a week.

S&A: I've heard that your mother passed away when she and Bill were on the road.

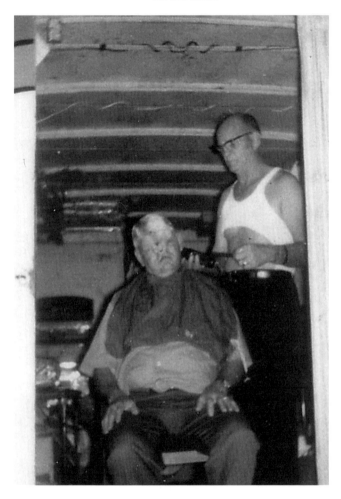

DH: They had just come off the road from York, Pennsylvania, because they didn't have the freaks on the show. So Mel Burkhart said, "Let's go home for a couple of days. Let's go home." See, Pennsylvania, when you drive like they did, that was nothing to drive to Florida. So my parents said, "Good, let's go see Dotty."

S&A: So they came back to Florida from York to see you?

DH: Yeah. They come home and Mel had a sore throat and my mother started to have an asthma attack. Melvin was going to the doctor to see about his throat, so they took him and put my mother in a chair and my mother had a heart attack and passed away right there in the hospital.

S&A: What did Bill do at that point?

Burkhart the Barber takes a little off the top.

DH: What could he do? My mother was gone, they gave him time off from the show but, what could he do? Stay home? I said to Daddy, "Let's use common sense. You'll only grieve yourself to death. Go back on the show." He said, "Everybody's going to hate me!" I said, "What do you care who hates you? I don't hate you." So Daddy went back on the show. When he went back on the show, my aunt and I fixed a little cottage up and when he come home, that's where he lived—with us. Daddy and Bill Burnes, the ticket taker, and Wally lived in that house when they were home. Wally was not a showman. Daddy didn't drink that much when my mother was alive. After my mother died, though, he and Bill Burnes drank and Wally drank and I used to pour it down the sink and pour water in it. But he didn't dare gripe because he wasn't supposed to drink. It was really sad because his best buddy now was gone, his sidekick.

S&A: How long did Bill live after your mother passed away?

DH: He must have died in '73.

S&A: So he didn't outlive your mother by much, did he?

DH: No, and when Daddy passed away, I kept him in the closet over there.

S&A: Excuse me?!

DH: You know—how people are when you cremate them. I told Daddy before he ever got sick, "If you want to be by Mother, you're going to have to be cremated, 'cause I can't take you until I have a vacation." See, I'd have to wait until I had time off from work to go to the cemetery in New Jersey.

S&A: New Jersey? That must have been an adventure.

JH: You know, I had this great big dog, a leader dog, and we had Mr. Durks in the back of Dotty's little Hornet station wagon. And with this dog, he took up the whole back. I had the window cranked down at a gas station and we were talking about Durks and everything and the guy looked in there and said, "I don't see anybody in there but that big dog." And Dotty says, "No, Bill Durks is back there." And he says, "Look lady, I don't see no person in that car but that big dog." I said, "You better look again. He's back there in that box." That guy, Dotty said, he turned about three shades of white. He said, "What?! What?! You cremated a guy?!" And he turned and got out of there. So after Bill Durks is dead, he's still scaring the public! If he were alive, he would have just roared.

And in the Kingdom of the Blind (be it Biblical or Carnival), the one-eyed man is King.

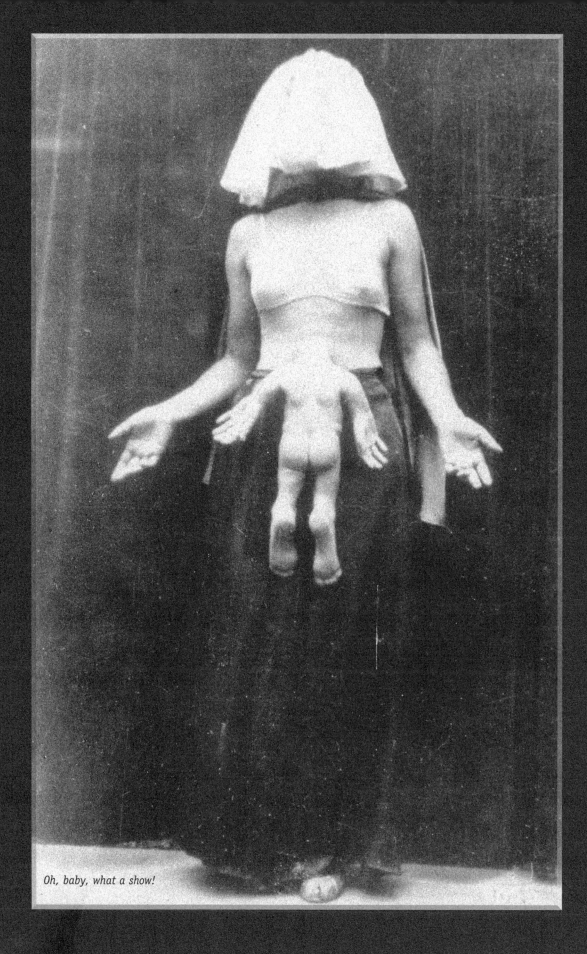

Oh, baby, what a show!

I Am Not A FREAK

Who knew? Well, apparently every carny between here and Barnum's grandfather; the only ones in the dark were us suckers. And damn well we should've been too. Here you see Margurete Clark, renowned sideshow freak in all her glory, her parasitic twin drooping from her abdomen, its arms and legs splayed out limply, Margurete's own held out from her sides almost in imitation of her twin's, and her head covered by that enigmatic veil. What an icon.

What? An icon? Certainly the image is. It's appeared in virtually every freak and sideshow book both in and out of print. What you have to ask is not why the photo appears everywhere. That's obvious. It's like that oft-repeated photo of "Lobster Boy" Grady Stiles as a boy, his hands held out to show you his claws, the look on his face already hard and cold; or that full-face shot of Bill Durks, "The Man With Three Eyes." Margurete's photo is just too incredible to ignore. Like the Stiles and Durks photos, it sucks you in in a way that supersedes even the performers pictured and drops you whole into the subject matter itself.

So try Margurete on for size and see how she fits. Margurete Clark was not one half a Siamese twin, her parasitic twin hanging from her gut. That twin was a rubber baby doll, and a damn ghastly looking one at that according to the showmen who knew the act. Hell, Margurete wasn't even female. You see, the world famous freak Margurete Clark was really Billy Logsdon, himself a pretty popular half-and-half. In a business where you get paid for the number of acts you perform, there's a distinct advantage to being multifaceted, let alone multi-bodied (not even to mention ambi-sexual). I suppose you just had to know something was up when all you ever saw was that one pose of Margurete/Billy, and she/he always kept his face covered. The better to see *through* you with.

Front of Billy Logsdon's show.

the ANATOMICAL wonder

P hotographer Joel-Peter Witkin has taken a few arresting shots in his day. Just a couple tons of work for each image. Make-your-hair-fall-out or make-your-teeth-move-around type images. How to pick a favorite? Simple, Pick the only one whose subject an speak for itself.

Arguably, Witkin's *Blockhead—Melvin Burkhart, Retired Circus Performer,* is the best image Witkin ever made. And—Mother of God in Heaven—it does speak for itself. No need for dead babies nor the medico/autopsy bric-a-brac so common in Witkin's images. There's this guy, see, with an aviator's cap, welder's goggles (that's the arty stuff), and he's driving this goddamn railroad spike (it looks that huge) into the middle of his face with a hammer! Go ahead: Lie to me. Tell me mere art can beat that!

But that's just another day's work for Burkhart. Doing something to make everybody back up every time he does some stunt. Even that damn Witkin photo of all things. That image hung in a New York museum not that many years ago, along with a number of Joel-Peter's other pieces. Melvin, having a day off from his job with the sideshow on Coney Island's Sideshows by the Seashore (back when it was on the boardwalk), took himself up to the Witkin show and found himself pretty quickly in front of the shot. After all, he had to see himself displaying proudly his craft for the art crowd, any crowd. On that day, it was a crowd of kids, probably a class trip uptown to "see some pictures." And there's Burkhart and this kid, both staring at this horrific image of . . . well, Melvin. "Do you think that looks like me?" It was a question he had to ask. The kid's answer, of course, just had to be "No way!"

What followed was pure Burkhart: out comes the driver's license. More disbelief. More kids involved. Arguments over

Opposite: Melvin was never fully dressed without his smile.

145

whether the photo is or isn't of Burkhart. Finally, the guards come over in the midst of the din and ask him to leave for creating "a disturbance." Joel-Peter Witkin should be so lucky.

Actually, though, it isn't just "anything to create a scene" with Melvin, though that makes him happy enough. He's also more than willing to put up with the shenanigans of others. When I took my associate editor, Kathleen Kotcher, to meet Burkhart the first time, after he'd run through a number of pretty decent card tricks, she had to show him the only one she knew. (Don't ask me why; wacky circumstances generate wacky behavior in some people.) The trick was not her invention and, truth be told, it wasn't a trick so much as a gag, from an old segment of Taxi. In the show, the victim of the trick is asked to pick a card, does so, then is told to shuffle the deck then place it face down on the table. After some appropriate mumbo jumbo over the deck, the magician then asks what card was picked, is told, then asks to have the top card turned. Of course it's not the card named but the magician's line in the face of that is, "You see, your card had been magically turned into the [insert appropriate card name here]!" Baboom.

Melvin Burkhart and lucky seven.

So Kotcher pulls the trick, Melvin follows through, she drops the punch line, and Melvin laughs. But then he comes back with, "You know, I thought when I told you my card, you were going to say, 'Right you are!' and go to your next trick." That may have been his way of letting her know that he and she were both on the square. Earlier he'd looked hard at her while she laughed hysterically at one of his routines, and he mugged, "You like to laugh at freaks little girl?" and it was clear he was unsure whether she understood he was just joking around. Then again, leave it to Burkhart to put up with such silliness as her card trick, then compound it. I suppose that's the least you can expect from the man who took a pretty gruesome piece of fakir performance, made it even more gruesome, and then made it comic.

S&A: What was your first work in entertainment?

MB: I was working as a Western Union boy when I was about 15 or 16, and I used to hang around the back of the theaters because I could get in free and see the show free because of my Western Union uniform. One time Louise Lovely, who was a very famous movie star in the '20s from Australia, she was making a tour through the vaudeville circuit. Every town had vaudeville, four or five houses. Anyway, she was fading in Hollywood (she was getting old) and this was her way of making a living by playing in the top vaudeville houses. Her husband was Art Welch, a director. Now, they had the hand-held cameras in those days—you're talking way back— and they would call people up out of the audience to come in and appear on the stage and she would direct them, and they would photograph them, and the next week they would show the film back to the whole audience.

Wild Mel Burkhart.

That was the whole idea. You would get people to come back and they would have their friends come to see them on the big screen because they were actually working in a movie. But she sold it as a "talent hunt": they're looking for talent to send out to Hollywood and, "We have to give you these auditions here on the stage to see how you work out." That sold me, but I had caught on right away. So when she asked for someone out of the audience, I marched right up there with two or three others from the audience. She was going to have a scene—"You go over there and you take this gun and go over into the wings there"—and this girl was going to be his wife making love to this man when the husband comes in. "You take the gun and when you point the gun, the man in the pit is going to make a BOOM! Like that and shoot the guy making love to your wife."

And they laughed at the fellow trying to make love to the girl, and I'm supposed to come marching in like the jealous husband. I come in and I tripped over a wire that was laying on the stage. "Cut! Cut! Cut! Do it over again." I went back there and I started over again and the gun goes up by my head. "I'm sorry," I said. "I'm very nervous." "That's okay. Try it again." This time I come out there, and I can't get the gun out of my pocket and the guy in the orchestra pit looked up

The Anatomical Wonder

and thought I had it out of my pocket and BOOM! By that time they were just getting a big bang out of the audience. It was just in my head to do that. When the act was over, and we all went backstage, she got me over and she said, "Can you come back for the 7:30 show?" So I got to come back four or five times that week, see, and I would pretend like I was part of the audience coming in there and I would pull some of the same things. I had a ball with the other acts all week long. That was my first time. Now the second time, they had an amateur show in an outlying theater and they had all amateurs on and they would come out and vie for prizes—$15, $10, $5—and everyone that showed up

Melvin Burkhart with the Doll Family.

got a dollar. In those days, that was no hay, y'know. I had to ride the streetcars to get to this place, and I was late getting off from where I was working at and I jumped off the streetcar and went rushing up the block. I knew they were going to have something like an amateur show where they would call members from the audience up, and I got out there and I went to the ticket box and I asked where the amateur show was. "Oh, it's right down through that alley and around the back, the stage door. They're waiting!" So I went around back and there's this guy standing with hair in his hands and I walked up. He said, "Do you want to be on the amateur show?" and I said, "Yes," and he said, "Come on! Come on!" and grabbed me and he actually run me in there and pushed me right out on the stage! So I said, "What am I supposed to do?" See the audience they had been waiting for the acts to show up, but there had been a bus accident with the dance studio where the singers and dancers were coming from, and they hadn't shown up because of the accident. I'm the only one that had shown up, and the audience was stamping and hollering out there because they thought there was going to be a show. So he pushed me out and I said, "What do you want me to do?" I looked at the audience and I said, "Just a minute." I asked the guy again, "What am I supposed to do?" and he said, "Do anything! Get out there and do your act! Do whatever you do!" You can imagine being in a place like that—it's funny when you talk about it now—but me, I didn't know what the hell to do! All of a sudden I said, "Hold on now. I'll do something for you." And the guy is standing there hiding from the audience going, "Go, Go, GO! Do any-

SHOCKED AND AMAZED!

thing!" I said, "Ladies and Gentlemen! He made me come out here and told me to do something, and I don't know what do to." And they're eating this up and they're yelling, "Do anything! Stand on your head! Do anything!" And I said, "Well I do a few tricks with my body. Would you like to see them?" And they were yelling, "Yeah, Yeah, Yeah!" and I said "Bring me out a chair and I'll do it." He slid me out a chair and I did a couple of handstands on the chair because I was very athletic in those days. I belonged to an athletic club. All of a sudden I got the idea to do the Anatomical! And I just did it right there and I got first prize! Anatomical is very simple you see. I told them, "You've all seen the ads that appear in magazines about how easy it is to get your muscles. All you have to do is clip the coupon, mail it, and you get your muscles in the mail. And you become a great big he-man like I am. One chap took the course of exercises and before long this is how he looked," and I sucked my stomach in. I can't do the act like that anymore, but the contrast is hard to believe. I told them, "This is the way the guy looked before he took his exercise." And I'd push my stomach out. "After he took his exercise, this is the way the guy looked." And I'd suck it in. "One chap thought he'd like to develop his neck. He had a long, skinny neck. You might say that he developed a rubber neck." One of the things that Mr. Ripley [of *Believe It Or Not!* fame] found so unusual was that I could do the two-faced man. It is unusual muscle control. I could smile on one side and frown on the other and I could breathe through one lung at a time. It's amazing. I would call a person up to the stage and tell them to put their hands right there on my chest. I would usually try to get a girl. What am I doing?

S&A: [with hand on Burkhart's chest] Breathing.

MB: Breathing. Anybody could do that couldn't they? Now what am I doing?

S&A: Breathing out of one lung!

MG: Then I'd say, "Now let's see if you can do that." And the girl would start shrieking, "No! Don't do that!" Big laugh from the audience, and I could pull my stomach way back in, which I don't do anymore. The doctor told me not to do that anymore.

S&A: Did you know you could do those stunts before? It didn't just occur to you when you went out on stage?

MB: I used to go out to parties and found it was stuff that I could do. Just fooling around. I was a boxer and when we went to athletic meetings it was lots of, "Can you do this? Can you do that?" and I found out that I could do so many things that the coaches used to get me to

The Anatomical Wonder

show other coaches. "Show him how you do this. Show him how you do that, Melvin." And all of a sudden it just blossomed out into an act. Well, I worked all of the amateurs after that and I even made a little money. They even sent me all the way out to Indianapolis and Cincinnati from Louisville—I lived in Louisville, Kentucky—and they paid me $25 to go there because they needed acts and I was a good audience person. That's the way the Anatomical Act started. But I had to quit it in 1989.

S&A: What happened in 1989?

MB: I barely made it home from Coney Island. I drove 1,200 miles and the doctors wouldn't believe me when I got home and told them I had made a 1,200-mile trip. "You couldn't have in your condition!" But I did.

S&A: What was wrong?

MB: I had a pulmonary embolism. Blood clots formed in my lungs. You could die, but I was lucky.

S&A: You've said elsewhere that you worked up the Human Blockhead routine after you watched doctors operate on your nose following your accidents in boxing. Had you watched other people do something like the act before?

MB: I saw a fellow years and years ago doing it, and he had a little nail like this and I said, "Good God! I could do better than that." I remembered sitting in the doctor's chair when they were going in and out and cutting in there. And I said, "I can do better than that. Damn!" Later, we needed an act real bad, and I said, "Well, I'll make up one." So I got me a nail and a hammer and an icepick and I got up there. Down through the years, I don't know how many performers I have taught, and they say, "Melvin, you're not mad that I copied your act?" and I say, "Why should I be mad? If you can do it, and you get paid for it, that's the main thing, and you're not doing it next to me when I'm doing it. And besides, when people see the way that you do it, they'll appreciate the way that I do it!" I never did care, and I did show several of them— young fellows trying to get by, then get on with another show—'cause there was a lot of sideshows roaming around the country once. At one time there were about 150 sideshows. You could pick up the *Billboard* and there was always ads, "Acts Wanted for Sideshow. Acts Wanted for Sideshow," and they could pick up the Blockhead and that was an extra sideshow act. Every carnival nearly had one. Now of course...

S&A: ...the rides make all the money.

MB: Well, the rides don't eat anything and they don't talk back to you. And they don't cuss you and they're not as much trouble as someone sit-

ting up there miserable and sick or drunk. But I have taught a number of young fellows who want to get into show business how to do the act because it doesn't make any difference to me if they're doing it. Who sees them? When people see me, they are surprised because I don't go out for the element of shocking you. I go out there for the element of entertaining you. Everything that I've done has been to entertain.

S&A: But your family wasn't in show business at all?

MB: No, no one in my family was in show business and they were so damned glad to get rid of me! I was so much trouble to them, especially during the Depression. I was always getting in trouble. I was going out with people that was stealing cars. Young punks.

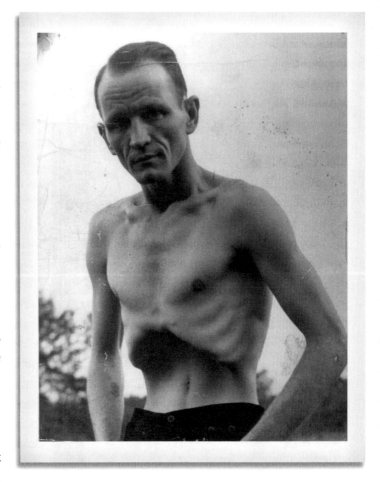

Melvin Burkhart: The Man Without a Stomach.

We lived right next door to the assistant chief of police, and his son and I used to get in trouble, you see, and he'd get us out of it. After I got in the shows, that was the main thing with me.

S&A: How did you end up "under canvas"?

MB: Things got really bad during the Depression and I got a job on the Conroy Brothers Circus. They had fourteen acts, and pretty soon I was working in nine of them.

S&A: Nine out of fourteen acts? What were you doing?

MB: First of all we had a sideshow out front. Just a little tent. It cost a dime to get in. First I would be outside selling tickets, then I would run inside and show them a "horned rattlesnake." We used to buy them out of Texas where they would take and make a slit in a rattlesnake's head and put a spur coming out of it there. A "horned rattlesnake." I'd show them "The Happy Family," which was a dog over there with its kittens, and that was the sideshow. Then I would run inside and put on my make-up real quick and do what they called a "clown walk-around" while waiting for the rest of the people to get in. One large tent wouldn't hold over 150 people. It was a tiny tent but only six of us ran the whole damn one-ring circus. They were well-known throughout Iowa and Nebraska. That's where we worked, in the small towns. In fact, we only did one show a night and during the day they would give me a big bullhorn and I would walk down mainstreet yelling, "Big show tonight! Conroy Brothers Circus!" in clown costume. I would do that two or three times in the afternoon, then after the sideshow I would do a "clown walk-around" in clown costume. I would have a stick and on top of the stick was a tray nailed onto the top of it with a whole bunch of tin cans piled on the top of that. Then I'd walk around and act like I was going to juggle it. Then when I let go, all the cans would fall and make a terrific noise and get the attention of the audience and I'd laugh and run off. I'd run back then and wipe off some of the makeup and get back there in the act then. We had a buckin' mule act. Little guys, those mules, but those sons a guns would buck and I'd go out there and act like I was going to ride one and it would buck me off. Well, you just kind of slide off. Every night there was some young punks out there that thought they were going to ride it and they would get bucked off and if they really annoyed the animal they'd

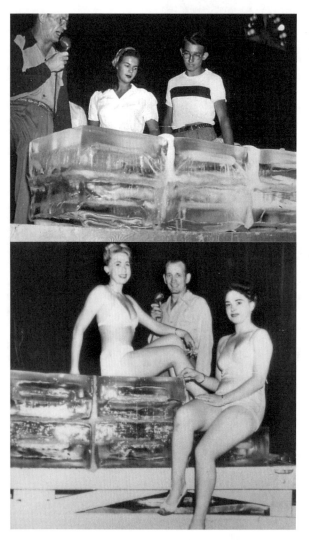

The lady encased in ice (top) warms for the crowd (bottom).

get the devil kicked out of them, too. In those days they didn't care. None of the shows had insurance and things like that. Then I'd run off and I'd get ready to do the Anatomical. The first time the circus owner saw me with the act, he just about run me down the road when they sent me out to do his show. Damnedest thing I ever saw.

S&A: He didn't like that act?

MB: NO! He thought I was a "kinker." When they sent me out from the booking office in Kansas City to join the show in Iowa, he thought,

"Damn kinker!" He gave me the dirtiest jobs to do. He wouldn't let me do a damn thing. "Cost me over $15 to get you out here. Goddamnit, I'm going to work it out of you!" I was scared. The guy swung at me and nearly hit me, but I went out and did my part because I thought that I was going into the circus and that was good. Curly Easter was his name. I'll never forget. One time his son was sick, and I had to fill in for Sonny. He did a Roman ring act where they go up and turn and twist and so on and of course he was very good and I'd go up there and clown it, and we had another act on the bars where you would go up there and hang from your feet and I was pretty good at that. They had a trained goat act. I'd never seen that before or since. Curly was a good circus man. He'd been out there with the big ones. Sonny also did a slack wire act and juggled on the slack wire, too. He was very good.

S&A: How did they have the trained goat act set up?

MB: They had them pulling little wagons, jumping over each other. It was like a trained dog act. He had five trained goats and he had some dogs at the end. Finally he said, "Go out there and do something. I'm not ready." And the audience was out there clapping, so I went out there and I took off my shirt and I told them I was going to show them tricks with my body. I didn't know in those days how to present what I do, but I wasn't bad at it. I had the idea. Anyway, I go out there and they are applauding and clapping and carrying on. When I go back in there Curly goes, "I'll be damned. You'll do that next show, too." That was it. After that I was in his good graces because I worked in all the different acts he put me in and I helped put up and take down. I worked two years with the one-ring circus, and every time I was with any show, even when I was on Ringling, any time I was on another show, it was like taking a vacation compared to the one-ring circus.

S&A: Still, you did a lot of acts in most of your shows, didn't you?

MB: I used to do about five acts in the show. I was the magician, I was the Anatomical Wonder, I was the Human Blockhead, I worked the Electric Chair illusion, and I was the emcee. I developed a way of doing the Electric Chair by getting kids out of the audience. A kid and a girl up there. It's just terrific the way it worked out. We used to do an act wrasslin' snakes. I have a picture of the snake here with seven or eight of us holding him.

S&A: That's a big snake [looking at photo]. That thing is bigger around than your neck.

MB: You're telling me! That was a good show we put on. We called it "The Wild Snake Show." People would pay an extra quarter to see the snake in the back—that was our blow-off. We would have a snake wrestling exhibition. I would get the snake and I would get him right behind the head, and he would wriggle around, but he couldn't reach around and bite me. If you control the head and the snake doesn't get aggressive, it won't bite you. But it will coil up around you. I'd act like I was talking away a mile a minute giving them all of the details.

"Ladies and gentlemen! The snake has the strongest digestive tract. It can digest any animal it swallows whole, including the hide," and I'm talking away a mile a minutes—"The shark is the only other animal known to digest the leg of a horse cut off and thrown into the water, but the snake digests anything!" And all of the time the snake is just draping itself around me, and I act like I didn't notice it and all of a sudden "Ugh!?" And the audience looks up and I'm hollering, "I got him, I got him!" and it looks like the snake is throwing me all over the place. "I got him, I got him!" I had a trick, see: When he would get up around my waist, I'd expand my chest. I had a great big chest expansion. And when we were done, I'd exhale and he'd loosen his grip to get a tighter one on me but I'd just slip out. People would be running out of the show. They'd run out and talk about it, and we'd get more people and that was the show. But I've lived so long and hear so much. A lot of people ask my why I don't write a book. You have to feel that you have the ability to write a book in the first place. I never got out of the sixth grade. There's a heck of a lot that sticks with you if you're erudite though, such as I am. What does erudite mean anyway?

S&A: Very knowledgeable.

MB: I know a lot about nothing. You know when you get old, the first three things to go, you know, are memory and the second one is . . . I can't remember what the second one is! That's an old joke that I've used many many times on the bally. Now that I'm old it works good. When I was the emcee and I would introduce this act and that act, and I could sell their acts for them, introduce them and then jump down and let them go into their act. The boss appreciated that, and that way, I didn't have to go out front and work like the rest of them did, leaving me more on the inside. I never did have to work the outside of a show. I was always the inside man. Out there, it's either cold and miserable or sunny and hot. I didn't like it. Inside, they actually needed someone—an intermediary you might say—between the audience and the acts. Sometimes an act would come out they'd be surly and mean and grouchy. I got pretty good at handling that, so that's why I stayed on the inside.

S&A: How did Ripley pick up on you?

WONDERLAND MUSEUM
JULY·24·1935

COPELIN
PHOTO

MB: In 1936, I was working the Ringling Brothers Circus and we worked Madison Square Garden. That was the Ripley's headquarters, but Hix, of *Strange As It Seems,* come over and visited with me and said he'd like to put me in his column. I said okay, but I had to leave and go out on the road after '36. I left and went to go on the carnival and so I didn't see him. In '39, Ripley and Hix had a feud going on between them and when Ripley heard that Hix had asked me to perform, he sent a fellow over and said, "You know, we're opening up a big show on 39th Street in New York here and would you like to work?" I said, "Sure." The salary seemed good. I had been working at Hubert's Museum on 42nd Street and Broadway.

S&A: What was Hubert's like?

MB: It was a rat race, but it was good. They had damn good action, acts that were off the road and needed some work. I would go down there and work during the winter. We had our regular rounds we would make. Philadelphia and Newark and Patterson and New York and you could fit in

Wonderland Museum line-up. Melvin is holding the linking rings, front right.

The Anatomical Wonder

several weeks that way. I lived in New York during the winter time. This guy from Ripley's said, "Let's go over and talk with him," but I never did get to talk to Ripley himself. He was always busy. They had a good show there. They put me right to work, but when I was supposed to go out to Treasure Island on Ripley's show, I heard they were trying to get some-

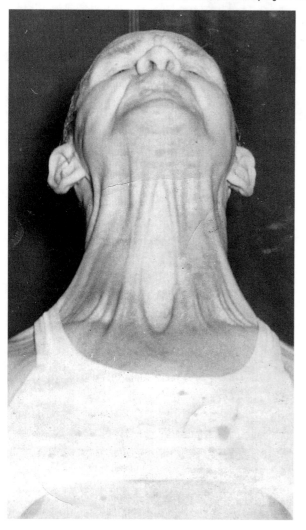

Long neck Burkhart.

one else. Hix came up to see me at my hotel and he said, "How would you like to be in my column?" I said sure and that made it twice I was in his column. That made Ripley so mad. He said, "Just for that, you don't go to Treasure Island." I had two men come and talk to me then. I said, "Look, you said I wasn't going to Treasure Island anyway." He said, "I said no such thing!" And I said, "Look, I heard you hired another man, Ed Hayes." He was a good Anatomical Wonder, and he worked for Ripley in 1933 at the Chicago World's Fair when I was working in Chicago. Anyway, they got me mixed up with him on several occasions because he was on Ringling Brothers; I was on Ringling Brothers. He was on Ripley; I was on Ripley. So I told Hix, if you aren't going to have a show, I'll go out with Ringling Brothers because they asked me to go out with them again. I was with them in 1940 and '41.

S&A: This bouncing around between shows happened to you guys all of the time, didn't it?

MB: You went between the shows for the one that would give you the best deal. The one that wanted you the most would give you the most. After all, there wasn't no really big salaries in those days. You worked with Ringling Brothers, you got $45 a week. That was good money. You could live on it and get by and even save some. You traveled with them, and they furnished the meals and expenses were included, you see. And you had the prestige of traveling with "The Greatest Show on Earth." You could say in later years that you had been with the Big One. I was supposed to go out with them the year they had the big fire. A chap I had worked with told me, "Melvin, I'll give you a better deal. We're going up to Canada. I'll give you a hell of a good deal if you go to Canada." He had been the assistant manager on Ringling Brothers, and I went up there instead.

S&A: That was the Hartford, Connecticut, fire that killed so many people, wasn't it?

MB: Yes. I was so glad I wasn't there. The fellow that was the Indian act said it was a terrible thing, that it affected him the whole rest of his life. Seeing children laying out there all burned and people burned and dying and you couldn't get away from it because it was everywhere. I was glad I was up in Canada. So anyway, I never had a season that I didn't have an offer to go work. Not only that, but good offers. The last show I was with was the Strates show, the James E. Strates show, thirty years straight and I never missed a show. In fact there was a fellow from the *Guinness Book of World Records* that come to Coney Island to see me and he said, "Melvin, I understand that you were with the James E. Strates show for thirty years straight and never missed a show. Is that right?" And I said, "That's right. Why?" "Because I would like to write that up and enter it as a world's record." I told him, "Fine with me," but they had no place in the book for that kind of a record. They had no classification for it. He came out to me and said he was still working on it but he needed some affidavits because he couldn't just go in there and say, "Take my word," because he had taken my word. He was mixed up in the book some way and he was a very nice guy and visited me the last time I was in New York. He came out and said, "You know, I never could get that damned thing to work, but it's still on the boards." It didn't make any difference anyway. I would have liked it, but it didn't make that much difference. It never did get published to my knowledge. One reason was it was so hard to get the affidavits. Old man Strates had died, and his son had taken over the show and many of them over there remembered me. They would come in with their little kids and say, "I remember you when I was a little kid!" Now, a number of the magicians remember me from Ringling Brothers Circus and that was over 50 years ago. And you know they've got to be pretty old to remember me! They had to be young at that time. I had a pretty nice run.

S&A: It sounds to me like you were constantly working. Was there anytime when you weren't?

MB: There were times when you weren't working. When the circus would close, you'd have to go back to New York to work at Hubert's Museum; and there would be times—two or three weeks—in between opening up the acts they had booked already waiting for you to come on. You'd

The Anatomical Wonder

spend much of the winter there then go to Madison Square Garden to open up for the circus. I found out I could do better with carnivals, you see, do more on the program and get paid more than just doing the one act on the circus. That's why I stayed with the carnivals so long. They would do better for me than any of the others were doing.

S&A: I guess it's like the saying goes, "It's all about money."

MB: I have a sliding scale when it comes to that: I get whatever I can.

S&A: I'd say that was sliding.

MB: I did a show for my chiropractor's wife. Her son goes to the Tampa Academy School here and she wanted to give a surprise party for him— cake, ice cream and so forth—and I was going to be the surprise entertainment. When it started out, she had called me and said, "How much would you charge to come out and do a show?" And I said, "Well, I usually charge about $500." She said "Well! Oh! What?" I said, "I work on a sliding scale though. You can't pay $500? I'll play for $300. You can't pay $300, I'll take $200. What can you pay?" She said, "Oh, Mr. Burkhart, I can pay $75 if you can come out and play for that." I said "That's fine with me." So I go out there and she gave me $75. On that basis, you know, you don't have any "How much?"

S&A: You've appeared in a lot of books and TV over the years in connection with the business.

MB: Oh yes. I got a call from a producer, Madeline Smith, asking if I would be interested in being on the *You Bet Your Life* show. "Why would they want me?" "To be a contestant. That's what we need—people who can get up there and talk about their lives." "I wouldn't have to perform?" "No, we have performers. If I put you up to them, would you be interested?" "Sure I'd be interested." They paid expenses up and back, and that way I wouldn't lose anything and it would sure break the monotony of my day. So I sent them a copy of my video, but I think one look at the Human Blockhead act was all they needed. You don't know who's deciding those things when you go to do a show like that one. I was supposed to be on a show and two days before I was supposed to leave they called and said they had to cancel because they were worried that someone in the audience might faint and hit their head and they'd be sued. And they couldn't take that chance, their legal department advised them, blah, blah, blah, blah, blah. That's understandable, I suppose. They don't want to take too many chances. But I see so many things on TV, so many of the blow-'em-away movies. TV eats up so much. You just have to feed it. Just like that *Springer* show.

S&A: When you were on the *Jerry Springer Show* with Capt. Don Leslie

[Ed. Note: tattooed sword swallower] and Jeanie Tomaini [The World's Only Living Half Girl]?

MB: Yeah. Not so long ago you'd be amazed to find anything like me on there. I was on the *David Frost Show*. I was on *Showtown, USA*. I was on there twice. I had to do the Anatomical Wonder. That was back in '64. They came to where I was living, out in Tampa—I wasn't living here then—and I made a very good friend out of one of the associate producers. Later, we went out to Hollywood to visit my son in L.A., and I called up this chap and asked him if he remembered me. "Sure, I remember you, Melvin."

S&A: So he got you back on TV?

MB: The upshot of it was they wanted to get me doing the act, rehearsing it. But I said to him, "I do another trick that no one else in the world does." "What is that Melvin?" "I do this big dice trick." Pretty soon I had the crew saying, "Come here! See this!" I'm doing my trick and all of a sudden somebody taps me on the shoulder and I turn around and there's David Frost standing right there watching. "I say, couldn't we put that in the show you know?" and I said "Sure. I don't mind," and he asked the director, "Couldn't we put that in?" and the director said he could. So I got in the show with the dice and the Anatomical Wonder. In fact, they showed that program six months later again

Ring-a-ding-ding.

and people out on the West Coast when I went out there had seen it and many of them remembered seeing me. When I went out to Magic Castle, I called up this chap again who had been the associate producer. I had my son and his wife and my wife and me and he called up the *Johnny Carson Show*. We'd already been to a couple of shows, but you had to get in line and wait in order to see anything. When I told him he said, "I'll get you into the *Johnny Carson Show*. When you go up there, just walk to the door and tell them what your name is and who you have in your party and they'll take care of it." So my son and his wife and my wife and I were bopping around. There was a line a block and a half long, and they opened up and let as many as they can in and then they close it off. Anyway, I looked down by the door and people are looking and gawking. "Who's that? Who's that?" and I knocked on the door and the fella comes running over and says, "Yes?" I said, "My name is Melvin Burkhart. Do you have me on the list?" and he says, "Let me see." He ran back and got the book. "Oh yes, Melvin Burkhart and party. How many? Four?" And he let us right in. When we went in, it was a big amphitheater and down here is the stage and there was already some people down there, friends and so forth, just sitting around. Here he had taped off four seats with our name around it and marched us down there and took the tape off and said, "Here you go." We sat right down there and people were gawking. "Who the hell is this?" We got a big kick out of it. Then after that we went out to the Magic Castle. We were invited in there by my friend Pat. I've known him for fifty years. He was good friends with the owner of the Magic Castle, so he sent up a note in there for me and we showed up. He arranged for us to have dinner, and then afterwards they have little rooms off to the side, a hall where the local magicians set up to do magic and people stop and watch them. I went up to one of them and I said, "Do you know anyone here that does a trick with a big set of dice?" He looked up at me, and he's so blasé because people have asked them the same set of stupid questions before. "What do you mean 'big dice'?" I said, "I saw a fellow do this with big dice like this and I want to get me some." "What did he do?" I said, "Well, [Melvin pulls the dice out of his pocket] five and two on this side and six and three on the other. When he turned it over it was only four and one and six and two." "Do that again." One of the fellows who knew my friend Pat got me up to do this, you see. His friend was standing in the back just laughing. "Do that again!" so I did the trick again for him. "Goddamn it! I know you! You're Burkhart aren't you? I heard about that damned trick," and he called over all his friends. They came over there and I had to do it. By that time they had the whole hall blocked up with people who wanted to see it. I had to do it over and over again. Pretty soon the manager came over. "What the hell is going on over here? We have to keep this hall open. You'll have to get moving." I got the biggest bang out of that. We were all up to having dinner later on, we're eating up there, and some woman stopped by and she said, "Hey, hey, look who's here! He was the best one of all." Boy, my son looked up at me because we had seen some wonderful tricks done by the other magicians. But those things happen. Just like one time I was doing the Anatomical Wonder routine in a nightclub and we had to work on a small stage back up against a wall. The entrance was over here. There was no entrance to the back. You had to walk through the audience to get up on the stage to do the act. So I'm working up there and I did the Human Blockhead and I had to get down off the stage and walk back through to get back out again. As I was going by a table, two ladies were sitting there, one of them grabbed me by the arm and she said, "Mr. Burkhart, that's a trick that you do with pounding that nail?" I told her, "No, the nail's real.

It's my head that's fake." Those things I keep to remember, something to brighten your day a little bit. Wherever I go people know me. A lot of people know me. I'll whip out the dice "Want to shoot a quarter? Did you ever see the dice trick? I'll show it to you right quick." Pretty soon they'll call over to this one or to that one to come see the trick, too. The manager of this one store where we go do business, every time I go in there he's got somebody else in there and he'll call, "Melvin! Melvin! C'mere a minute. Got your dice with you? Show it to this one." And you get a lot of good deals that way. A lot of people will treat you better because it's something they

For goodness snakes!

remember pleasantly, and it's a way to pass the time. I get a lot of fun out of it. I'm the only person that I know of who does the trick.

S&A: How many people have you shown your tricks, the ones you have worked up yourself?

MB: Any number. I've shown them to several.

S&A: Did you ever get word that anyone was using them?

MB: I don't know of it. I've tried to teach the big dice trick time and time again to friends of mine and I'm glad to show them. "Melvin," they say, "you know you didn't tell me something right," or, "Come on Melvin, you know you're holding something back." Any number of them come back to me and say, "I'm still working on that damn thing, Melvin." None of them have ever got the big dice trick to my knowledge. Not a person. I wouldn't be surprised some day to see somebody do it though. Here's the explanation for it. Do you want to see what it evolved from?

It's amazing to see where it comes from. I was working in the Wonderland Museum in 1933, and the magician got sick and I had to stall and take over in his place.

I wasn't doing magic then, and they had a good magician there, Gravityo. He went out to lunch and he took a solid hour for lunch, regardless. He was an older fellow and he said he needed that relaxation, and if the show went around to him and he wasn't there, you would have to skip him or go on to someone else. They didn't like to skip him because they had a three-way girl show blow-off in the back. Because they wanted a certain amount of time in between each show and the girls didn't want to be working all the time, they wanted time in between each show. The boss told me, "Melvin, the magician's not back, so go up there and do something, and maybe he'll come back and take over from you then." Anyway, the magician got sick and they told me I had to take his place. "You go down to the trick store and get some tricks." They gave me $25 to buy some tricks with because I couldn't use Gravityo's. I come back with a load of stuff that they had hauled off the back shelves loaded with dust. I didn't know what in the hell to do with it or anything. I worked out a few things—Chinese Magic and the Linking Rings—and got to working on that pretty good, and I get up and I said, "Ladies and Gentlemen! I'm the world's *worst* magician." I dropped this and dropped the cards. "Take a card, take any card you want." This was for comedy. When he stayed sick I had to keep going as the World's Worst Magician.

One day, one of the shills (we had five shills working in the audience) come up with the dice and he said "Melvin, I've got one for you. What's that number?" "It's a one." "Are you sure?" "No, that's a four. Wait a minute. That's pretty good." The next show, I was out there with "What's that number?" I got the dice out and I was doing that. One day, I'm up on stage and the people are out in front of me. I'm up on stage and I kept asking a guy out in front what the number was and he said it was changing, but this guy on the side kept saying "Five. Five." The number never changed for him! It got me so mad, because I wasn't getting over with the trick, so I turned the dice over like that and I said "Are you sure that's five?" "No, it's two." "Are you sure it's two?" "No, it's five." And pretty soon there I was out there doing it like this again, you see, and then I got the two dice together. That was the way the trick was born. It took me quite a while to do the routines that I do with it. Now it works. You can look as close as you want to and you don't see anything. I got pretty good at it, and the boss gave me a five dollar raise to keep me on. Gravityo wasn't able to come back. He fell down some steps—he had a stroke or something—and he couldn't come back to work, so I became the magician.

Pretty soon I was working and I was working mechanical tricks you could buy in the store and I got some cards. Then I got the idea of doing my own tricks that I'd seen magicians work and I'd try to do. Then I got some tricks that no one else could do and I got the dice working, then I worked out a routine on the rings. Pretty soon I had a magic act, you know. Then the good part of it was that it was *my* act, not somebody else's. Right down through the years I got better and better and the dice got bigger and bigger. Now, if I try to teach somebody, it's too obtuse! I wouldn't be surprised to see someone do it, though. On the carnival you did show after show, day after day, season after season. I was on that one show for thirty years, and people still come up to me and ask me if I'm going to do the big dice and the rabbit trick. They want to see the same damn things! Pretty soon, I got so good at it, I never had to change the act. You become an unknown celebrity: People have heard of you but don't know you. I can get up and do a show for magicians, too, because every trick you see had to be made up by somebody out there, then it's taken up by others that see him and they want to do that trick and maybe they polish it up a little different. For some reason or another though, nobody's been able to do my tricks.

Don't get me wrong when I say that. I have never seen anybody be able to do it, and I've tried to teach any number of them. People are amazed when they see this. I always have a pair of dice in my pocket. I'm known all over the city for having a pair of dice in my pocket. Because wherever I go and I'm standing around, I'll pull the dice out of my pocket and say "You wanna shoot for it?" and I start a little conversation and have a little fun. Make people laugh. People at stores, it doesn't make any difference to me. It's just a way to pass the time. I don't drink or smoke, you see. It's a shame. I could get all the free drinks I wanted! When you stand around with magicians and do it, they want to see it again. They've never seen anyone else do that trick before. That is a pocket trick that I carry around with me. I can take any number of magicians and I don't know one of them that can do it. They all get discouraged. I made up that trick about 60 years ago. I've gotten it down in that time. Magicians may have never heard of me. Actually, I'm an unknown celebrity in the magic circles too! Many of them have heard of Melvin Burkhart and the big dice, but they've never seen me because I don't go to any of the conventions, and unless they have come to see me they haven't seen

> I always have a pair of dice in my pocket. I'm known all over the city for having a pair of dice in my pocket. Because wherever I go and I'm standing around, I'll pull the dice out of my pocket and say "You wanna shoot for it?" and I start a little conversation and have a little fun.

anybody else do it. You want to see another trick that I do that gets a kick out of magicians? Watch! It was made many years ago by Gene Gordon. He and I used to play the fair together. He would come out and spend half the day with us. He's in a nursing home now. He's in bad shape. He was a good friend of mine, and he came up to me one day and said, "Melvin, here's a trick of mine called The Professor's Nightmare done with three pieces of rope. It would be good for you up on the platform there." He did the trick for me. The trick was very simple at that time. When I say simple I mean it was the bare bones of the trick. I had to take it and work it up. As I say, it's a common trick, but it's the presentation. It's what you do with it. Here's a trick that I made up [does knot trick with scarf]. I've taught some of the magicians how to do it, but I haven't seen any of them do it good yet, but I've tried to teach them. When I go out to magic shows I have to do these tricks because they're what they've heard about and want to see. Now I saw a wonderful magician name of the Great O'Keith—he's been dead a number of years—and he was doing a show for a birthday and he did this. Tied a knot in there, see, then he blew on it and it would disappear. And I thought, "That would be good for me up on the stage there—a good, quick trick." I went home and I figured he had to get a slip knot in there somewhere. That's the main idea of the trick: Blow on it and it disappears. I must have worked on that thing for two or three months. I'd pick up the string and I knew damn good and well it's a simple trick, but how in the hell did he do it? One day I was doing it and I ended up with the trick you just saw, to my surprise and amazement. That's the greatest trick that I do now. I'll have some wonderful magicians standing around, and they won't ask you how you do it. A good magician never asks you how you do your trick, but if you want to know how to do it, I'll show you how to do it. There are so many damn card tricks out there too. I'll show you a couple of card tricks that I invented. Don't get me wrong. I've got books over there full of card tricks, wonderful cards tricks. I can't do them. It takes too long to get the trick down! So I made up my own tricks. When you do a trick, you don't try to fool people; you try to entertain them by fooling their eyes. [Melvin does his card tricks]

S&A: I suppose it's a function of practice, too.

MB: A funny thing, I never really practice much on anything. Take a golfer. You know, if you can't hit the ball down the fairway or in the hole, you give up after a time. But if you send that thing out there sailing— "Hey! Man, that's all right!"—and the next time you go out there, you're doing it better, see. Because some people have a penchant for certain things and it falls right into the milieu of what they are doing or what they can do. That's the way with me. I never practice a lot. Doing the dice trick down through the years, I slowly graduated from doing the small dice to doing the large ones. It's a very good sleight of hand trick because it takes people by surprise. I've had a lot of fun down throughout the years. When I would go to a magic meeting and pull these tricks, I would get the attention of the news media and you'd have a lot more fun. If you do something fast enough and funny enough, then they like it. Most magicians try to drag things out for too long. That doesn't register with the audience the way that it should. They open up the book and see that "this is supposed to be a hot trick." I close the book then. These are linking rings. Every magician I know knows ten tricks to my one because they read the books, they study the books, and they practice the books. I don't. It would be a waste of time to me because I would never get a chance to do those tricks on any show that I'm in.

S&A: Other than the TV and magazine exposure we were talking about, you were also featured in the *Freakards* set of trading cards. It's really sad they're out of print.

MB: [rifling through his personal set] In the *Freakards* set they've got me down as "Ed" Burkhart because there was that guy doing Anatomical Wonder and his name was Ed "Anato" Hayes. I was confused with him several times. I worked with several of them in that set. Yvonne and Yvette, the Siamese twins. They're the ones that just died. Laurello, the man with the revolving head. Here's the Ossified Man who traveled with us for a number of years. Of course, he's dead a long time ago. They're all dead! Robert "The Two-Faced Man" Melvin. Pete Robinson. I have a story about Pete Robinson.

S&A: The human skeleton.

MB: About 1933 or so on Ringling Bros., as a joke, the publicist married Pete to the fat woman. We were playing in that area so they went to Niagara Falls for the honeymoon. There were four pinheads on our show. There was also Eko and Iko. Lentini was a good friend of mine. The lion-faced boy. The Gibbs—the Siamese Twins. The Ubangis. They were on Ringling Bros. In 1939. Rasmus Niellson.

S&A: Who lifted an anvil with his nipples.

MB: Yeah. It was made out of aluminum. It was heavy, but it wasn't a steel anvil. Frances O'Conner.

S&A: The armless wonder.

MB: Zip the Pinhead. I used to work with him. I worked with Zip and the Giraffe Neck Girl when I was on Ringling. I worked with her for many years. She's still alive in Jackson, Mississippi, I believe. The Alligator Skin Man—

that's Emmitt—and his wife the Monkey Girl, Percilla. Daisy and Violet Hilton. They were dolls. I liked working with them. They were very pleasant people, but some of them aren't. I have always got along with the freaks I have worked with because I understand that freak physicalities can cause freak mentalities. Some were so sensitive. Many of them were thin skinned, very sensitive to what they might have thought was a barb thrown at them. But if you know how to get along with them, it was all right. Sealo. He just died. He had one hell of an act. He'd take a piece of clay and make the damnedest things right before your eyes. He'd take that ball of clay and boom, boom, boom, boom you'd have a horsey. Switch it around and have a goat and a pig. He was just amazing.

S&A: Who would you say was the most incredible act you ever saw?

MB: Me! No, I don't know. They're so damn many of them it would be hard to say. When you associate with them all of the time you just look at them like your friend. You don't stop to figure out that this is an unusual person in that respect no more than if somebody would see me working and then go out and see me as a freak because I look perfectly normal to them. Even though I was a big freak! But, you know, I went to work in 1956 on James E. Strates show. We had about eighteen acts in the show, and we had two owners, Whitey Sutton and Slim Kelly. But there is not a soul alive now that was performing when I joined that show. First of all Slim died when I was there about eighteen or nineteen years, then Whitey Sutton died and then his wife and son took over. Every act out of the eighteen acts—I'm the only act that's still alive. Other acts joined us later on and worked with us. Sealo was on there and he's gone now. Dolly Regan and she's gone and fat people and sword swallowers—all gone. And at my age I don't feel so good most days. My future is all behind me! When they gave me that write-up in the *Parade* magazine, the fellow that wrote that spent two or three days with us out there and hung around with me mostly. One time we were

Melvin is really two-faced. Cover the left side of his face to see the "Sad Melvin"; cover the right side to see the "Happy Melvin."

talking there and I told him, "Well there's nothing that's good or bad that thinking it won't make it so." And he said, "What?" and I repeated it and told him I thought it was one of Confucius's sayings. They I said, "You know, the way I figure it, yesterday never was, tomorrow will never be, but today is always," and he asked me if he could quote me on that. I told him that I guessed so, and he wrote it in the article. As far as I know I made that up on the spur of the moment. So don't worry about yesterday or tomorrow. Just worry about today.

◆ ◆ ◆ ◆ ◆

I'd already been up since dawn, and above and beyond Burkhart's interview that day (my first with him), I'd interviewed another show-man in the morning and been driving maybe three hours. So here it is midnight, and I'm finally finishing up Melvin's interview (more so, I think, because he could see I was falling asleep in his living room than because he had nothing else to say). On the metal steps to his and his wife's home, I was saying my last, yawning goodbye, when he got serious. Or so I thought. "You know," he said, "I don't drink, gamble or run women. What am I living for?" And then he winked. I should've seen it coming.

Once a blockhead, always a blockhead.

Blockhead Memories

Melvin Burkhart is widely credited for inventing the performance known as "The Human Blockhead." Not that people hadn't been sticking spikes up their nose for some time; they had. It had just been part of a larger series of Torture/Pain Proof acts somewhat akin to fakir performances. Traditionally, blockhead acts put audiences in slack-jawed awe of the performer's ability to withstand excruciating pain. Melvin was different. In addition to inventing the name most commonly associated with the act, he turned it into a comedy routine. The stories that follow—some funny, some horrifying—are all told with the spirit of Melvin's Human Blockhead: You're too busy laughing to run away screaming.

Doc Swan

A performer (not an every third Thursday open-mike performer but a real dyed in the wool one) knows that everytime you appear in public, it's a show. You're on. For Doc Swann (magician, fire eater, and yes, human blockhead) the venue may not be the Broadway stage or a platform underneath a sideshow tent. It may be (and lately is) as a pitchman for steakknives in a warehouse club store. Wherever, the show must go on.

It happened when I was working for Ward Hall in the Meadowlands. For the first time in all of the years that I have done the act, I just wasn't paying attention and I drove the nail right past my nostril and right on in and lost the head of it right in there. I thought, "What happens now?" I had a good crowd and I was pounding it with a microphone and I thought, "I'll just add this on." I'm really hitting a lot less hard than I make it look, but it just sort of slipped right through there. Actually it came out a lot more smoothly than the three or four milliseconds that I thought, "OK where is the closest hospital that removes nails from nostrils?" I just kind of hung my head down low and shook my head a little and reached around there and finally blew real hard and got it out. That was the first time that had happened, and I'd been doing the act for 20 years.

Johnny Meah

Johnny Meah shies away from being called a "Human Blockhead." It's not because his act is fundamentally different from others who use that name to describe their act: It's out of deference to Melvin. It comes from a sense of reverence about the creative spirit only a fellow artist could possess. Once you create something (a banner, a bally or a book) it's yours and Johnny would never feel right calling himself another man's masterpiece.

I had just finished a show, and a rather unlikely looking woman—unlikely as in she didn't figure at the event much less in my audience—came up to me with a rather concerned look on her face and she said, "Could I ask you a couple of questions?" And I said, "Well certainly." And she said, "Did you—you know the thing that you do with that spike—did you have any type of operation to enable you to do that?" And I said, "Yes. It's called a lobotomy."

D.C. Collins

D.C. Collins, as part of the Palace of Wonders, has to be one of the youngest show owners/performers on any midway. Youth equals tireless energy and enthusiasm, both of which are crucial for a life as arduous as a showman's and traits D.C. possesses in spades. Youth can also mean making mistakes. Stupid mistakes. The difference between youth

and stupidity is being able to learn from your mistakes. D.C. is young, but he's a real fast learner.

U P D A T E

Melvin Burkhart died November 8, 2001.

I was quite fresh, probably six months, and the blockhead was still a novel trick to me and I was so ecstatic over this great sideshow trick that I knew. I was "Mr. Sideshow." I was "King of the Sideshows" because I knew how to stick a nail up my nose. I thought I was somebody. I was just learning how to talk on a microphone and do it productively.

I was still young and dumb and liked to flirt a lot. So I'm sitting there on the bally stage and I take a nail—a sixteen-penny nail—and I prepare it and I give a spiel about, "All steel. All real. American made." And there was a couple of gorgeous little things standing there in front of me, at least I thought so, and one in particular I was trying to impress a little harder.

I set there and I took my microphone and drove the nail into my head with it, which has been kind of a standard routine for lots of people. It wasn't original to me; I copied it from somebody who taught it to me. But I made a BIG mistake, a mistake I have never made since.

I leaned down a little closer to show everybody what I had done and this young lady was in front of me and she was just ecstatic over it—she was wild—and she said, "That's not real!" When you hear that, it can either strike fear in your heart or it's what you're asking for. Well, the nail was in my head, but what struck fear in my heart was that little girl I was trying to impress was not impressed.

So I lean down on all fours, lean off the bally stage. Right into the crowd. With my little bean head with the sixteen-penny nail stuck in as deep as it will go, right into my head. I lean down and she's looking at me and she leans over and I said, "I'll tell you what you do. Why don't you pull it out for me."

I leaned down and she starts to pull it out and she's fine. She gets about this far away from my body and her hand starts shaking and her eyes get big and her lips are quivering and about this time she screamed. She realized it was real and in my head. When she did she resigned herself to get it out of there as fast as she could.

She grabbed my face and grabbed as hard as she could to get the nail out. Well that set me on fire. It hurt! We've all been hit in the nose. Anybody attacks you, hit them in the nose. Their eyes are going to well up in tears, they're going to feel sick to their stomachs, and this was inside my nose!

It really caused an effect. It went like crazy. It drove the nail into the back of my head, but it was not as bad as it could have been. She actually pulled the nail out and I pulled away and the nail fell out.

I bled for days afterwards.

The Anatomical Wonder

WAINO AND PLUTANO.

Weight, 45 pounds.   Age, about 50.

City of Humbug

by John Strausbaugh

There's a Heritage Trail plaque on the iron fence at old St. Paul's Chapel, the Revolutionary-era church on Manhattan's lower Broadway at Vesey Street. It says that George Washington prayed there, and Lord Cornwallis; points you to the historic sites of Trinity Church and the Woolworth building, a couple blocks in either direction.

There's no mention, here or in the church's pamphlets, that P.T. Barnum's original American Museum, the most popular attraction in America, once stood directly across the way at the corner of Broadway and Ann Street. But I guess that makes sense; as a neighbor, Barnum was St. Paul's worst nightmare for nearly 25 years. And the rest of New York wasn't too sure about him either.

The one thing that everyone knows about P.T. Barnum is that he said there's a sucker born every minute. Like most everything everyone thinks they know, it's wrong. The full quote is "There is a sucker born every minute, but none of them ever die," and Barnum never said it. According to A.H. Saxon's *P.T. Barnum: The Legend and the Man,* it most likely came from a notorious New York con man, "Paper Collar Joe." It was probably one of Barnum's circus rivals, Adam Forepaugh, who pinned that saying on him.

That it stuck is a sign of how ambivalent people have always been about Barnum. You can see it in how poorly New York City treats his memory. Barnum is one of New York's greatest, most colorful figures. In terms of his influence on New York as a capital of theater, mass marketing, advertising and media—New York as the biggest hype fac-

Opposite: Waino and Plutano, the Wild Men of Borneo.

171

tory in the world outside of Hollywood—he had far more impact than most of his contemporaries whose houses are historic shrines, their statues attracting pigeons in the parks. Yet you can do a walking tour of the many Barnum sites around lower and midtown Manhattan and it's almost like he never existed. I think it's a sign of how ambivalent New York is about its role in American culture. Because it is, undeniably, a P.T. Barnum town. Now maybe even more so than when he was alive.

The Man, the Myth, the Legend: P.T. Barnum.

Ask Barnum scholar Jonathan Hall. "Talking about Barnum's influence on modern culture," he says, "is like talking about the influence of the printing press on western civilization."

Hall is part of a Barnum revival, or renovation really, that's been going on among historians for the past few years. Saxon's influential reappraisal, first published in 1989, has been reissued in paperback by Columbia University Press. Several new Barnum books have come out since, most notably *P.T. Barnum: America's Greatest Showman* by Philip Kunhardt.

Most still focus on Barnum as the quintessential showman and humbug artist. Hall argues that he was much more than that: he was "the first person who understood the modern world, and understood how to use it, in the business sense."

And where else could he have done that but in New York City?

Our tour of Barnum's New York begins in lower Manhattan. Born in Bethel, Connecticut, in 1810, Barnum first saw New York City as a boy of 12, helping a man drive some cattle down from Danbury. He moved to New York in 1826, at 16, to take a job as a clerk in a Brooklyn grocery store. The following year he was a clerk in a porter house at 29 Peck Slip.

After a couple of years, he returned for a time to Connecticut. He married there, started a family and clerked in a Bethel general store, learning the art of the dicker and the deal, the hard sell and the humbug. He started his own newspaper at age 21, and was promptly jailed for libeling a local clergyman. In an early flourish of p.r. genius, he used his paper to whip up such sympathy for himself that on his release he was greeted by a brass band and cheering crowds.

He moved back to Manhattan with his young family in 1834. Now the tour sites are scattered all over lower Manhattan, as Barnum restlessly searched for the key to fame and fortune. He rented a house somewhere on lower Hudson Street. He opened a small boardinghouse at 52 Franklin Street (now a parking lot), bought into a grocery store at 156 South Street, and honed his chops writing florid ads for the Zoological Institute (on the east side of Bowery, just north of Bayard Street, in what's now Chinatown). He went briefly into a bootblacking business at 101 Bowery. There's no 101 anymore; 101 is a Chinatown flophouse, World Hotel, between Hester and Grand Streets.

Along the way, he traveled a lot, peddling *Sears' Pictorial Illustrations of the Bible,* and began to dabble in his true calling, show business. He went on the road throughout the South with an Italian juggler and a touring variety show. In 1835, Barnum made one of his most controversial moves: he bought the rights to manage Joice Heth, supposedly a 161-year-old Negro slave who'd been "Little George" Washington's nurse. She'd played to middling crowds under other management in Philadelphia, but Barnum made her a superstar. He plastered New York with posters, flyers and the brand-new illuminated transparencies. He plied the newspapers with puff pieces he wrote himself—a career-long strategy. Some papers ran them because it was good copy, others because he also bought ads.

Barnum's American Museum: Before the fire.

It was his first all-out p.r. blitz, and a great success. He "displayed" Heth in a room near Niblo's Garden, the famous entertainment hall and beer garden at the corner of Broadway and Prince Street, in what's now fashionable Soho. Thousands came. Some thought Heth was authentic, others were skeptical, and they all paid to confirm their opinions. When everyone in New York had seen her, Barnum put her on tour. She died at his brother's house in Connecticut in 1836, but even then he wouldn't let her quit the stage. He ballyhooed the hell out of her autopsy—which was supposed to finally prove or disprove her age—and charged admission to it.

Even after she was buried he kept it up, planting rumors with gullible newspaper editors that her death and autopsy had been hoaxed. One of those taken in was James Gordon Bennett, publisher of the *New York Herald*. Realizing later that Barnum had humbugged him, Bennet became a lifelong enemy. Forever after, the *Herald* vilified Barnum's every move and later refused to run his ads. Barnum always joked that he was very grateful for the free ink. "Especially was it profitable to me," he wrote in his autobiography, "when I could be the subject of scores of lines of his scolding editorials free of charge, instead of paying him forty cents a line for advertisements, which would not attract a tenth part so much attention."

Beyond the pale:
An albino family.

He didn't coin the saying that there's no such thing as bad publicity—he just invented the idea.

If Heth made Barnum famous, his next move made him rich. In 1842, he bought—with "more brass than gold," he later winked—Scudder's American Museum, at the southeast corner of Broadway and Ann Street Typical of museums in its day, including Charles Wilson Peale's famous museum in Philadelphia, Scudder's was a cross between "a rather stuffy, earnest, educational" institution, as Hall puts it, and a cabinet of curiosities, much like what we'd consider a sideshow today. It was filled with stuffed animals, shells and crystals, antiques, ethnographic artifacts, knick-nacks, curiosities, and the occasional human freak.

The notion that Barnum's version of a museum was less dignified, more freakshow than standard for his time, is false. "The [only] real difference was he sold it better," Hall says.

Barnum's ad copy had a distinctive "self-deprecating humor," Hall adds. "There's sort of an in-joke between him and the reader." This is a crucial point for Barnum fans. He would never have called his customers "suckers." What he did say was, "The people *like* to be humbugged" (my emphasis), which more accurately reflects his conviction that the public was actively, consciously collaborating with him in his spectacular publicity stunts. And in fact, on more than one occasion when he'd pulled one of his finer gags just

this side of hoaxing his customers, the crowds would hail him like a hero—and shout, literally, "Three cheers for the humbug!" The masses, if not always the press, got his jokes; they appreciated Barnum as a master prankster.

Pitchbook from the first Circassian Beauty.

Barnum always pointed out that he didn't invent hype, he just perfected it. "It was the world's way then, as it is now, to excite the community with flaming posters, promising almost everything for next to nothing," he wrote in his autobiography. "I confess that I took no pains to set my enterprising fellow-citizens a better example. I fell in with the world's way; and if my 'puffing' was more persistent, my advertising more audacious, my posters more glaring, my pictures more exaggerated, my flags more patriotic and my transparencies more brilliant . . . it was not because I had less scruples than they, but more energy, more ingenuity, and a better foundation for such promises."

He drove the folks at St. Paul's crazy in the process. Literally overnight, he had the entire exterior of the five-store American Museum painted like an enormous banner, with giant snakes, lions, bears and such in rampantly gaudy colors. It was like a circus had sneaked into town overnight and camped right across the street from the venerable old church. He put a band out on a balcony to serenade passersby (and churchgoers) with "Free Music for the Millions." This band was made up of the very worst musicians Barnum could hire; his idea was that the terrible din they raised would drive people off the street and into the museum.

At dawn on July 4, 1842, Barnum directed his people to string a line of American flags across Broadway, "for I knew there would be thousands of people passing the Museum with leisure and pocket money, and I felt confident that an unusual display of national flags would arrest their patriotic attention, and bring them within my walls." One end of the line was tied to a Museum window, the other to a tree in St. Paul's churchyard.

By 9 A.M., "Hundreds of additional visitors were drawn by this display into the Museum"—and a couple of St. Paul's vestrymen were drawn into the street, angrily demanding that Barnum remove the "sacrilege." Raising his voice for the milling crowds, Barnum cried, "Well, Mister, I should just like to see you dare to cut down the American flag on the Fourth of July; you must be a 'Britisher' to make such a threat as that . . . " Facing bodily harm from the patriotic mob, the church folks wisely slunk off, and never bothered him again about hanging his flags from their tree.

JRMA LOUSTAU
FEMME PANTHÈRE AGÉE DE 24 ANS

Leopard-Spotted Woman.

It's often forgotten now that Barnum backed up the ballyhoo with solid product. If he rarely gave customers precisely what he'd promised, he always gave them their money's worth in other stuff.

He vastly expanded Scudder's collection, amassing a trove of exhibits and attractions crammed into every nook and cranny of the building. The New York Historical Society has catalogs listing the astonishing amount of stuff that was typically on display. In Barnum's own recollection, this included "educated dogs, industrious fleas, automatons, jugglers, ventriloquists, living statuary, tableaux, gypsies, Albinoes, fat boys, giants, dwarves, rope-dancers, live 'Yankees,' pantomime, instrumental music, singing and dancing in great variety, dioramas, panoramas, models of Niagara, Dublin, Paris, and Jerusalem, Hannington's dioramas of the Creation, the Deluge, fairy grotto, Storm at Sea . . . "

And the "Feegee Mermaid"; General Tom Thumb and Commodore Nutt; Anna Swan, "The Nova Scotian Giantess"; Grizzly Adams and his trained bears; William Henry Johnson, the original "Zip" the pinhead; Dora Dawron, a singing half-man/half-woman act; Mme. Josephine Fortune Clofullia, a Swiss bearded lady; the voluptuous "Circassian" beauty Salumma Agra; and relics from the Holy Land, and a campaign hat donated by Ulysses S. Grant (a big fan of the museum), and a guy who made music with his nostrils, and phrenologists, pet taxidermists, sewing machine salesmen, daguerrotypists and photographers.

Oh, and there was an oyster bar and a rifle range. A day at Barnum's was so full he had to devise ruses to get people to leave.

Barnum made other additions Hall considers "very important culturally." At a time when New York theaters were little more than places for men to go meet whores, Barnum made theater safe for families. In his Lecture Room (actually the best theater in town), he put on "moral entertainments" like *Uncle Tom's Cabin* and the temperance melodrama *The Drunkard* (he was a teetotaler and temperance lecturer himself).

> "Without Barnum," he continues, "it's hard to see how [New York City] would become the theater capital of the world, because the middle class wouldn't have come...And how could you imagine Hollywood without Barnum?"

"He created middle-class audiences for respectable entertainments," Hall says. "It was the one place in town they could go. People now think of him as this vaguely disreputable character, but what the name Barnum meant then was like Disney. It meant wholesome family entertainment. Yes, they had a whole different definition of what was 'unwholesome.' Now we might be queasy about putting people with birth defects on stage, or bringing in people from Africa and having them dance around. But that was regarded as perfectly respectable then."

"Without Barnum," he continues, "it's hard to see how [New York City] would become the theater capital of the world, because the middle class wouldn't have come . . . And how could you imagine Hollywood without Barnum?"

Another Barnum addition was live exotic animals. Menageries had been popular since Colonial days; Barnum's Barnumesque expansion on the theme was the mid-step toward full-fledged zoos. (He would later consult in the creation of both the Central Park Zoo and the National Zoo in D.C.)

Along with lions, tigers, monkeys, rare birds and such—many of them captured during expeditions Barnum sent to the far corners of the earth—he built the first public aquarium in America. It was in the basement of the museum, where in addition to the first hippopotamus displayed in America, he housed, incredibly, white whales trapped for him by fishermen at the mouth of the St. Lawrence River.

It says a lot that the Smithsonian and the American Museum of Natural History fiercely competed for Barnum's favor, so that he'd donate cast-offs to them. They're still trailing him today. When a museum adds an IMAX theater, or plays off pop-culture icons like *Star Trek* and *Jurassic Park* to attract customers, it's doing nothing but "Barnumizing" itself. (Tom Thumb coined the term.)

Of course, there are always critics who object that these museums are prostituting their educational mission. "And there were similar objections to Barnum in his time," Hall notes. "There will always be purists who think that if it's not boring it's not good for you." Then again, he smiles, "It certainly is true that you lose a certain amount of subtlety when you Barnumize something."

Saxon estimates that in its twenty-three years some thirty-eight million tickets to the museum were sold. That's more than the total population of the United States, estimated at thirty-five million in 1865. It's a better sales record, proportional to the national population, than Disneyland would rack up in its first quarter-century.

On July 13, 1865, a large crowd thronged Broadway to watch the last great show at the original American Museum: it was completely destroyed by a spectacular fire. Newspapers around the country ran accounts like the *Tribune*'s, describing the "horrible howls and moans" of the trapped animals, the monkeys "perched around the windows, shivering with dread and afraid to jump out," the corpses of the two white whales boiled to death in their tank. There were stories of exotic escapees roaming Manhattan's streets for days afterward.

Standing in front of St. Paul's nearly 140 years later, it's sad not to see even a mention of the museum on that Heritage Trail plaque. No plaque either on the building that's now at Barnum's old site, an anony-

> It says a lot that the Smithsonian and the American Museum of Natural History fiercely competed for Barnum's favor, so that he'd donate cast-offs to them. They're still trailing him today.

mous white office building from 1961. There are still trees in St. Paul's churchyard, some of them pretty tall and old, but I don't suppose any are old enough to be the one he once tied his flags to.

When the disaster struck, Barnum's friend Horace Greeley suggested that he "take this fire as a notice to quit and go a-fishing." Instead, he immediately leased new premises at 535-539 Broadway, on the west side between Spring and Prince Streets, and opened "Barnum's New American Museum" that November. It too would burn down, in the winter of 1868, on a day so cold that the water froze in the firemen's hoses.

Since 1889, that block has been dominated by 555 Broadway, the white monster of the Charles Broadway Rouss Bldg. (recently renovated for hipster Soho retail and office use). I have a feeling Rouss must have known he was building next door to a former Barnum site. A Southerner and self-made man, he slapped up a huge sign while the building was under construction. Its message was irrefutabley Barnumesque: "He who builds, owns, and will occupy this marvel of brick, iron, and granite, thirteen years ago walked these streets penniless and $50,000 in debt."

"The show business has all phases and grades of dignity," Barnum wrote, "from the exhibi-

2 Headed Girl, MILLIE CRISSIE.
(Copyright secured.)

Two-Headed Nightingale: Millie-Christine.

tion of a monkey to the exposition of that highest art in music or that drama which entrances empires and secures for the gifted artist a world-wide fame which princes well might envy. Such art is merchantable, and so with the whole range of amusements, from the highest to the lowest."

(I'm quoting from an 1871 edition of *Struggles and Triumphs: or Forty Years' Recollection of P.T. Barnum, Written by Himself*. I found it a few years ago for $15 at the once-famous, now closed, Barnes & Noble

Annex store on 5th Avenue. *Struggles and Triumphs* is the revamped and expanded version of the *Life of P.T. Barnum Written by Himself,* originally published in 1854, when he was only forty-four. He continued to update and revise it until he died. At least a million copies, an astronomical figure then, were sold during his lifetime. It's been said that the two most-read books of the era were Barnum's and God's.)

The tour doubles back now, heads all the way down Manhattan island to the Battery waterfront. Castle Clinton, a circle of fortress stones now run by the National Park Service, is one site where the brass plaques and guided tours openly acknowledge Barnum as about the biggest thing that ever happened to it.

Jenny Lind, the Swedish Nightingale, "was an existing phenomenon in Europe" when Barnum heard of her in 1850, Hall explains, "And even with mediocre promoters over there she was doing quite well. It was on the basis of that reputation that Barnum basically said, "I don't know if you can sing, but I know you can sell tickets.'"

Barnum went deeply in debt to bring her to America—and, to protect his investment, whipped up the most massive, most successful publicity campaign ever launched. Without hearing her sing a note, the entire nation was gripped by "Lindomania." It spun off an entire industry producing Jenny Lind memorabilia: Jenny Lind hats, Jenny Lind parasols, Jenny Lind face cream, etc. (The New-York Historical Society has a large catalog of these novelties.)

"It was a masterful p.r. campaign—partly because it had only just become possible to do that," Hall says. "Barnum came along at the moment when you could start to talk about 'mass media.' The telegraph changed everything. You have papers across the country stealing one another's stories. So when you have a story like Jenny Lind's arrival at Canal Street—which was carefully choreographed by Barnum, of course—it's covered by all the papers and becomes a national story." Eventually, "it becomes a national story if Jenny Lind takes a walk."

An enormous crowd met Lind's ship when it made the Canal Street dock, then it followed her carriage over to the Irving House hotel, on the west side of Broadway at Chambers Street Broadway was thronged all night; around midnight, a brigade of firemen showed up to serenade her.

Her first public concert in America was on September 13, 1850, at Castle Clinton, then known as Castle Garden (built as a fortress in 1808, but already converted into a concert hall by the 1820s). Leaving nothing to chance, Barnum lashed the public into a ticket-buying frenzy by auctioning off opening-night seats to the highest bidders. It was not a gimmick he invented, but he added his own twist. He tried to set up a deal whereby a friend would be the highest bidder, setting the

tone for the auction. But his friend couldn't understand how that would benefit anyone but Barnum. Barnum then went to John Genin, a hatter whose shop was next door to the American Museum. Genin understood exactly what Barnum was offering him. The day after the auction, newspapers across the land ran front page headlines about how "Genin the Hatter Pays $225 for One Jenny Lind Ticket!" Genin's business skyrocketed—as did bids for tickets.

To Hall, these two guys—one who just thinks Barnum's trying to rip him off, the other who gets the joke and profits—are symptomatic of how the culture in general reacted to Barnum's ploys. "You see it in the newspaper. Some of them are very shrewd and see what he's about." Others, like Bennett's *Herald*, keep thinking he's either a con man or a fool.

John A. Kouwenhoven's *Columbia Historical Portrait of New York* reproduces a great cartoon lampooning Lind's opening night. Called "The Second Deluge," it depicts the concertgoers as a horde of well-dressed animals—people with heads of dogs, asses, turkeys, etc.—rushing into Castle Garden, "The Modern Ark of Noah." Barnum is depicted as a crafty monkey, grinning in a nearby tree.

The monkey and his Nightingale went on to make fortunes from their partnership.

Barnum introduced Tom Thumb to tiny Lavinia Warren in 1862, and they were married later that year in what the press called "the grand national event of the season." Barnum staged this "Fairy Wedding" in Grace Church, then Manhattan's very most fashionable, at Broadway and 10th Street One of the officiating clerics was Grace's Robert Taylor, a man of the highest society, able to dictate who received invitations to the most exclusive balls and parties. Congressmen, governors of several states, grandes dames and captains of industry attended. Rev. Taylor later got an angry letter from a parishioner who denounced this "marriage of mountebanks"—because he couldn't get in.

That the crème of Manhattan jostled for invites to what was, after all, a wedding of sideshow midgets, shows again how schizoid New York was about Barnum. He was jeered at as a tricky-dealing Yankee peddler while at the same time he was hobnobbing with presidents, crowned heads and industry barons.

Barnum, Hall says, "was schizophrenic about it himself." He often said he preferred opera to his own music-hall acts, and loved to hang with the literary giants of his age, including Thackeray (to whom he gave financial advice) and Mark Twain. "He kept hoping that a Barnum-like character would turn up in one of Twain's stories," Hall tells me. "It seems natural." But Twain, oddly, never granted him this wish—unless one cares to read a little Barnum into the *Connecticut Yankee*. Melville, however, did parody him to a series of magazine articles, and seems to have lifted a scene in *The Confidence Man* straight from Barnum's autobiography.

Bearded lady Annie Jones.

"Clearly he had his finger on the pulse of what the average person wanted," Hall explains. "If you were an upper-crust person you might not like that. On the other hand, he's so clearly successful at what he does, and any kind of success has its own magnetism."

The Thumbs' wedding reception was held in the fancy Metropolitan Hotel, at the northeast corner of Broadway and Prince Street (now 568-58 Broadway, home to Eddie Bauer and Armani outlets). According to the 1866 *New York As It Is, or, Stranger's Guidebook* (which included an ad for the American Museum), the hotel was "furnished throughout in the most splendid and costly style, having all the accommodations and conveniences that the most luxurious taste could devise."

Meanwhile, not everything Barnum touched in New York turned to gold. In 1851 he bought an interest in a new fire-fighting invention, "Phillips' Fire Annihilator," and helped arrange to demonstrate it to potential investors in Hamilton Square. This was an unusually uptown site for Barnum, an open space between 66th and 68th Streets, from 5th to 3rd Avenue. In twenty years it would be eaten up by new streets and houses. Phillips failed to annihilate the staged fire, and the project died of humiliation.

Barnum was also involved in the ill-fated Crystal Palace, the large hall of iron, glass and wood built in 1852 for America's first World's Fair. Barnum was elected president of the stockholders' association in 1854, and they begged him to take over the limp programming of it. He staged a few spectacles there, "But it was a corpse long before I touched it, and I found . . . that so far as my ability was concerned, 'the dead could not be raised.'" It went into liquidation soon after—and then burned down in 1858. The site is now Bryant Park, behind the New York Public Library.

The other thing everyone knows about Barnum is that he pretty much invented "the Greatest Show on Earth." It's true that no circus before or since was ever the giant three-ring spectacle Barnum created; it's less known that this "was really sort of an epilogue to his career," Hall notes. "He was semi-retired, in his sixties already, and had basically given up show business and retired to Connecticut."

At first, he simply rented out his name to William Coup's circus, and he never ran it on a daily basis. "He used his connections to get the animals and the acts," Hall says, and of course he applied his genius for publicity, "but what he liked the most was going around to the circus and having everybody cheer him, 'You came to see Barnum? Well, I'm Barnum.'"

Barnum's Museum, Menagerie & Circus opened under canvas in Brooklyn in 1871. It toured the country to thunderous success. In 1872, Barnum bought the rattletrap Hippotheatron, at 14th Street and Broadway, and installed the circus there for winter performances. Only five weeks later, on Christmas Eve, it burned to the ground in yet another spectacular fire, taking a large part of the neighborhood with it. Once again, many of his animals perished horribly in the flames.

The following year he leased a site for his last famous venue in Manhattan: Gilmore's Garden—later named Madison Square Garden—and Barnum's Roman Hippodrome. The golden-spired New York Life Building of 1928 now stands on the site, between Madison and Park Avenues, from 26th to 27th Streets. Another of the few bronze plaques in the city to mention Barnum is on the wall at the building's Madison Avenue entrance.

It's true that no circus before or since was ever the giant three-ring spectacle Barnum created; it's less known that this "was really sort of an epilogue to his career," Hall notes. "He was semi-retired, in his sixties already, and had basically given up show business and retired to Connecticut."

Lionel the Lion Man.

Barnum may have gotten the idea from Franconi's Hippodrome, which had stood nearby, 1853-1856, facing Madison Square from the northwest corner of Broadway and 23rd Street. Franconi's was a faux-Roman arena, with brick walls and a canvas tent roof; "a short-lived attempt to introduce spectacular pageants, gladiatorial contests, and chariot races to New York audiences." According to Kouwenhoven, it seated 10,000.

Franconi's was torn down to make way for the ritzy Fifth Avenue Hotel, one of several top-class places (including the Murray Hill Hotel, at Park Ave, and 40th Street) the aging Barnum and his second wife stayed during frequent visits from their permanent residence in Bridgeport. *New York As It Is* notes that the Fifth Avenue's rooms were all accessible via remarkable "perpendicular railway," which I take to mean some sort of elevator or escalator. The hotel was torn down at the turn of the 20th century.

Barnum's hippodrome was a massive affair, with a quarter-mile track running around the infield performing area. The circus played there for years. Redesigned by Stanford White and rebuilt in 1889, Madison Square Garden continued over four decades to be one of the best-loved buildings in New York City's history, until it was torn down in 1925 to make way for New York Life.

In 1882, Barnum bought Jumbo, the African elephant, from the London Zoological Society, and brought him to New York in a truly jumbo publicity blizzard. Jumbomania was nearly as big as Lindomania had been, with a similar flood of products and novelties.

"Jumbo was one of the greatest product spokesmen there ever was," Hall says. "He was the Michael Jordan of his time." By the time Jumbo was killed in a tragic train accident in 1885, he had entered the English language as a synonym for "big." As Hall puts it, "Jumbo shrimp would not be jumbo shrimp if it weren't for Barnum."

Like Joice Heth, Jumbo continued to produce for Barnum even in death, touring with the circus for a few more seasons—his skeleton standing at one end of the big top, his mounted hide at the other, like doleful bookends. Eventually, Barnum sent the hide to his favorite college, Tufts University (where, characteristically, it would be destroyed by fire). Despite fierce bargaining from the Smithsonian, Jumbo's skeleton went to the American Museum of Natural History.

And that's the end of the tour. Though, if Barnum had had his way, Jumbo's name might have been permanently associated with one more site. Foolishly, however, the Brooklyn Bridge company's directors spurned Barnum's offer of $50,000 to let Jumbo be the first creature to cross the bridge when it opened in 1883.

Barnum died in 1891 in Bridgeport, where he'd lived most of his mature life, and which he always liked better than Manhattan anyway. Bridgeport likes him back; the Barnum Museum is its chief attraction.

Still, Hall argues, if Barnum's legacy in New York is less touted, it's more important and pervasive. When I ask him if he thinks Barnum was a good influence or a bad one, he shrugs and says, "It's sort of like judging the weather . . . Certainly he raised the decibel level in American culture, and made it less genteel. Which is both good and bad. It definitely became more difficult to get any sort of subtle ideas across."

"I'm ambivalent about Barnum myself," he concludes. "If the question is 'Barnum—thumbs up or thumbs down?' I don't know, I guess I'm thumbs sideways."

City of Humbug

Percilla Bejano:
A spit-polished sideshow
sensation.

Monkey Business

Percilla Bejano, aka "The Monkey Girl," famous from the Ringling Bros. Circus and some of the most prominent carnival sideshows of this century, doesn't have hair one on her face anymore. She shaves now. As she put it to me years ago, when she and husband Emmitt "The Alligator Man" retired, she'd decided the beard would go. No more veils in public. As she told me then, "Show's over."

Of course that's only partly true. She's still the center of attention pretty much wherever she goes, hairy face or not. She's under five feet tall with black hair as dense as steel wool. She's thin as a yard stick, and the dark, coarse hair on her hands draws your eyes the minute you catch sight of them. When I've taken her shopping, it seems half the people in the supermarket know her, say hello, ask how she's doing, how her dogs and chickens and ducks and goat are doing. Though she misses Emmitt dearly (he died a few years ago and she grieves still), hers is still a busy house.

In a trip to Florida not so long ago, I took Percilla to the Extravaganza, the annual trade show for the carnival business held in Tampa, so she could visit and be visited by friends from the midways of yesteryear and by others who want to meet the premier attraction they've seen in assorted documentaries and movies and have read about in countless books on the biz. Later, I took her to dinner

Percilla and one of her "babies."

at a local buffet where we could sit around for hours if we felt like it and no waiter would be giving us the hairy eye. As she puts it, "I don't eat real fast," not exactly a news flash given the dentition problems which follow from her hypertrychosis.

Hers is—and has been—a troubled life, filled with more than your average showman's share of thrilling joys followed chockablock with abject sorrow. The fact that she's physically, psychologically and emotionally whole, by the standards of the average non-show biz citizen, is no small miracle. Hers has been a life of petty (and not so petty) annoyances she's had to address in a number of ways, as often as not by unexpected generosity. In the first conversation we ever had, Bejano told me she loved the old homestead she and Emmitt had bought near Tampa as she could go out to her pool, dressed in her swim suit, "and there's no chumps looking," unlike her days in the shows, when looking, might be the least the chumps thought they'd be able to get away with. By the same token, I've been told countless times—by others, seldom by her—of Bejano's lengthy chats with fans, especially children, who came to the shows to see her.

Percilla in Canada, 1946.

Show historian Robert Houston told me that, as a child, he'd gone to the sideshow only to be sent on a prankish wild goose chase by one of the performers after he'd asked too many annoying, vexatious questions (hey—he was a kid; whaddaya expect?). Where'd that performer send him? From pillar to post, one carny to another, to get "the key to the midway," a prize which never occurred to the young Houston was as elusive as winning big on one of the flat stores. Well, by the time he'd gotten to Bejano, she'd seen just about enough of that little game, and she not only stopped his hunt for the faux golden fleece but talked to him for the longest time. So long, in fact, that the discussion (intermittent and by mail now) is sill going on. And Houston's retired! No, talking with Bejano's not a problem.

Percilla on Dancing & Music

Emmitt, I taught him how to dance. In a little trailer in the trailer park before we got any property. He would get up and turn around and look at me and shake [his hips]. See why I miss him? We weren't married too long when I taught him to dance. He wouldn't before that. He wouldn't.

He said "I can't do that crap. My legs won't go this way or that way." And I said, "Yes they will. You just count—one, two, three, one, two, three—to learn." But he learned quick because he knew the music. He loved music. He loved *Margie, Dipsy Doodle, It's a Long Way to Tipperary.*

I know all the music, but some of the words I forgot. I used to yodel and sing. I can't sing no more. But I taught myself. I went to a studio once after I was married and [the instructor] says, "There's nothing I can teach you. You've got it all right there." But we loved to dance (after I taught him). Before that he set there and watched everyone have fun. He said "I ain't gonna get up there." The girls came up there—I could see when I was dancing—and try to get him to dance. "C'mon," they'd say. "No. Can't dance." He set there and said, "I'd make a fool out of myself. No way. If I step on their feet . . . "

But I was dancing from when I was five years old. It wasn't part of my act; I just did it. I taught myself. I'd be

PERCILLA

Percilla Bejano pitchcard.

down there [at the girl shows] looking behind the stage, watching the girls doing the steps. I would count the steps. So I taught myself. Do you remember Carmen Miranda? She wore those big shoes, so I went out and bought me some, and I would dance on the stage in them. Karl Lauther, my [adopted] father, would look for me to work. He would be talking the inside of the show, "Now look at this little girl here. Her name is Percilla, and . . . where is she?" And when he found me [he'd ask,] "What are you doing?" [I said,] "What do you care as long as I get my can filled?" He'd laugh, "How much you make today?" They used to throw the money up to me on my blanket, you know, a rug. Well, as long as they threw money at me, Karl was okay with that.

Percilla on Other Acts

The Laurel brothers, they blew glass. They sold stuff just like the joints. They had cards and they had shills. They were on my dad's show sometimes. A father and mother and then they had their own show. They had three boys, and they had shills. They'd be out there in like a ticket box and they would be blowing glass with fire. You know these magnifiers—they make things larger by filling it up with water? They made those. There is a picture of me doing it [blowing glass], but I wasn't good at it. They made ships and like glass over the ships, you know, in bottles. And when they break the glass they'd say, "There goes another one." [laughs] They had these cards in a box—ships, dogs, magnifying glass—and people would pick cards to win. Most didn't. But that's how they ran that joint.

Feliz, Tampa, Florida.

Laurello [the man with the Revolving Head] could put his head all the way around. He was a Nazi. And he didn't like the American flag. You meet all kinds on the sideshow, worse than me!

[Nabor Feliz] Felix, the Indian clay modeler, spoke seven languages and read and wrote them. He was very educated. He told me what the Indians used to do years ago. I wanted to go wherever Felix went. You would say, "Make me a cow," and he would make you a cow [out of clay]. He would bronze them when you would ask him and they sold. He never advertised. He made beautiful things. He was almost 100 years old when he died, but he still had his brains, and he had all his own teeth, and he never shaved; if he had a hair, he would just pull it out and he was just as smooth. He never ate meat. And he could go out there and pick up dandelions on the ground and eat them. "You see this," he would say, "you don't eat that. You eat this." And he would eat them. I told him, "I'm not a grass eater," and he'd laugh at me. He worked for my dad when I was little. Karl Lauther put him in the show when he was a young boy.

Years ago, they didn't have [geek shows]. A man come in the show and said, "I've got to get some air." I said, "Why you come in here? Don't you know what's next door?" Well, I didn't know. I didn't leave the show when Emmitt and me set up. Anyway, the man said, "You'll fall out. Woman next door pulls the heads off chickens and eats the chickens with the feathers and all." I said, "No wonder they come into my show and faint." It was nice soft ground to fall down on. But I couldn't sell no tickets on our show because they're all falling down in the geek show.

[Sword swallower Alex Linton] used to write me, after he worked for Karl. All the way from California. He asked me, "When we going to get married?" Big red letters—this big—I wrote back, "Never."

Flip and Pip, the pinheads, they weren't ours. We rented them. A woman had them. She'd change their diapers, see that they eat. You have to put diapers on them or they'll mess up. They're like kids. You have to walk them, take care of them. They didn't like the police either. They didn't like them. They didn't like the pants they wore or something. Every time they saw them, "Goddamn cops."

He put rats, mice, you know, down his throat [the Great Waldo]. He'd swallow them and then bring them back up. He ran everybody out of Pappa Karl's show once. His mice got loose and ran everybody down the hall. A whole box of them. Mice was everywhere. He was next to my stage, right next to me. It made me sick. I told him, "Can't you put them somewhere else?" That's the only time I ever got sick on a show.

The first time I met Grace McDaniels was at the store show. She took my place when I had my two weeks vacation at the farm. I went down to the museum, sat down and started to eat my breakfast and across was Grace McDaniels. She almost made me sick, first time I saw her. Nobody told me that she came. She was nice, though. The next day, they sent me to [Karl Lauther's] farm. They changed acts every two weeks. For Grace they had a painting of a mule with a mountain, a beautiful painting, hanging in the show.

Percilla and Mule-Faced Woman Grace McDaniels.

We used to drive right past [restaurants] when we saw that Popeye stopped. It was terrible. He'd put his eyes out, you know. Pop his eyes out. They'd come and wait on him, he'd say, "Thank you," and pop his eyes out on them. They'd run back and tell the boss, "There's a man out there losing his eyes!" [The Great] Waldo told him not to. He told him, "You're not on exhibition. You don't do that where you eat." One time [a waitress] run out to her car after, run out and drove away! She did. Guess she wasn't going to wait on him again.

I'd get them [new performers] into swordswallowing and pin cushion. I'd tell them, "Don't gag. Don't eat—swallow and then eat." If you swallow those [neon] tubes and you lean over and it cracks, you get a belly full of glass. Pin cushion is easy. You put alcohol on first and pull up the skin. And you put the pins in overnight in alcohol.

Mortado was the crucified man. One week in Karl's [Oddities on Parade] show, he done the crucifixion. The next week was Palm Sunday. They put him last in the show. I thought he was kind of odd. His wife dressed as a nurse. She took the bandages off his hands and feet every show because they [the holes in his hands and feet] were wide open. They had to be, to put the spikes through. His wife was a registered nurse. The week he done the crucifying, they put the cross up there and they put the nails right through his feet. I never seen him walk. People would faint in the crowd. Buy tickets and come in and faint.

Cuckoo. Cuckoo the Bird Girl. First time I seen her she got up and started climbing a tree! She scared me; she really scared me, and I never was scared of people at all. She was really something. But she wasn't wild: She got paid to be wild. She retired and got a store in Connecticut when she got home. Hartford. A beautiful store.

The Igorotes were Filipinos. Dog eaters. That's what we told everybody anyway. The head guy, chief, used to act like he was going to take my dogs, I used to run! [laughs]. After Karl lost most of the Igorotes, he put the one who stayed in his own sideshow. He'd take the orange wire—like cable—and then you put it in the fire and make designs, and he made his own walking canes with handles and they sold just great. "One dollar! One dollar!" He could say that so easy. I was teaching him English. So I said, "Fifty cents"; he said, "No, two. One dollar." He knew the money. They gave him pennies, he'd give them to me. He didn't want to keep that money.

Percilla and her mother, 1941.

Percilla's Origins

I'm from San Juan, Puerto Rico, and my father was from the old country. From Spain, my father. He was born in Spain and my mother went to visit and met him and they got married. They got married in Puerto Rico. So I'm full-blooded Spaniard. Hot blooded.

Karl [Lauther, my adopted father] didn't meet the whole family right away. My dad come over here with me when I was a baby. He heard about the show and thought he could put me in a show. But he didn't know how to do it because he couldn't talk very good English. He came over with my mother, but my mother didn't like it here because she couldn't speak English. I found that out after I found her [in Puerto Rico] when I was older. My father met Karl and Karl seen me in his arms and he just fell in love. This was not show business; he just fell in love. "What a sweet baby." My father said to Karl, "Could you in an exhibition?" Because he couldn't speak very good English.

But he spoke more than my mama. She couldn't talk at all, and she wanted to go home. So he took her back home and come back and got in touch with Karl. He loved Karl. And all Karl wanted was me. He stayed with me and Karl hired a maid—a white maid—to take care of me, to see that my clothes was clean and I had a clean body for the show. I wasn't wearing a diaper then, just little white panties. She took care of me. My father seen that Karl Lauther cared for me, because he hired that woman to take care of me because he couldn't do it. See, he liked Karl. He was German, very strict. He knew how to use his belt; he had an alligator-skin belt. Anyway, he stayed, and he got shot in Gainesville, Florida. My own flesh and blood. They never caught the man. He was walking home with me and Felix—the Indian clay modeler, who was working for my dad. Felix was interpreting for my father in Spanish, and he was trying to teach him English. So my dad died, and Karl went through his trunk and there was this paper in there it said "If anything happens to me, you take my daughter and raise her as your own." That's how Karl adopted me. His sister was a lawyer, and that's how he got me quick. I was a real little baby. I was holding onto my dad when he got killed. We were working some little still

Percilla: The kid on the midway.

date and Felix had a boarding room, and they did a lot of gambling there. We were coming home, me, my dad and Felix—Felix always came with us because he could talk English—and my dad was shot in the back. There were two of them. The next month or so, somebody else got shot. Like they are doing now. They never caught who did it. Nope. My dad never hurt anyone. He didn't order a whiskey or anything. Couldn't. He spoke Spanish. But he wanted Karl to have me forever.

Percilla —Kid on the Midway

[When I was a kid] they made me bally. I'd climb up the steps with that veil on. My dad would stand on the edge of the stairs and watch me like a hawk. And his wife would work the Electric Chair. We had pits; it wasn't a geek show; it was a sideshow. A 10-in-one. Then Karl had a panorama show that would move around. Like miniatures. Men and women dancing, animated. He had a lot of gadget shows.

I'll never forget there was a guy across the street that had a grab joint and I could smell the onions on the skillet. I got so hungry. Karl Lauther had his own cookhouse and his own toilet and none of us could go on the midway to eat. None of us. But that guy at the grab joint, I'd crook my finger at him to get his attention. The talker would say, "I'm trying to make an opening and get people in here. Will you stop whatever you're doing."

But we would go to work at seven in the morning and be ready. Those country people would come out so early; I would get so mad. I'd think, "Why don't you people go back to bed?" I just wanted to sleep. But we had fun. We slept in tents—we didn't use trailers in the old days. And we rode on trains. See, they'd put the girls at one end and the boys at the other on the train, you know, on the cars. With a partition between. I loved it. I did. Oh, I couldn't do it now, oh no. You're young, you can do anything. Anything.

Menagerie Sideshows line-up. The Bejanos are on the top left.

Percilla on her Show Name

I was billed as the "Little Hairy Girl" before they called me the "Monkey Girl." Karl didn't like it, but somebody said it and he went along with it. He learned to live with it. He didn't like the name "freaks" either. "She's my daughter, not some freak." Karl was protective.

Percilla Gets a Brother

Babe [Karl's first wife] handed me something, said, "Here's something for you." It was Karl Junior. I thought it was one of those moving dolls, that walk. I said, "It's moving." I told her, "Here. You take it. I don't want it." [laughs] Karl, he got a kick out of that. She had that baby in Miami; I was thirteen I think. That was my baby brother, Karl Junior, Babe's son, Babe, died—fever—but she raised me. She was Italian, from Cleveland, Ohio.

Percilla on Freak Show Man Harry Lewiston

We worked for him, Harry Lewiston. He owned a museum. Cold! We had to walk from the hotel, Emmitt and I, and the dogs (we had two Pekingese). He was nice. "Good morning, Miss Bejano. How are you? Cold isn't it?" I said, "Tell me about it! We had to walk: you ride in a Cadillac back and forth. Why don't you pick us up?" [laughs]

The fire department, they wouldn't allow no cooking. But we still had meals downstairs; if we seen the fire department, the cook would cover it up. But people had to eat. We had two meals a day, including breakfast. Get up real early and go down the museum and eat your breakfast and then be ready. I had my costume on—I dressed at the hotel—and I had a dress over my costume. When I got to the stage, I just took it off. We'd open early, to get the people going to work. They have money on them. They were coal workers, factory people. You should have seen those people come from the coal mines. All the coal places, coal towns. Money. They all had money.

Percilla on Ray Marsh Brydon

Roy B. Jones was our press agent when Karl had a museum. He had a big museum, acts every two weeks. New acts. Just the winter. It was called Karl Lauther's Oddities on Parade. Roy B. Jones, he would go ahead and see about the building and get the license and go to the fire department. We had a fire eater, but he couldn't use gasoline on account of the building. They were very strict. You had to get permits, licenses; you had to go to the courthouse.

Roy B. Jones was busy all the time. Anyway, when we were traveling the next year, Roy B. Jones had a hard time because [competing show owner] Ray Marsh Brydon was skipping the license, and he would send the people out the window. They'd get in the car and take off. Roy B. Jones would say, "Well, there's a beautiful building here, Mr. Lauther, but we can't get it!" "Why?" "Because somebody skipped." Ray Marsh Brydon, that's who. He got free rent: When it was time to pay, they were gone. People and all skipped, and we couldn't get a building. Beautiful building. We had the lumber and everything to put the stages up. Nope. Nice buildings that we would rent if we got there before Ray Marsh Brydon. Roy B. Jones made sure it was paid in full the next spot before we moved in. To beat Ray Marsh Brydon.

He had some big shows, but he never paid them. They were working just for food. He'd feed them good, that's it. No money. He told the fat woman once he was going to pay her $200 a week, and he got her. Then his fat girl wanted me to get something at the 5 & 10—she just wanted bobby pins and some makeup—but she didn't have any money. He never paid none of them.

Percilla Takes a Vacation

The first time I ever had a vacation, you know where it was Karl sent me? Put me on a farm. All I could see was trees. Jesus. Cold weather, the wind's blowing. First time I seen his farm. Big farm. I think it was 80 acres or more. It had timber, redwood, cherry wood, oak wood. Francis'—Karl's [second] wife—uncle stayed there and took care of things. He had chickens in his room! Eggs hatching. He wanted me to come in and rub his feet. I told him I wasn't there for that: I was on vacation.

The first thing I said, because I was movie crazy, "Where's the movie house?" He said, "What are you looking for?" "Where you go to the movies." "Thirty-five miles up the road." Richmond was the closest city. Tappahannock is where they were from. That's where Karl is buried. I walked up and down that road many times. I rode the mule there once. That damn bony mule just sat down. The blanket slipped off and I went on my rear.

Emmit and Percilla's Daughter

I had a baby at Karl's farm with a country doctor. Emmitt and I had a little girl, Francine Lauther Bejano. Karl wanted to take us out on the road right away. So we were in Washington, D.C., downtown, and it was cold as hell. She caught a cold and died of pneumonia. Couldn't save

Percilla and her newborn, Francine.

SHOCKED AND AMAZED!

Percilla guarantees she is for real.

her. Stayed in the hospital two weeks. If I'd have stayed at the farm another month . . . Emmitt cried too. She's buried in Pittsburgh. She was so beautiful—long curly hair. I miss her so much. We tried to have more kids, oh yeah. Couldn't have them. That's why we adopted Tony.

We were married in '38. Karl sent us to the farm to have the baby. Country doctor. He had a goat with him. He come and said, "Percilla and Emmitt, you're going to have a baby pretty soon, but I have to go down and pull a tooth from a horse." "What?!" "I'm not just a people doctor; I am an animal doctor for the whole county here. You should be having pains, but by the time I come, the baby will be born." He said, "Give it a push, Percilla, give it a push." And I screamed and Emmitt ran out on the farm! There's this big window and I screamed. "Emmitt!" He was long gone! He never forgot that either. He said, "You screamed and I run. I run like hell." He wasn't there to help me. Now Tony helped his wife, April, deliver. He went to that Lamaze whatever. Tony and Emmitt and I were talking about birth once, and Tony said, "I helped my wife. Did you, Emmitt?" Emmitt told him, "No, I run like hell. I heard that yelling and I couldn't stand it. . . I run like hell." You know it's the hardest pain for a woman to have and the easiest pain to forget.

Monkey Business

Percilla's Brush with Cuban Adoption

The Enquirer had a piece on that. Karl Lauther had a sideshow in Cuba. She was the richest woman in Cuba. She come over to see me; she had heard about me. Karl had to go back on the boat to New York for a fair meeting. While he was gone, she come over and talked to me. She said, "You want to see my place?" Karl Lauther's brother was there and he said he would take me. He wasn't supposed to let anybody take me anywhere.

We went all through her house and went upstairs. She had her own church, her own doctor. She had chimpanzees, gorillas. . .running around loose in her yard! I looked over there and there's a big alligator coming. Clarence said, "Where you going?" "Look behind you." He took off running. That thing had its mouth wide open. It was hungry. I said, "No way will you eat me." Clarence said, "You're right, Percilla. Lets get the hell back to the fair."

She wanted to adopt me and I'm already adopted. She wanted to adopt me. She even called Karl Lauther. Clarence gave her the phone number to get in touch in case anything happened to me, so she called. "I'm Rosalia Olbraya." Karl said. "Who the hell is this?" "I seen your daughter. Can I adopt her?" "She's already adopted. Right from the family. Her flesh and blood. She's my daughter. Nobody takes her." "But I'm going to have her teeth fixed." And she did.

She was the richest woman in Cuba. She had her own dentist. You know I've got two rows of teeth? I still have two. You take one out and another comes out. Went to the dentist up north and I had a toothache, and there was a dentist right outside the gate [of the show] and he looked at my mouth and shook his head, "I've never seen this before." Emmitt said, "Well, strange things happen, you know."

But I was really young when I was in Cuba. She said, "Look at all of these beautiful animals." She had one of those orangutans—those monkeys I don't like. Ugly animals. All loose. She had gorillas and goats, pigs, marmosets.

Years later *The Enquirer* had that I was going to be mated to a gorilla by that woman. All she wanted was for me to be her daughter. Her husband died in the Spanish American War; on the wall was all pictures of soldiers. Her son and daughter got married and left. She had nobody but all of these animals. She was lonely. She had her own dentist, her own doctor, her own church on the property, but Karl wouldn't let her have me. "No way. She's my girl. When we leave here, she's going to be on the boat with me." Oh, I was so sick on that boat. All that water. Coming and going. They had a band, a calypso band. They were all dancing and having a ball and when that bell rang, dinnertime. Blech.

Percilla Lauther Meets Emmitt Bejano

I met Emmitt when he worked for Karl, him and Larry. Larry was a talker. They come on the show and worked for Karl Lauther. Before that, he worked in Texas for his father. He was adopted because his father died. He was born in Pinto Gorda, Florida. His father took him on the road to make money. He used to make money on pocketbooks, you know, from snakes and alligators. Emmitt was good because of his skin, but his mother tried and tried to get that skin off. She didn't want it on him at first.

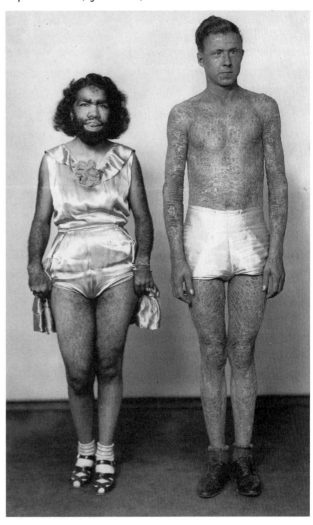

Emmitt came to visit us in Dallas—he had a week off—and he came in the show. He said, "See that girl, I'm going to have her one day." He told me that after we were married. I said, "Oh, c'mon," when he told me that. He said, "Remember? You waved at me." I said, "Yeah. I always waved when people came in to see me." He said, "You waved at me and I waved at you and I blew you a kiss." "Oh, you're *that* jerk, huh." But he said, "I'm, gonna have that girl.

He left before he got fired by Karl Lauther. He played it smart, Emmitt did. I used to sneak him letters through a book, and the girls on the show would come in and bring me the book. Then we eloped. 1938. It was midnight, Karl Lauther was sleeping safe and sound; even the dogs didn't bark. I wanted to go back to get the dogs. Emmitt said, "No way. I'm not going back there and getting shot. No way. For a dog? I'll get you one." So he got me a beautiful Pekingese with long hair. The next day Karl asked one of the show girls, the sword box girl, Audry, where I was. She told him, "She went to get me some sleeping pills," which I didn't. She said that so he wouldn't know where I went. "I'll fire you!" He bawled her out. "I'll fire you!" [She told him,] "Okay, I want to go home anyway." Just like that.

Percilla and Emmitt Bejano.

Emmitt lectures
on his wife.

Percilla on the Art of the Humbug

Emmitt's father, he had a couple of shows, just like Karl. He had a snake show and a hagy-bagy. You know, anything goes. You never heard of that? You get a couple of black people up there and cut their hair and you have a pinhead. You make your own pinhead. And you tell them don't talk to the people. You know, dummy up—you're a pinhead.

We had a pinhead; his head was really in a point. Karl said, "We're going to shave your head." He wasn't stupid; he was smart. When he left Karl Lauther, he had a grip; he had new shoes he bought himself. He put his money in checks and would send them to his mother. At the end of the season, he went back to his mother in New Jersey. He could read and write; he was smart. He said, "Why do they call me a pinhead?" "Because your head comes to a point." But he was smart. Some guy asked, "You can't speak English can you?" He said "Not a word." [laughs] I told him not to talk to nobody, dummy up. "You're supposed to be wild from Africa or somewhere." Karl Lauther said, "I told you not to talk to people."

People come out of the shows sometimes complaining, "That's a fake: they're all fakes in there. That little [monkey] girl has glue hair." We had a woman—the one who came down to the farm to help me—she had leopard skin and leopard hair. We had her in the store show and she wasn't supposed to speak English. She wasn't supposed to speak at all. She was really from Alabama or Georgia, big fat girl. She made a good wildwoman. We had a wig on her and she wasn't supposed to talk to no one, but people can't help themselves. So I would say, "Ida. Ida." She would say, "Yeah?" I'd laugh and say, "You're not supposed to talk to me; you're supposed to be wild." Someone came out of the show and said, "You know those people, they're supposed to be wild. They're not wild, but they smell wild." You know why? My Buddha Flukem. I put my foot down in Flukem—it developed the Buddha papers to tell the fortunes. You know, it develops the writing on the paper. We buy the whole pad of Buddha papers with fortunes and pictures on them. Buddha Flukem develops the pictures. I put my foot down in it and went up there and the whole museum stunk. I laughed; I wet my pants laughing.

Percilla on Keeping Busy on the Show

My act with Karl wasn't long. Not long. But the crowd would hang in there. At the end we had an act for the family, the glass blowers. After they left Karl's show, he had made the cages for the monkeys at the end so the crowd could look at them. The blow-off was down at the other end, and you would send the kids down to look at the animals.

We had Punch & Judy, too. We had a woman do Punch & Judy when she was sober; and when she wasn't, I'd go in there and work Punch & Judy myself. I had to have boxes to stand on because I was so little. I'd call out "Judy! Where are you?" I even blew the [Punch] whistles and I made them.

I would make the boxes you would look through and "see what little Johnny had seen": a naked woman. I did all that. I would make whistles and the little boxes for the magic man. If I wasn't crocheting, I was making whistles. You were on that stage from early in the morning, and you had to do something to fill the time.

The Monkey Girl and her wild stage.

Percilla on Health and Electricity

We had to take all the show lights and wrap them up; otherwise they would go on a flat and you would have broken lights. Saturday was pack-up day. There were *lots* of lights on the show. With them arches? A lot of lights. But I don't like electricity. That's how I got knocked down. Knocked down twice. Karl got a doctor. He wanted me well. I told them, "You aren't sticking any needles in me; I'm alright." Do you know what Karl believed in? Castor oil. I could have a nose running and sneeze and here he would come running with orange juice and castor oil. He believed in that, castor oil.

Percilla on the Dangers of the Midway

One guy he pulled on my leg and, when he did, I brought my shoe right up under his chin and he bit his tongue. This was around 4 o'clock. The idiots, the chumps and the drunks would fall out of the bars and come round to the fair. There was only dirt back then; now they have cement. Now when they fall out, "splash!" and get their brains all over the cement. I was older when that happened. Emmitt'd say, "There goes the meat wagon. Another guy fell out of the Ferris Wheel again." Sure enough. Nailed right on the head. We seen them come and go. They would rock and they're not supposed to rock and then they would blame the people that the rides were not working. It was the *people* that weren't working right. Idiots. Well, they fall out of the bar and they come to the fair and they want to ride the biggest ride there. But they don't know how to act up there. It's a shame.

Emmitt would close up, and we'd get something to eat when they're on the midway. That gave time for the families to come out. You get families at night. Not so many chumps. But it wasn't bad in the old days. It's not like today. I could go down the midway at night and take my dog. Maybe the ride guys would be under the ride, sleeping. And they'd holler, "Hey, how're your doing? How's them babies?" They were being fresh. I'd say, "Nope." and keep going.

Percilla on Emmitt

They asked Emmitt, "How come you married her." He said "Love is in the eye of the beholder." They asked Emmitt one time in the show, "Did you have college education? You talk like a college man." He said, "Yeah. I went in one door and out the other." They got a laugh. They would come back just to talk to Emmitt. They all loved Emmitt.

Percilla on Her Chimp Josephine

Josephine was my chimp, my baby. Papa Karl gave her to me. She'd sleep with me and Emmitt, between us. That's how I broke her, you know, from going—messing—in her clothes. We'd put pajamas on her, and when she'd mess I'd point my finger at her, "You know what you did? That's bad! You get that potty and do it right." And she'd go under the bed and get her little potty.

Karl Lauther, Josephine, and Percilla.

We did army shows—during the war—and they really loved her. We trained her to ride a bicycle and smoke. She smoked cigarettes. We went to hospitals; they all wanted to see her at the hospitals. Walter Reed, we worked there. And all the boys wanted to give her cigarettes, "This is for Josephine; take this home for Josephine." Cartons of cigarettes, different ones. That's how Emmitt got all his cigarettes.

Percilla on Karl Lauther's Last Days

We hadn't seen Karl in about three years, something like that. See, Karl Junior came and picked us up when Karl was in the hospital. He said, "Percilla, get dressed. We are leaving in the morning." I said, "We just got here." Karl Junior said, "Lock up. Take your two little dogs. Emmitt and I will take turns driving to the hospital." "But Francis said she had him at home." Karl Junior told me, "That woman is a lying bitch."

See, Karl made a lot of money in his life. A lot of money. I could have had that farm, fifty or more acres, and I told Karl Junior, "I have this place now [in Florida] and I don't want that," the farm in Virginia, thirty-five miles outside of Richmond. And you got snow, so Emmitt said no way. He [Karl] never did see this place [Emmitt and Percilla's home in Florida]. He saw the other one; he stayed there with his wife,

Francis, the Queen. She wasn't as nice as Babe. No, Babe was a sweetheart. She wanted me to take care of the baby, Karl Junior.

Anyway, we went there, and Karl was still in the hospital. We didn't tell anyone we were coming. First thing Francis said when we went in was, "What did you bring *them* for?" Karl Junior told her, "Well, they're family; Karl Lauther is her dad." The next day the doctor let him come home and he died at home, after we left, you know. I think it was a month after. At the hospital he grabbed me, the first time he ever kissed me on the mouth. Grabbed me, said "My daughter." And I cried and cried. He said, "You came to see me." "Yeah," I said, "Karl Junior is here too. We're your kids. We came to see you. Brother and sister."

Bejano's told me many outrageous stories over the years, but the tales don't have to be shocking or amazing. Sometimes they only need be . . . well, like this one. She told me that, in the old days of the carnivals, at season's end, all the show bands—from the girl shows, the Harlem reviews, bagpipers from the sideshows—all of them came out onto the midway on the last night, after all us marks had been swept out at closing time, and all the show bands played and marched and danced for the fellow carnies. A grand, final performance to mark the end of the season. They played all the forbidden songs (*Home Sweet Home*, for example, and *It Ain't Gonna Rain No More*, songs forbidden during the season by the carnies' fear of false hope, not unlike the "legitimate" theatre where you never say "Good Luck!" but "Break a leg!") And they played them well into the night. All the show people knew what this was about: After this late-night show for those who were "with it and for it," most wouldn't see each other for another four months or more. Some knew they'd never see their old friends again after the party. As Bejano put it to me over her German chocolate cake there in the diner after the Extravaganza, "It made us laugh, but it made us cry too." It did the same thing to me.

Percilla Lauther Bejano. RIP.

Final curtain: *Shortly after the completion of this piece,*
Percilla Bejano passed away in her sleep, February 5, 2001.

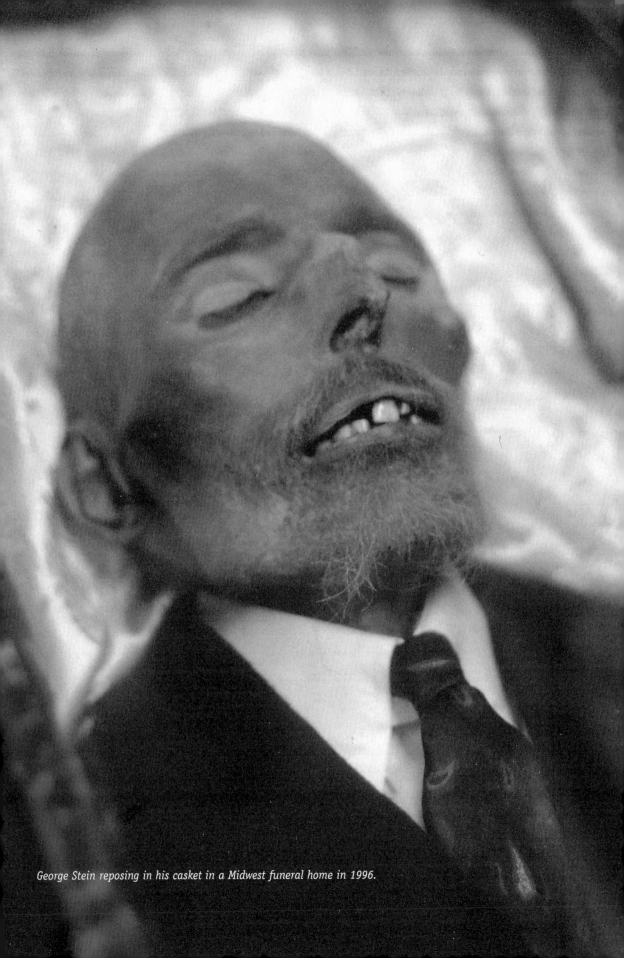

George Stein reposing in his casket in a Midwest funeral home in 1996.

MUMMY
Dearest

BY CHRISTINE QUIGLEY

Read about the preserved bodies of the famous and the infamous, the well-known and the unknown! Be on a first-name basis with people who died decades ago! Learn how bodies may circumvent decomposition naturally by dehydrating or becoming soap! Become more familiar than you may want to with several ways to prevent nature from taking its course: embalming, salting, tanning, freezing, pickling, petrifying, and freeze-drying! Find out the whereabouts of the mummies still on exhibit so you can plan your next vacation!

The Embalmed Bandit
(Died October 7, 1911 / Buried April 22, 1977)

Elmer McCurdy had many occupations before his death: soldier, plumber, miner, drinker, bank robber, train robber. He also had a few afterward: He appeared in the Great Patterson Carnival shows, Sonney's Museum of Crime, Dave Friedman's movie *She Freak*, the lobbies of theaters showing Dwain Esper's film *Narcotic*, and the Laff in the Dark funhouse at the Nu-Pike Amusement Park. Masquerading as a mannequin, Elmer was living a peaceful, posthumous existence in California until he was exposed as "The 1,000 Year Old Man" by the crew of *The Six Million Dollar Man*. He was forced out of his semi-retirement and was featured in the *National Enquirer* and on the *CBS Evening News*. He was confiscated, autopsied, x-rayed, identified, and grudgingly released to Oklahoma for burial next to fellow outlaw Bill Doolin.

Hazel the Mummy
(Died December 20, 1906)

All Hazel Farris wanted to do was buy a hat. Being thwarted by her husband provoked her to kill him and the four policemen who tried to intervene. Hazel escaped out the back and supported herself on her back until her boyfriend sold her out for the reward money. She chose to take poison rather than be captured and some say the poison—not embalming fluid—is what has preserved her to this day. Hazel entered show business shortly after her death, under the direction of O.C. Brooks. Still in remarkable condition and owned by Brooks's nephew for the past 47 years, Hazel does occasional shows at the Hall of History in Bessemer, Alabama, where, during her years as a fugitive, it is likely she bought a hat.

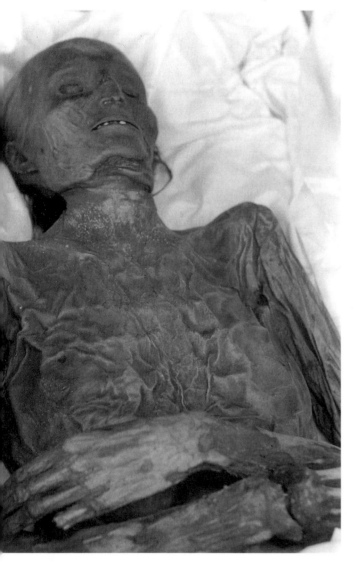

Hazel Farris,
fashion victim.

Evita
(Died July 26, 1952 /
Buried October 22, 1976)

Eva Peron was a showgirl of another sort. Certainly more famous than Hazel Farris—and some would say more ruthless—she was made immortal in more ways than one by her husband, who just happened to be the president of Argentina. Actually, the handiwork was done by embalmer Dr. Pedro Ara who is revered to this day. Dr. Ara's initial embalming allowed Evita to be viewed by the public for more than two weeks. His second treatment—arterial injection of the body, followed by immersing it in a preservative liquid of debated contents for the better part of a year, and finally coating it with several layers of plastic—preserved Evita so well that he was accused of having perpetrated a hoax.

During its twenty-four posthumous years above ground, the beautiful body was prayed to by her adorers, visited by her family, stolen by revolutionaries, hidden in a military storeroom, buried secretly, exhumed and returned to Colonel Peron, displayed next to Peron's closed casket after his death in 1974, and finally released to her family who buried her in the family tomb. The tomb, by the way, was made by a company that builds bank vaults and is said—like her body—to be indestructible.

Spaghetti
(Died April 28, 1911 / Buried September 30, 1972)

Cancetto Farmica is best known for being profiled in Arthur Lewis's book *Carnival,* but Lewis's research fell short of actually visiting the mummy, according to the embalmer's grandson. Thousands did over the years, not all of them residents of Laurinburg, North Carolina, where "Spaghetti" (as they called him) was exhibited upon request, but never for a fee. Spaghetti, ironically a carnival worker at the time of his death, had been killed with a tent stake and had never been claimed. He subsequently dried out on the wall of the embalming room, where he was suspended so that he wouldn't take up any floor space. Subject to a very political burial in 1972, Spaghetti was given what for some was a suitably respectful and for others a regrettably irreversible burial by the funeral home he had called home sweet home for more than sixty years.

The Stone Man
(Died October 25, 1902)

George Stein became a local attraction after he died of natural causes out in the Midwest. An immigrant from Germany, he settled contentedly in America and made his living selling insurance, working in a planing mill, and later acting as porter in a saloon. Like Spaghetti, his body was never claimed by family members after his fatal heart attack, and he became a resident of the funeral home in which his remains were prepared. Reclining in a glass-topped casket, Mr. Stein requires little maintenance: the casket lining has been changed once and he is provided with a new suit every couple of decades. The previous owner of the funeral home was offered $10,000 for the mummy, but refused to sell Mr. Stein to the carnival. Instead, he showed the mummy to interested parties himself and good-naturedly put up with holiday and after-hours pranks by teenagers. The present owner has been urged by his younger staff members to lay Mr. Stein to rest (and has been offered a free plot by the local cemetery), but he has refused to part with the man who now qualifies as an old friend. Mr. Stein's residence at the establishment continues above ground, but both he and his custodian keep a low profile.

The Amazing Petrified Man
(Died 1913 / Buried 1973)

Anderson McCrew has the distinction of being the subject of a song recorded by Don McLean, although McLean admits he changed McCrew's first name to "Andrew" for a better rhyme. McCrew, who only had one leg, lost the other one, and his life, when he fell out of a boxcar he had hopped. Since he was indigent, his body was used to test a new embalming fluid. The experiment was a success and McCrew was purchased by a showman and exhibited but he was warehoused when the carnival disbanded in the 1930s. The mummy was rediscovered in Houston in 1964 and was stored in the basement of a nurse, who lost her job (partly due to her housing the body of McCrew, an African American) and could not afford a funeral for him. When McLean heard about the story, McCrew had already been buried, thanks to the owners of a Dallas funeral home. McLean's song, released in 1974, brought belated attention to the mummy's plight and resulted in the purchase of a headstone and the reinterment of "The Amazing Petrified Man" in Dallass' prestigious Lincoln Memorial Cemetery.

Speedy
(Died May 30, 1928 / Buried August 5, 1994)

Charles Henry Atkins was given his nickname during life because he was a fast worker at the Paducah, Kentucky, tobacco factory. He may have been an efficient employee, but Speedy was a pauper when he drowned in the river while fishing. His friend A.Z. Hammock happened to own the local funeral home and used the body in an embalming experiment. Due to the secret recipe of the fluid (the ingredients of which were never revealed), Speedy mummified and his fame grew. The mummy, dressed in a tuxedo and cleaned three times a year, was the pride of the funeral home, which Hammock's widow Velma continued to operate after his death. Sixty-six years after Speedy's accidental death, Velma decided it was time to lay him to rest. The whole town turned out to pay their respects to (and take one last look at) Speedy before he was buried in 1994.

Deaf Bill
(Died 1915 / Buried June 24, 1996)

William Lee was hard-of-hearing, hence the nickname, but that didn't stop him from barging into the church of his choice on a typical Sunday morning and conducting an uninvited guest sermon. The subject of the sermon is unrecorded, but he would have been a hypocrite to preach on the dangers of drink. Deaf Bill lived and fished in "Dogtown" outside Alton, Illinois, until his health failed him. He died at the poor farm and would have been buried in the potter's field but for the actions of the local undertakers. Hoping he would be claimed (and they would, therefore, be paid for their services), the undertakers embalmed him, but never did undertake him. When the owners of a traveling curiosity show offered them cash for Bill's preserved body, they realized the fame the mummy might bring to their establishment. He was relegated to a closet, but the door was opened again and again as his notoriety spread. When management of the funeral home changed a few years ago, Bill's cheeks were rouged and he said his last goodbyes to the townspeople before being belatedly consigned to the ground.

Floyd Collins
(Died February 16, 1925 / Buried March 24, 1989)

Unlike other mummies, Floyd Collins did have family and they did claim him—although it took several years. Floyd's life ended nightmarishly and he did not rest in peace. He was trapped by a boulder in the cave he had been exploring in an attempt to find a connection to Kentucky's Mammoth Cave. He survived for nearly two weeks, but was dead by the time the well-publicized rescue efforts reached him. Floyd became a folk hero and a funeral was held, but he

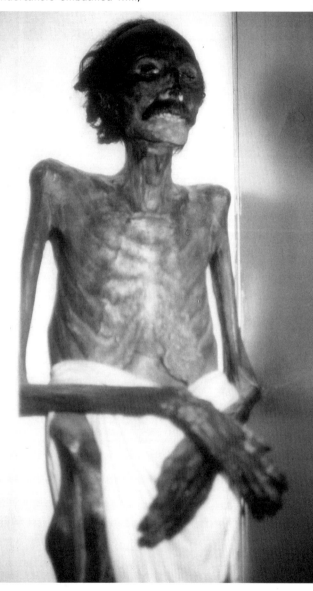

William Lee, aka "Deaf Bill," prior to his burial.

remained pinned in the cave until two months later. The recovered body was embalmed and buried, but the land was sold by Floyd's father along with the rights to disinter his son's body! After some remedial work, Floyd was placed in a glass-topped casket in Crystal Cave from 1927 until 1989—on full public display for the first two years. During that time, Mammoth Cave became a national park, Crystal Cave was purchased by the National Park Service, and the connection between the caves that Floyd had hoped for was found. It took decades and a lawsuit against the federal government for Floyd's family to recover his body. It took three days for that body to be removed from the cave and reburied with forty of those family members present and Floyd permanently sealed from view.

Mr. Dinsmoor
(Died August 21, 1932)

Samuel Dinsmoor is a permanent resident of the "Garden of Eden," and you can gaze on his remains. In addition to admiring his cement sculptures, you can peek in at the face of the artist himself in a mausoleum of his own design. Dinsmoor was—at his own request—embalmed with his children present and placed in a glass-topped casket made from the same medium as his statues. "It seems to me," Dinsmoor explained in his writings, "that people buried in iron and wooden boxes will be frying and burning up in the resurrection morn. How will they get out when this world is on fire? Cement will not stand fire, the glass will break. This cement lid will fly open and I will sail out like a locust." Until then, Dinsmoor remains cocooned in a film of mold, but still visible, and his sculpture garden has been listed in the National Register of Historic Places.

John Wilkes Booth
(Died January 13, 1903)

The whereabouts of the mummified body of David E. George are unknown except to a privileged few. The remains of George may or (more likely) may not be those of presidential assassin John Wilkes Booth. Nevertheless, they were exhibited as such for half a century until the body was taken out of circulation. The idea that Booth had survived was championed by Memphis lawyer Finis Bates, who wrote a best-selling book after taking possession of the body of the man he insisted had confessed his identity to him. Bates occasionally rented the mummified body out to sideshows over the years, but "Booth" returned to the entertainment business full-time when he was sold after Bates's death. The mummy underwent a well-known examination by doctors in 1931, but disappeared during World War II. Researchers are eager to find the mummified body (and others purported to be Booth's), since they have been denied permission to disinter the body assumed to belong to Booth in Baltimore. They would be willing—with the help of x-rays, photographic superimposition, and DNA testing—to put the rumors to rest one corpse at a time.

Notorious Marie O'Day

(Died circa 1925)

Not as notorious as John Wilkes Booth, Marie O'Day did have the distinction of being exhibited in her own "Palace Car"—after she was dead, of course. While she was alive, she entertained in a nightclub until she was killed by her common-law husband. According to the legend, he stabbed her, slit her throat, and disposed of her body in Utah's Great Salt Lake. Due to the action of the salt, when she washed up on the shore some twelve years later her body was intact from her red hair to the "corn upon her toe," as the promotional literature read. She was exhibited in thirty-eight states and Canada by several showmen, including Charlie Campbell, "Hoot" Black, and most recently—minus the long-gone Palace Car but with a special place in the "Palace of Wonders"—Captain Harvey Lee Boswell. Like him, Marie is on the verge of retirement. Want to buy a mummy?

UPDATE

Hazel Farris was autopsied, cremated and buried in 2002.

Capt. Harvey Lee Bosewell—the exhibitor of Marie O'Day—died January 22, 2002.

Marie O'Day as she appears today.

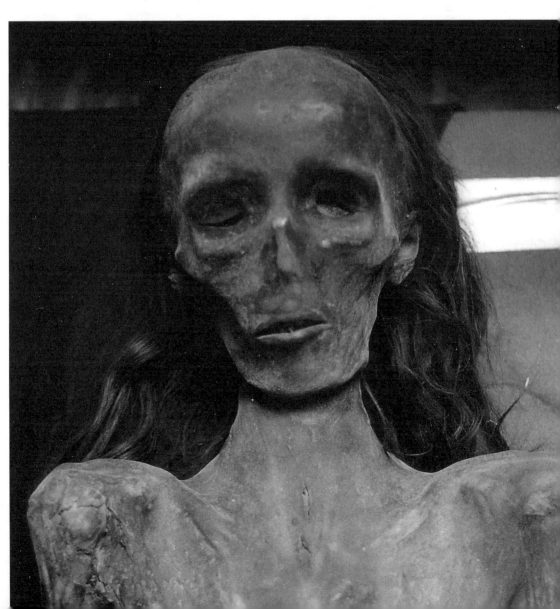

Two Heads Are Better than One

"James Taylor? This is Bobby Reynolds, greatest showman in the world." That's the way nearly every phone call I've ever gotten from Reynolds has started. Once, in the same half-joking manner in which he announces himself over the phone, he asked me whether I thought it "presumptuous" of him to title himself so. More serious than joking, I assured him it wasn't. Showmanship, and success as a showman, you see, isn't accurately measured by money (though they'll all assure you it is). Certainly Reynolds has had his share of the green, and lost his share, too. Rather, showmanship is what it takes, in Reynolds's case for example, to mount two two-headed baby shows in Coney Island and expect them both to make the nut. Both on Surf Avenue. Both within one block of each other.

Of course both were decent, "educational" shows. I suppose you could say that about Reynolds' giant rat show as well. All right all right all right, so it was really a giant guinea pig, aka a capybara, standard "killer" or "giant" rat material for as long as the shows have existed. The scariest thing about that show, when you think out it, was that Reynolds convinced New Yorkers to pay to see a rat.

But nothing beat those babies. John Hiner's glorious banners were on the front of the tent show; the baby carriage was just beyond the ticket box in case the twins needed to take the air (a substance they likely never breathed or breathed only shortly, and that would have been nearly 100 years ago, "grandfathering" them beyond virtually any statute prohibiting exhibition). The extra kick in the tent show was a second set of newly showcased twins joined at the head, displayed in front of their own special inside banner. And then there's the other, trailer-mounted two-headed baby show just a block away, the girls, as lovely a set of bottled specimens as ever faced daylight.

Opposite:
Fiji does it.

213

Bobby ballies on the International Circus Sideshow

But that's just the grind shows. Reynolds's museum was another act of showmanship entirely. Oh, he groused and complained about the accommodations. There's a lot to be said, though, for a sideshow museum (with live act Frank Hartman, probably one of the best fire acts I've seen and a damn good sword swallower) set up in a turn-of-the-century bank building with 50-foot ceilings, a mezzanine skirting the entire show about three-quarters of the way to the roof, all of it baroque within an inch of its life, an architectural wedding cake that must have seemed right at home amid the likes of Luna Park and Dreamland. Upstairs, dogs patrolled the offices and there's a vault with a foot-thick door where Reynolds held court, as much a king of sideshow heaven here on "the Island' as anyone could be anymore. (Since the departure of Reynolds's grind shows and museum, Dick Ziguns's Sideshows by the Seashore, just across from the bank, has become the last of the permanent shows there.) Not so long ago, Reynolds ushered me and my associate editor Kathleen Kotcher to that aerie, his quarters near the museum's roof, overlooking the island where he got his start and the museum some three stories below. After telling us hours of stories, he confirmed for Kotcher that the one show her mother remembered as a child from her visit to Coney Island was indeed his: the horrifying Giant Kentucky Redwood Bat . . . which, of course, turned out to be a pretty large Louisville Slugger. And then, Reynolds sang us *Join the Circus* from Barnum, the music coming from a cassette in his boombox sitting next to his Fiji mermaid. It was a very Bobby moment.

SHOCKED AND AMAZED!

S&A: Why don't we begin at the beginning . . .

BR: I was shining shoes—I used to shine shoes when I was around ten years old—and I went over to New York and I seen this guy pitching Chinese horn nuts. A horn nut looks like a buffalo horn, and they used to put a single bloom of a gladiola in it and some greenery around it and submerge it in water and they'd say, "Poke a hole in the top and one in the bottom. In three days you'll have a green sprout. Before a week, you'll have a beautiful Chinese water lily."

S&A: And of course . . .

BR: They never worked, but they were ten cents or three for a quarter. So I shined this guy's shoes and he says, "Do you think you can do this, kid? I want to go across the street for lunch." There was a bar across the street so he went over there and got lushed a little bit. I put the shoe shine box under the tripe and keister. (You know what the tripe and keister is? Tripod and the keister. That's what the guys on the street called them—tripe and

Appealing to women of all ages.

keisters. A keister was a suitcase and a tripod held the suitcase. That's how you pitched, off of that. Tripe and keisters.) I was selling horn nuts. I was doing a good job. Then this cop came up and asked for $3, the guy that walked the beat, and I gave him $3. And the Mickey Mouse took $2 or $3, I forgot what the figure was. That's what we called the police cars, Mickey Mouse.

S&A: So I guess the pitchman wasn't happy when he got back from lunch.

BR: The guy comes across the street and says, "You didn't gross very much money." And I said, "The cop took $3, and the Mickey Mouse took $2." He says, "Oh, you paid the rent." I says, "Guess so." And he said, "Well, you didn't do that bad," and he gave me $3. He says, "You want to be my helper everyday?" And I said, "Terrific!" I threw the shoe shine box away and I went home and cleaned up real good the next day. I got a shirt at the Salvation Army and I slicked my hair down. Do you remember this green gel called Wave Set? It would make your hair just like cardboard. I slicked my hair down with this crap and I went to work with this Irishman. I was doing quite well. I was getting $5, $6, $7 a day and this was right at the end of the Depression.

S&A: That was good money for a kid.

BR: Oh yeah. It was so good my mother thought I was over there killing people with the gangsters. Finally, one day the Irishman says, "I'm going over to Jersey to see my sister (or mother or something). I'm going to be back late, but stay over here until I get back." I paid off the Mickey Mouse, I'm grossing money, and he never shows. It was nighttime so I grabbed the tripe and keister and the horn nuts and I went home to Jersey City. I came back the next day, and I started work-

ing and I paid off the Mickey Mouse and the cop and the guy never shows up and I'm starting to run out of stock. No more horn nuts. I don't know where the hell to get them. I know there's a guy uptown pitching these things, so I go uptown and I say, "You know where the Irishman is? I'm running out of horn nuts." He says, "Go down to Chinatown to Gung Fung Lou's," and he gives me an address and I go down there. And the Chinaman says, "You worka street?" And I says, "Yeah. I worka street." He says, "How much you want?" I says, "Well, give me $35 worth of horn nuts." These things are very light, they're almost like Styrofoam, and he comes out with this enormous bag of horn nuts and I gave him the $35 and I get on the train to Jersey City and I keep them in my room under the bed. And that's how I started.

Bobby surrounded by potential customers.

S&A: Didn't you ever get in beefs over these things? I mean, three days later they're supposed to do something. Instead, they just float in a glass of water and stink pretty bad, too.

BR: Yeah, once in a while they would come back and I would say, "I guess you didn't make the hole deep enough. You didn't fertilize it. You didn't make the hole deep enough so the water gets in there and germinates the nut."

S&A: What was the pitch like for that?

BR: You'd use a grind pitch. It wasn't a high pitch. It's called a grind pitch. You stick the single bloom of a gladiola on top of the nut and you stick some green around it and it made it go down in the water like a Chinese water lily. You had to go buy a gladiola each day, a nice fresh one. Sometimes they were pink, sometimes they were all different colors. It depended on what was happening that day. Ten cents each, three for a quarter. I was making so much money, my mother thought I was over here with the gangsters. So she came over one day from New Jersey with a bag of sandwiches, and she watched me sell these horn nuts. She went and got a big thing of orange juice—they didn't have paper cups in those days—and she comes over to me and she says the things she always said to me all my life. "I'm not too thrilled about what you're doing, but don't get in any trouble." That was her answer to everything. Once I'm working the Smithsonian Institute for the Folklife Festival back in the early '80s. And my mom's down there and my brothers and sisters are there and she's walking around and in a very serious moment, I says to her, "Ma, what do you think, Mom, I'm at the Smithsonian Institute. I'm going to be in the archives. They may do a book on me. What do you think of this?" "Oh, I've seen you work." I felt like punching her.

All alive on the inside for one small dollar.

S&A: I suppose it's a good thing you loved her.

BR: Yeah. She was never impressed by me; she wanted me to get a steady job. You know what used to infuriate her? I'd tell her, "Ma, don't die during the season 'cause I'm on the road." And she'd say, "I'll die when I wanna! You don't tell me when to die!"

S&A: I know you learned magic early on from Al Flosso, the Coney Island Faker. Was that when you were selling horn nuts?

BR: Well, I was on 14th Street and then on 34th Street selling these horn nuts—I changed my location once in awhile—and I finally went up to Al Flosso's, which was the oldest magic shop in New York. It's called Hornmann Magic Shop. I was up there buying magic in his shop—I used to shine his shoes, too—and he used to say, "You wanna be a magician, kid? Sit in the corner, keep your mouth shut, and your eyes and ears open." He used to have a funny voice, "Stay out of the

Two Heads are Better Than One

Bobby presents the really Real Frog Band.

back room, kiddo. Sit down there and keep your mouth shut." I used to make up Punch and Judy whistles for Al, you know, the little whistles the guys used to sell on the road for the slum packages of magic. I used to make the whistles up and I used to make cootch dancers up. You know what a cootch dancer is? You put a match behind this little silhouette and you folded it up and it made a lump in it and you put a match behind it and it made the little figure dance. I used to make up cootch dancers and keyhole cards.

S&A: Keyhole cards?

BR: I used to have a rubber stamp and we'd stamp keyholes—it looked like keyholes—on an index card. So you dip it in the water, go into a dark room, hold it up to a bright light and "see what little Johnny saw the night his big sister got married."

S&A: And what did the marks see?

BR: It was nothing! The ink would roll off. Something crazy like that. I ended up pitching that because Flosso taught me some of the magic pitch and I learned the magic. I used to hang out in Hubert's Museum a lot, too, learning magic.

S&A: So you were working Hubert's pretty early, too?

BR: I worked Hubert's when I was thirteen. I used to stick for Albert-Alberta, the half man, half woman. Albert used to give me ten cents a show. I was deathly afraid of Albert. He was a weird person. He used to get me into the dressing room there and he'd say, "I want you to go down to 8th Avenue there and I want you to get me," he used to raise Pomeranians, "beef kidneys—don't get pork kidneys—for the little doggies. On the way back, go to the Horn & Horn and get me a big coffee with four sugars and a little piece of cake or something." I was deathly afraid of him because he had this shaved leg and this false tit. It just scared the hell out of me. I used to go schlepping off to get these kidneys and stuff. And I used to stick in his show and he'd give me a dime a show.

S&A: What was he selling? Pictures of himself?

BR: Yeah, and I used to say, "I want one of the pictures." He would say, "Little boy, you don't know what to do with these. You're too young." He used to embarrass me in front of the tip. That was my shot, but I got to keep the dime. But I knew everybody down there. I knew Charlie Fallon, the strong man, and I knew Eddie Mareno, the lecturer. Roy Heckler with his flea circus. I knew Roy Heckler very well. There was a man by the name of Jack Elkins, very gaunt, very twisted mustache. Looked like something out of the Moulin Rouge. Very tall and gaunt and an excellent talker. I was working as a magician at this time, working seven days a week, twelve hours a day for $21.65 a week. That was a hell of a cut from the horn nuts, I'll tell you that! One day Jack says to me, he says, "Bob, I'm going upstairs for a bowl of soup. You make the opening on the flea circus." I says, "I don't know how to make change too good." He says, "Well, you'll learn." So I made the opening on the flea circus. The admission was nine cents.

Magical Mr. Reynolds.

S&A: Nine cents?

BR: Nine cents. It was the thing at the time that if you paid a dime, you had to pay two cents sales tax. So they charged nine cents. Since it was below ten cents, you didn't have to pay tax and you could get away with it. The first opening I ever made was on a flea circus. Roy was the manager of the show. He would make the payroll up and pay everybody and he was kind of in charge of all of us. He used to change the signs upstairs and change the pictures and stuff. He was the manager of the show downstairs. Then there was Wofo and Woogie. And Wofo would jump on a bed of nails and Woogie would dance with a snake. Then there was Jean Carroll, the tattooed girl. There was Suzy the Elephant Skinned Girl. Sealo was there.

S&A: Sealo the Seal Boy?

BR: Yeah. There was Alex Linton, the sword swallower, and Laurello was there, the guy with the revolving head. He was there, and once in a while before I came in there was a magician by the name of Roger. He taught me how to palm coins. Then Walter DeLens, who was a pitchman who pitched a package of magic, came down and I was smitten by him. He gave me my first Punch and Judy whistle and showed me how to do the Punch and Judy whistle. Then I ended up being a pitchman for the package of magic.

S&A: As a teenager you were working Coney Island as well, weren't you?

BR: Yeah. The first job I had in Coney Island was doing magic and I made openings on the blow-off. Alzora Lewis the Turtle Girl was one of them and Johanna the Bear Girl. Then we had Serpentina. She was in the blow-off and I made openings for her, too. I used to do a blind opening. No one ever used it, but I did. It could have been for anything. One time, in one of my own shows, I had a hermaphrodite pig in the blow-off. Everyone went in there under the blind opening and there is that pig laying there with two sexes. This little lady come out, and she says, "Young man, you did a good job. This is the first time I have ever paid a quarter to see a pig's ass." When I was with the wife on the road I was doing magic and eating fire and swallowing swords; I did everything in the damn show. I made openings after a while. I was on the road, and that's where I really cut my teeth as an entertainer.

S&A: Were there any of the acts that you didn't do?

BR: I can do every working act in the show. I can eat fire, swallow swords, pound nails up my nose, do the electric chair act, jump on broken glass; I can lay on a bed of nails; I'm a knife thrower and a sharpshooter. And I'm a ventriloquist. I do Punch and Judy, too. I swallowed swords for a long time and then I heard that shit could affect my voice, and I made more money from my talking than I ever did swallowing swords, and one of the things had to go. I can still drop a blade if I have to.

Bobby at the Smitty's.

S&A: How did you get into ventriloquism?

BR: Roy Douglas, the guy that taught Shari Lewis how to do vent, he had a little shop in Greenwich Village. We were drinking partners. He was brandy and I was drinking scotch and we would get whacked out every night. So we ran out of things to talk about and he says to me, "Well, why don't you become a ventriloquist?" I says, "That sounds interesting; I'll become a ventriloquist." So he taught me how to become a ventriloquist. I probably know more vents and can do more things than most ventriloquists can. I had a MacElroy figure I got from Al Flosso. The same guy that carved Charlie McCarthy, put moving eyes in this MacElroy figure. Al Flosso says, "What do you want that thing for? You're not a ventriloquist." I said, "Yeah, Al, I am." "You're fulla crap. You're a pitchman." You know what his thing was always to me? He said, "Be an entertainer and learn a few tricks." Most people got it wrong. They do great magic, but they're about as fun as a bottle of glue. I do nothing and I'm entertaining. So I became a ventriloquist and I worked exactly one week in a nightclub and that was it. I didn't want to talk to myself anymore.

S&A: You've got quite a reputation for your pen pitch. How did you get into that?

BR: The pen pitch was near the end of the '60s. I was kinda broke and I was living in the Village with one of my wives and I learned the pen pitch from a friend of mine. Milty Levine, who was a talker down on Coney Island. I learned his pen pitch and I was very good at it. That saved my ass. There were times I went out and pitched pens to make the payroll on the sideshow. I have made lots of money off of the thing. I still do. I still make it. I wanted to go into Canada this year and I decided to go down to Baltimore selling pens in the GC Murphy after I had a little trouble getting into Canada. I was in my motor home and they looked in and there were shrunken heads and snake skins, magic props, and they didn't know what the hell to make of me. It was a little weird. They were looking for drugs and they came up with all this shit. They figured, "This guy's nuts! We don't want him in Canada." But the stuff's just part of the ambience of my motor home. What can I tell you?

Bobby and a pint-sized Palliachi.

S&A: When did you have your first show?

BR: The first time I had a sideshow was with a guy named Artie Steinhardt and he was out of Coney Island. I was on Rosen's show as a talker. Artie's father came over to me and he wanted me to go out with Artie as a talker. I says, "I can't leave this here." And he says, "What do you want?" And I says, "Well, if I'm gonna go out with Artie, I gotta be at least a partner." And so he says, "Artie's got all the tents and the stakes," and this and that. And I says, "Well, that's good, but if you want me, I can't leave Rosen unless I'm a partner." So he made me a partner. That's how I got my first sideshow.

Bobby and a former competitor.

S&A: Who was in your first show?

BR: Well, we brought out on the show Johanna the Bear Girl and we brought Kokomo the Mule Boy out one time. We had the Electric Chair, the fire eating and I did sword swallowing and I did openings. I did everything, practically, and that was our sideshow. I ran the show with Artie about two seasons. Then Freddie Sindel made a deal with him to go into the Connecticut State Fair in Danbury every year, so we were up in Danbury. I spent my birthday every year up in Danbury.

S&A: I've heard that was a pretty good spot.

BR: In the early days, in the '50s, it was. That was the first sideshow I had that I got together. Archie McHaskel gave me a bannerline and a bladebox from his Hell's Belles show. Then we got booked over on World of Mirth. I was over there for two years with the sideshow and Milty Levine was my partner. He was one of the talkers from Coney Island. We worked the World of Mirth and they had the tents and we had the banner lines and I made some stages out of bars—some counters and stuff. And we had Kokomo and we had Albert the midget and we had Alzora the Turtle Girl and we had Eddie Carmel the giant work for us for a little while. And then I worked Ringling Bros. for awhile. I was down in the Garden there. I was a magician. I pitched a package of magic. The first time I worked there I got $50 a week and I was giving them fifty percent of my package of magic after the stock cost every day. I was doing about $400 or $500 a day pitching. I had everyone making those damn packages up. We used to get the slum from Waldrick Press in Waldrick, Rhode Island, and that's where you can get all that slum stuff.

I can make it, too, but you can buy it up there. I used to make the Punch and Judy whistles myself.

S&A: Did any of that stuff really work?

BR: Yeah. Some of it did. The whistles, they worked. The real ones were made of silver. But the kids, they enjoyed them.

S&A: When were you working on the girl shows?

BR: Girl shows? On Coney Island it was a small girl show. I worked for Terza, had a wine bath in Coney Island, and I worked there with Walter DeLens and Walter was pitching the magic inside and I was butchering the tip for him. There was a talker by the name of Billy Milton, one of the most fascinating talkers I have ever heard. He actually hypnotized the whole tip, and I learned a lot from him. Once in a while I used to grind for him when he went off—his arm was full of gangrene from shooting so much dope: That's the type of stuff I grew up in—but he was an excellent talker. Awesome. There was one thing in that show I used to love to do: They would exit them out the back door right near Nathan's, the hot dog stand—and there was a breaker door like a theater door. And they would go out and they couldn't get back in again. And what we used to do was, "Gentlemen, you probably seen Terza and she had a little net here and a little net there, but if you want to see the bare skin, we have back here the bare skin. Just the same way you see the palm of my hand, you will see the bare skin." What we would do was, it was a nickel more, we would get them all in this hallway that was outside near Nathan's, and it was a big hallway with very, very tall ceilings. The ceilings had to be at least fifteen or sixteen foot high. And then we get them out there and we had a microphone inside and we'd say, "Now gentlemen, if you will look straight up in the air," and they would look straight up in the air where we would have a bear skin nailed to the ceiling, "and now you have seen the *bear* skin." The ones that didn't have no sense of humor, for a nickel, what the hell.

> "Now gentlemen, if you will look straight up in the air," and they would look straight up in the air where we would have a bear skin nailed to the ceiling, "and now you have seen the bear skin." The ones that didn't have no sense of humor, for a nickel, what the hell.

S&A: You ding them for anything else?

BR: Walter used to say, "Gentlemen, in this envelope, in case you should meet some lovely girl this evening, I have three rubbers in here," and they'd come out and there would be three rubber bands. All kinds of crap. Then you'd have "a cigarette lighter that's guaranteed to work everytime" and you'd give them a package of matches.

S&A: Showman Todd Robbins told me a story that you told him a little while back, one about you and a girl show and a buxom lady who didn't like men.

BR: That was Camille. See, that year I promised to make it with every girl in the show. That was my goal for the year: to make love with every girl on the show. I even made love to Camille's girlfriend! I said, "Camille, c'mon! You're going to ruin my racket." She says, "C'mon! You know me. I'm gay. I go for girls." I says, "I got everybody except you. I'll tell you what I'll do. I'll put a wig on and fishnets and we'll make love that way." She says, "You'd go through all that trouble to go to bed with me?" I says, "Yeah." She says, "You go get dressed up and put makeup on—I want makeup, too—and I'll go to bed with you." I got dressed up in drag and went to bed with her.

S&A: You went through all that?

BR: I didn't want to ruin my rep. There was another time I was tapped out, and I'm waiting for the carnival to come in. I've got no money; I've got my magic with me, of course. And there's this big drag show in the middle of town at this bar. And I go in and I'm like, "Jeez, I'm tapped out. Can you buy me dinner?" The guy says, "Well, why don't you work the

Snakes Alive!

show? It don't pay much, but you'll eat." I says, "Okay." And they put me in this drag and I go up to do the magic and I nearly break my ankles going up. I was the ugliest drag magician you've ever seen in your life. I looked like the wicked witch from *The Wizard of Oz*. I worked a week and got a few bucks and went on my way. I pulled my testicles up so tight, I talked in a higher voice. It was weird. The things you do for show biz. Show business is my life. You know, I went out with a half-man/half-woman one time. Someone asked me if I had a good time, I said, "Well, yes and no."

S&A: At one time, you had a lot of shows out on the midways, didn't you?

BR: At one time I had fourteen shows going at one time. I had a museum, live circus sideshow, a thrill-sphere and then I had two rat shows and two midget horse shows and a freak animal show. I had a Chicken Little show.

S&A: Chicken Little show?

BR: I had all kinds of weird chickens in a barn.

S&A: Freak chickens?

BR: No, regular chickens like Polish Crested. Hippie Chickens, half-turkey, half-chicken and the bass-ackward chicken, which would be

The skull of Goliath.

frizzy and the feathers were going in the opposite way. Weird shit. Then I had the hairless dogs, "The Moon Dogs." All in all I had fourteen shows out.

S&A: How long did you have that many shows out?

BR: Two years, until I lost my sanity. Then I had the two-headed girl illusion. One of the girls I married was German, and she brought that illusion with her. It's a neat illusion. Both heads talk to each other. It's positively alive.

S&A: How is the show done?

BR: Piece of glass and lights. Similar to the gorilla show but backwards. One laying down and one sitting up.

S&A: So you lost your sanity and gave up on the midway?

BR: Nah. There are no shows in the carnivals because the real estate is too high. You know what makes the carnival owners annoyed? They spend a million dollars for a ride, and I set up the two-headed baby and out-gross the ride. They really get annoyed by that. They go crazy when the Giant Rat outgrosses a ride that cost them three-quarters of a million dollars. They just can't handle that, even when they're getting fifty percent of the act. It takes up a hell of a lot less space, too.

S&A: I saw your two-headed baby show at Coney Island and it was surrounded by newspaper articles about its being confiscated by the law.

BR: They confiscated it when I was in the Pomona Fair in California. They snatched it from me and I had to go to court. They won an autopsy on it and I found out that this particular baby lived for two weeks. (I have two you know. I have a little girl and a little boy.) The lungs were all inflated and the umbilical cord was all healed. What happened was, I won the case. They called it a museum piece and the specimen itself—being eighty-five or ninety years old—was older than the law, so they classify it now as a museum piece. I display them now without much fear. A lot of showmen are scared, but I don't care. As a matter of fact, at Coney Island one of the ward leaders said, "That baby is causing me a lot of problems." And I said, "It's causing you a lot of problems. Why? I'm telling them not to take drugs or alcohol." "It's causing me a lot of problems. A lot of people don't like it." And I said, "Well, as I stand here on the phone with you, I can see a guy selling crack to a kid and that's okay, that's cool, but you're talking about a two-headed baby causing problems." And he said, "You're talking about apples and oranges." I said, "I'm doing what I'm going to do, and if you want me out of here, you're going to have to go through a lot of trouble 'cause I ain't leaving. And if you want to call the sheriff or the police, make sure their insurance is paid up because I sued them the last time." They left me alone pretty much after that. But I've always had something. I've had bouncers. I had one that was wax and looked like a gingerbread boy. Flat wooden thing with water around it. It was horrible. That was the first two-headed specimen I had. The one they had at Hubert's—it was wax—was an exact reproduction of the one I have that's real. I always thought the one they had at Hubert's was real until one time I saw it in a corner and the leg was broke.

"I'm doing what I'm going to do, and if you want me out of here, you're going to have to go through a lot of trouble 'cause I ain't leaving. And if you want to call the sheriff or the police, make sure their insurance is paid up because I sued them the last time."

S&A: You've had all kinds of weird animal acts and shows. Didn't you have a dancing chicken?

BR: I would put Scotch tape on its feet and I would tap dance with this chicken. You put Scotch tape on a chicken's foot and it'll wave its foot one way and then it will wave his foot the other, trying to get the Scotch tape off, and here I am tap dancing along with the chicken. It would walk off stage with me and come back and do the Conga or whatever I was doing. That was my act. No one could remember my name. They would always say, "Where's the crazy kid with the dancing chicken?" I used to go into hotels and I'd have the chicken with me and he'd start crowing. I'd get thrown out of a lot of hotels because of it. I'd put a burlap tobacco bag, a Bull Durham bag, over his head and I'd put black velvet over it and I'd put this over his head and he wouldn't see light and he wouldn't crow. That's why I broke in hens to do this act, so they wouldn't crow. I went around the country like that for a while.

Two Heads are Better Than One

S&A: I've seen pictures and read about tattooed animals, but you actually had one.

BR: Do you want to hear about the tattooed dog? I'm pitching pens and I always had Henry with me. Henry was my hairless dog. It was a Chinese Crested. He used to follow me—he was like a human; he was never on a leash—and I would go into bars and I'd snap my fingers and he would jump on a barstool. He would drink beer out of an ashtray. We drank beer a lot. (I'm an alcoholic. I drank for thirty-two years and now I'm sober. I go to AA a lot and drink coffee and don't drink in between.) I passed by this tattoo shop, Iwo Jima Eddy was the guy, I looked down at Henry and I said, "Henry, how would you like to have a bathing beauty or an eagle on your chest? Would you like that?" So the dog is kind of looking at me like the RCA dog, like I'm nuts or something, and I'm half gassed anyway. So Iwo Jima says, "Who are you talking to?" I said, "Why don't we put an eagle on his chest, a bathing beauty on him, a clipper ship here and a 'Death Before Dishonor,'" and I picked out his tattoos. And he said, "Well, we have to take him to a vet. I know a guy who will knock him out while we do all the outlines and I can color it in the next day. You have to knock them out or you can't do it." I took Henry to the vet and they knocked him out and Iwo Jima Eddy brought a portable set, a battery set and tattooed him. That's how I ended up with a tattooed dog. He just had an eagle on his chest, a bathing beauty that went down from the end of the eagle and

The Greatest Showman in the World.

on one haunch he had, "Death Before Dishonor," and a clipper ship and a swabbie and a "Mom" in a heart. He had about nine or ten tattoos. I took him in the sideshow, that's when I was with Jack Waller. Waller painted a banner and Henry was the tattooed dog. "Now ladies and gentlemen, on the inside you are going to see little Henry, the tattooed dog. He's got an eagle on his chest, a bathing beauty on one haunch and "Mom" in a heart. Not only that, ladies and gentleman, this dog is unique: He barks in five languages." Such crap! Henry used to sit in a small crib on the stage and that was his bed. He knew when he was supposed to be on and what act was before his. When it was time for him to be on, he would jump out of his bed and run down and we'd show his tattoos. The ASPCA would come after me, the do-gooders, and I would tell them that I had bought this dog from a sailor who was afraid to get a tattoo, who was a coward, and every time he wanted to get a tattoo, he would tattoo the dog. I had rescued the dog from the sailor. I had paid him $300 and I kept him and he's been in my show ever since. I took care of him. And then they would say, "Well, you shave him?" And I would say, "No, he's a hairless dog. He's a Chinese Crested. And they would never believe that! They thought he had a bad case of the mange. I got a book that showed the breed of dog and we used to carry it all the time because people didn't believe it. But Henry's been gone for a while. He lived to be twenty-one years old. He was an old dog, but he was an alcoholic. That dog loved to get lushed as much as I did. I never brought him to any AA meetings. He died before I quit. He would have ended up drinking coffee with me too. He would have done all twelve steps and gotten a medallion and his chips.

S&A: Was he the only tattooed animal you had in a show?

BR: He was the only tattooed dog; I never had another tattooed animal. I had tattooed people. But, as a matter of fact, I have a pig out on the ranch. It was a pet pig, potbelly pig. He is all white. He was a pet and he grew, he's probably about thirty-five pounds. I'm thinking about getting him tattooed, but in this day and age, they would probably have me put in jail and I'd never get out again. It's horrible. Do you know what I call them? I call them the "Humaniacs." It's outrageous crap they come up with. They say, "You treat this animal bad." I make a living with them; it would be kind of ludicrous for me to treat them badly. The veterinarian sees them every month. They see more doctors than I do. My giant rat has a complete history and they look at him and they check him out. I have to do that for the state, and then I have the USDA on my ass, the federal one,

and then I have the ASPCA. I'm dealing with three people.

S&A: What kind of demands do they place on you for the rat?

BR: If there's cobwebs they want them down, they want the water changed and they want to know what I feed him. When I tell them Purina Rat Chow, they tell me there's no such thing. There is: It's called "Laboratory Rat Chow" and it has everything that a rat could use. And then you give them sweet potatoes and lettuce and supplement them with a little sweet feed and you have a little salt and then you throw hay in there. It likes hay every once in a while. I use capybaras; nutrias look better, but

Bobby sticks with his performers through thick and thin.

they're very vicious. They're very bad, nutrias. You get two of them in there and you could have a blood bath. And they will attack you. Capybaras are kind of mellow. You scratch them under the chin once they get used to you. Mine is almost a year old, so he's gotten so you can touch him now. They love to be scratched under the chin. They make two noises when you come in: the first noise is [coughing]. That's the one noise that they know you're there. The other one is if your scratching them under the chin and they're kind of content they go [chomping noise]. Those are their two noises. I have a five-legged cow that's working now at the flea market in Phoenix, too.

S&A: You're talking about a full-grown cow?

BR: It's a three-year-old cow. It's got a full size leg rolling out of its shoulder and it has another hoof off of it. So it has six hoofs. Interesting cow. "Elsie the five-legged, six-hoofed cow." I have a nine-acre ranch in California. I've had the cow for two years at the ranch and I had the show all framed, but I just didn't have time to bring it out. I keep the two elephant-skinned dogs there, Elsie and Ellie, and I have a bunch of chickens and the five-legged cow and a llama and I have a midget horse and snakes, stuff like that. I'm the Dr. Doolittle of the weird ones.

S&A: I guess that would include that two-headed cow I've heard you had. What's the story with that?

BR: Well, Al Moody has this two headed cow that he got from Archie McCaskill. It's an old cow, it's got to be seventeen and they only live to be eighteen and I'm working in Ohio at some fair, a big fair. It parallels with the Ohio State Fair, and he's got this grind show with a little barn and a trailer and a truck and this two-headed cow alive so I go and I says, "Al, what do you want for this show?" and he says, "Hey, Barbara," his wife was named Barbara, "he wants to buy the show. How much for the show?" She said, "$12,000 for the truck and everything. For the whole show." They acted like I didn't have twelve cents. I come back later on and I'm half-gassed again and I says. "Do I get the spot with it?" "Barbara, he wants the spot with it." So she calls out the trailer, "Give 'em the spot with it if he gives you $12,000." I went back to the trailer and I get $12,000 and I go over to Al and I says, "Here's $12,000. What does this thing eat?" It had to have a special bath and cortisone shots, shit like that. Friggin' cow was on its way out. So I got this cow finally (and after the $12,000 I think I ended up netting about $2,000; I was only out about $10,000!) and I went on Gooding's Million Dollar Midway and I had it all through the South. We brought it to Phoenix and every 100 miles it would get down and it wouldn't get up. It was a big cow, a big bull, and you had to walk him and exercise him. So here I am schlepping this two-headed cow around in the middle of the desert and this cop stops and asks me what I'm doing. "I'm walking this cow around." He says, "He looks different." "Yeah, he's got two heads." "Oh. Yeah." So then I put him back in the wagon and we schlep off to Phoenix and we finally get him in Phoenix and I'm feeding him and now he won't go to the bathroom. He's bloating and I go to the slaughterhouses to get fodder to, hopefully, create the gases so this thing will go to the bathroom. And he's eating and he's not going to the bathroom and he's drinking and he's not going to the bathroom. I figure any minute I'm going to have the most hellacious cleaning bill ever. I figure he's going to crap all over the tip one day. Then the fair is over and I send the cow out to the pasture and I says to my man, Buddy Thompson, I says "Do what you can to make this thing go to the bathroom." I figure any minute he's going to blow up and kill somebody. He didn't go to the bathroom and he finally died and I said, "Take him to the taxidermist and get him stuffed." So he took him to the taxidermist and had him done. It cost me $12,000 to have him done. So next year, I put him right back in there again and I go out to the barns and I'd take this shovel and I'd put some cow manure right on top of the straw so people, would say, "Oh yeah, it's alive. Look at the crap down there." Set right where we did the first time and he made more money dead than he did alive! "Does the cow move?" "No" "Why doesn't he move?" "Because he's dead." He looked alive. They did a beautiful job on him. He was mounted on a platform with casters and I put hay all around so you couldn't see the casters. He looked better dead than he did alive, too.

S&A: In Ward Hall's documentary, *The Last American Sideshow*, you tell an outrageous story from your show on the World of Mirth about an "Aunt Jemima."

BR: Carrie Adams. That was her name, Aunt Jemima. She put pillows on her breasts. She was a bally act. She took care of Kokomo the Mule-Faced Boy and the Bear Girl. I had Bobette, the bearded lady, on the road as the blow-off and she quit and went somewhere else in the middle of the night and I didn't have no blow-off. So I said to Carrie Adams, that was her name, I said, "Carrie, I'm gonna make you a star." She said, "Mr. Bob, when you talk like that, you're gonna do something bad to me." I said, "I'm not gonna do nothing bad to you. You don't have to dance on the bally stage. You don't have to walk up and down the stairs. All you have to do is sit there. That's all you have to do. You can sit there and listen to the radio. That's all you have to do. Once in awhile, you're going to have to be the blow-off attraction." She said, "What are you going to do to me?" "I'm going to make you the gorilla girl." I glued this crepe hair all over and around her face and her nose and I puffed up her hair in this big afro before afros were in. I put a scarf over her head and I used to say, "Half animal, half human. Her mother was human. What was her father? These things will be explained inside." They'd get inside and I'd say, "It started with a little hair on her face . . ." and I'd pull off the scarf. That was it. Everything was cool. So we're playing the Dixie Classic Fair, she's sweating like a hog, and the spirit gum that I used to hold the beard, the whole beard is laying underneath her chin almost on one side. And I'm going through the spiel and pull this thing off and there's this hunk of hair. And I'm saying, "This is the way she goes through life; like this," and I pulled off the scarf and she's going, "Bob, you a New York Jew and me a black lady down here. They're gonna tar and feather our asses. They're gonna kill us. You have got to get a better glue on here. I ain't gonna do this no more. I don't want none of the spirit gum. That shit don't hold. You have got to get a better glue on here." I don't know what to do, so I've got this Brown Bear—I put this Brown Bear on her and I stick up this thing. And she's grabbing and going, "This holds real good," and she's grabbing at it. "That holds real good." Then we learn she can't get this shit off! She's got alcohol and she's trying to peel it off with alcohol, and apparently she gets alcohol poisoning trying to scratch this shit off her face. Now I've got this black lady with a puffed-up face in the South and I take her along this street in town where they have all these doctors. They have these big white columns and the wrought-iron fence and I knock on the door and I go in and there's this doctor and I says, "Doc, you ain't gonna believe this." And he says, "Try me." And I says, "Well I have this gorilla girl." And he says, "You gotta what?" So I explain what happened to him. He says, "You all bring her in. I'd like to see this myself." So I go get Carrie and I schlepped her inside. He looked at her and put some cream on it and pulled it off and he looked at her and said, "Well, I wouldn't do anything for at least a week, and I wouldn't ever use that patching glue again."

A passionate plea to the patrons.

S&A: So that was the end of her blow-off days?

BR: No, I found this other thing—it was this liquid adhesive, like a latex—that was better than spirit gum. She finished the season out as half-animal, half-human.

S&A: But you've had hairy people who weren't gaffs?

BR: Yeah, but my bearded lady she shaved her beard off, so you know she doesn't want to be in the business anymore.

S&A: That's usually the first sign.

BR: Yeah. You get a feeling.

S&A: What was your museum like on the Island?

BR: I had a school of piranha fish, and I had a frog band. I got all these frogs from Mexico—I got this whole band—and they were playing wooden instruments. I bought this set of these miniature drums, clarinets and stuff—well, I got this whole band with a harp and a bass fiddle and clarinets and trombones and it's gorgeous. I had my painter, John Hiner, make this huge banner with "The Really Real Frog Band! Real Frogs!" down in the bottom put the Budweiser logo, like Budweiser was putting up the money for this crap! Everybody said, "Boy, is this going to be a friggin' heat score!" I had a fish tank with about nine or ten frogs in with all of them playing different instruments and one singing. That was my frog band.

S&A: And did it get you any heat?

BR: No. They'd look at it, they'd say, "Do these frogs play?" and I'd say, "Well, they used to." "Are they real frogs?" "They're real frogs." "Why don't they play?" "They're dead." You know what I did acquire? I have the real Fiji Mermaid. The real one.

S&A: You mean Barnum's?

BR: Yeah. This has been laying dormant for years and years. I got it from a family in upstate New York and the whole family was firemen. Like six generations of fire fighters. Apparently, when the museum caught on fire, somebody swallowed the Fiji Mermaid and this thing had been in the family for years and years and years and I finally bought it from this family.

S&A: So it wasn't destroyed in the fire?

BR: No, it wasn't destroyed, and they sold it to me. Then I had one wall that's nothing but photographs of freaks and stuff and then I had a school of piranha fish. It's a school of taxidermied fish. I had them on a wire and they look like they're swimming. And then I had the freak pigs and I had the cat with one head and two bodies and I had all of these wax figures of the Penguin Girl and the fat lady and Alzora Lewis, the Turtle Girl, and the ring-neck women from Burma.

S&A: They were all life-sized?

BR: Yeah, and I had the Ubangi saucer-lips. And the frog band of course. The Really Real Frog Band. Then I had great big Egyptian figures that came out of a movie set and wild crap like that. Then I had the kid in there. He eats fire and swallows swords and does magic and that's Frank [Hartman] and he did a little show down on the end.

S&A: I've heard that among all your other things, you've got a medicine show, too.

BR: I do a medicine show opening. I have a medicine wagon. I have a whole medicine show so when I get older I have something to do. I have this medicine show and it has "Dr. Reynolds" on it. It's a horse-drawn wagon. I do ventriloquism and I have this kid who swallows swords in an Indian outfit and I do magic and this and that and I do the metamorphosis. I stand behind the screen as I get into this high hat and a doctor's thing with a watch fob and then I say, "This is how P.T. Kelly used to do it." But that's when I get old and have nothing else.

S&A: Is the expression "going out horizontal" how you picture yourself leaving the business?

BR: That's probably what will happen to me. I'll be making an opening and then I'll drop dead on the stage, and just before I split, I'll say, "What was the gross?"

Hard by the City of the Angels and a far cry from the Island of the Conies (that's rabbits to the likes of you and me) is the tiny town of Fillmore wherein lies a ranch that's home to the weirdest damn collection of stuffed and pickled monstrosities extant, certainly extant in Fillmore. Not coincidentally, it's also home to Bobby Reynolds. By the front door of the house (nearly invisible behind the surrounding shrubs) is an elaborate cactus garden. On one side of the property runs a small stream at the base of a 30' gorge, a gorge Reynolds tells me the stream fills to the brim in "the rainy season" (read: January; otherwise, it's a desert). On the other side of the property is a small mountain, bone dry and the color of straw, a mountain Reynolds says was all aflame a few years back, a crisis that saw him and his help standing on the roof watering the house with garden hoses trying (successfully, as it turns out) to keep the house intact. In the distance the mountains go on forever.

It's a stunning view, one I have to drive through the evening I go with Reynolds to find Dave Twomey's FunTime Circus. Before we leave, he tells me he should drive. Thanking him for his generosity, I tell him thanks anyway, but my mother always told me to have my own accidents. When he keeps insisting, I keep pushing back, and I finally get my way. Big mistake. The drive over the mountains, all too many miles of it in darkness as deep as the inside of a cow, was as terrifying as any I've ever experienced. White-knuckle driving at its best. When I tell Reynolds I now understand why he'd been so insistent, he tells me a story about Jimmy Webb, the Ugliest Man in the World, how one time he and Reynolds had been driving through the hills, Reynolds at the wheel, when the brakes gave out. As the situation grew worse, with Reynolds fighting to control the descent of the huge truck, he'd asked Webb if he could do something for him. When Webb said, "Sure. What?" Reynolds, of course, told him, "Pray."

I suppose that story, full of the yanked-from-the-jaws-of-death flavor that fills so many showmen's tales, got Reynolds to thinking about Webb's passing, which occurred only a few years ago, mere days after another showman, a mutual friend of Reynolds and Webb, had also died. Reynolds told me that he'd been on the road and had gotten word of how bad off Webb was. He'd called Webb at the hospital, catching him literally at death's door. Webb, the Ugliest Man in the World, about to become the Ugliest Man in the Next. After a few words of uncomfortable small talk, Reynolds brought up the name of their mutual friend who had died recently. And in a move that was pure Reynolds, he told Webb he'd just talked to that showman and that Webb shouldn't worry. "Don't worry, Jimmy. I told him to get the lot all ready for when you get there." Jimmy Webb died that night. And, though I hope it's a long way away, I'm sure Jimmy will have the lot ready for Bobby Reynolds, the Greatest Showman in the World, when his time comes.

Bobby's Bally Lessons

You say you've always wanted to make friends and influence people but weren't quite sure how to begin? Well friends, have we got some help for you. Professor Bobby Reynolds has provided us with some of his choicest ballies. Guaranteed to turn any tip or your money back. You'll get people to agree to pay for any attraction—even when you're not sure what it is yourself. Remember, he convinced New Yorkers to pay to see a rat! You can learn to be a master pitch artist in a few simple lessons without going to the school of hard knocks. The line forms to the right and the main show will not begin until this sidebar is over.

Chinese Horn Nut Pitch

This is it! Have you ever seen one of these? A Chinese Water Lily. These are Chinese Water Lilies—you poke a hole in the top, one in the bottom and in three days you get a green sprout. Before a full week, you get an Oriental Water Lily. They come in three colors, the pink ones, the yellow ones, and [other colors as appropriate].

Flea Circus Pitch

Ladies and gentlemen, if you all gather down as close as you possible can, thank you very much, there'll be no show on these outer stages while this attraction is on. Ladies and gentlemen, once every hour, Hubert's Museum proudly presents none other than Professor Heckler's trained Flea Circus. In this enclosure you are going to see dozens of real, live, trained, performing fleas. Fleas that juggle, jump through hoops, play football, operate a miniature merry-go-round, tiny little fleas hitched to a chariot and they actually run a race. But the most predominating feature of the whole show is little fleas dressed in costumes and they dance to the strains of music. It is without a doubt the most fascinating sight the human eye has ever witnessed. Now if you would like to go, there will be no show on these outer stages until this attraction is over. There is a small admission, we don't apologize for it, it's only nine cents. So if you would like to go, you will see fleas that juggle!

Wine Bath Pitch

Gallons and gallons of wine over her entire body, ladies and gentlemen, and you see her inside taking a bath the same way you see the palm of my hand. It's a little bit naughty and a little bit nice. It makes the old feel young and the young feel foolish. Hotter than a cowboy's pistol shooting up the hill on the Fourth of July. We don't have any seats here, boys. You come in and you'll stand straight up.

236

Blind Opening for Blow-off

Ladies and gentleman, I have been in this business for a number of years and I've introduced a lot of strange people. People like Frank Lentini—a man with three legs, sixteen toes and four feet. Betty Lou Williams—a girl who had her baby sister growing out of her stomach and she had three arms, four legs and two bodies. [mentions many others] The attraction I have here this evening is equally as strange as those I just mentioned and, ladies and gentlemen, this act is not advertised outside and if I didn't tell you about it you wouldn't even know it was here. If you would like to see it, there is a small intermission and during this intermission we give you an opportunity to see this person. See this person the same way you see the palm of my hand. Positively alive. If you would like to go, there is a small admission, only a quarter—twenty-five cents.

Chinese Handcuff Pitch

How many of you throw a million baseballs? A guy would hand you one of these [shows item] and you would throw it the hell away. If you knew what this was, you wouldn't throw it the hell away. You say to your girlfriend, "Honey, I want to buy you a diamond ring. What size do you wear?" She would say, "I don't know." "Well, slip this on your finger and we'll count the squares" and when she slips this thing on and you count the squares, she can't get it off. She says, "I can't get it off." You say, "Well, put your arm around the tree and I'll pull." You put another finger in it. She can't get away from you, but if you don't know what to do, you call me.

Medicine Show Pitch

You're all dying. Every man, every woman and every child is dying. From the instant you are born, you begin to die and the calendar—yes, the calendar—is your executioner. That no man can change or hope to change. It is nature's law that there is no escape from the individual finale on the mighty stage of life where each of you are destined to play your farewell performance. So ponder well my words and ask yourself these questions: Is there a way to delay, perhaps at least for years, that final moment where your name is written down by a bony hand in the cold diary of death? Of course there is, good neighbors and that's why I'm here. [Go into the medicine pitch. Close with specific elixirs.] Ladies and gentlemen, if health were a thing that money could buy, the rich would live and the poor would die. But God in his wisdom ruled it so, when our time comes, we all must go. But an ounce of prevention is worth a pound of cure and how many bottles of elixir would you like, my dear?

Freda--Fred

HALF MAN and HALF WOMAN

HE   SHE   IT

Aside from what is it, a fat girl or a Seal boy, old mother nature sets one thinking, but after all, these people are the unusual, and as the unusual people are of decided interest, I will tell you something of myself.

I was born in New York City, February 22, 1908, of normal parents. At birth I was thought to be a boy and was named Fred, after my father, but at the age of 12 years and 3 months, a great change came over me. The left side of my body was growing out of proportion with that of the right; the left side was developing very small and the right side was getting large and muscular; my mother, being alarmed, called in the family physician (Dr. George Baker) of Brooklyn, N.Y. After an examination, he said I was neither boy nor girl, but both combined in one body. Up to this time I was dressed as a boy, and a week after my examination my mother dressed me as a girl and put me in a private school, my name was also changed from Fred to Freda.

And then when I was about 16 another great surprise took place, hair began to grow on my right side and on both sides of my face. Then all the papers of New York and other cities printed stories of my life, they would say, "Is it boy or is it girl?" and the doctors would come back at them and would say it is both, brother and sister combined in one body. So I was placed on exhibition as a double-bodied person or the Half Man-Half Woman, and I have toured the United States and Canada with various shows and companies.

A person of my type is called a hermaphrodite, the dictionary says a hermaphrodite is a thing having the characteristics of both sexes; bisexual.

The Greek poet, Aristophanes, relates an ancient myth that man was originally created as man and woman united in one body, until he aroused the jealousy of the Gods, who, for his vanity, separated him into two entities, man and woman. The cause of such an unusual birth is explained by many physicians as the union of two sperm, male and female, and forming two separate sexes in one body. Whether this is true or not I cannot say, although it sounds possible.

[Clippings from the Press]

Dorsey Bros. Circus in Town

The extra added attraction at the Empire Theatre tonight is Freda-Fred Van, part boy, part girl. See this girl-boy in person. Surely is one of Nature's puzzles.
—Lexington, Ky., *News*.

Freda-Fred Van, the wonder person of the age, has joined Dorsey Bros. Side Show, and is to give daily exhibitions. Freda-Fred is from New York City, is 20 years of age, and has the appearance of a woman on one side of the body, while on the other a well developed young man.
—Syracuse, N.Y., *Daily*.

Freda-Fred Van, double-bodied woman, returned from England today, along with ten other American attractions.
—March 10, 1927, *Billboard*.

Freda-Fred

Half Man & Half Woman
H E • S H E • I T

Aside from what is it, a fat girl or a Seal boy, old mother nature sets one thinking, but after all, these people are the unusual, and as the unusual people are of decided interest, I will tell you something of myself. I was born in New York City, February 22, 1908, of normal parents. At birth I was thought to be a boy and was named Fred, after my father, but at the age of twelve years and three months, a great change came over me. The left side of my body was growing out of proportion with that of the right; the left side was developing very small and the right side was getting large and muscular; my mother, being alarmed, called in the family physician (Dr. George Baker) of Brooklyn, N.Y. After an examination, he said I was neither boy nor girl, but both combined in one body. Up to this time I was dressed as a boy, and a week after my examination my mother dressed me as a girl and put me in a private school, my name was also changed from Fred to Freda.

And then when I was about 16 another great surprise took place, hair began to grow on my right side and on both sides of my face. Then all the papers of New York and other cities printed stories of my life, they would say, "Is it boy or is it girl?" and the doctors would come back at them and would say it is both, Half Man-Half Woman, and I have toured the United States and Canada with various shows and companies. A person of my type is called a hermaphrodite, the dictionary says a hermaphrodite is a thing having the characteristics of both sexes; bisexual.

The Greek poet, Aristophanes, relates an ancient myth that man was originally created as man and woman united in one body, until he aroused the jealousy of the Gods, who, for his vanity, separated him into two entities, man and woman. The cause of such an unusual birth is explained by many physicians as the union of two sperm, male and female, and forming two separate sexes in one body. Whether this is true or not I cannot say, although it sounds possible.

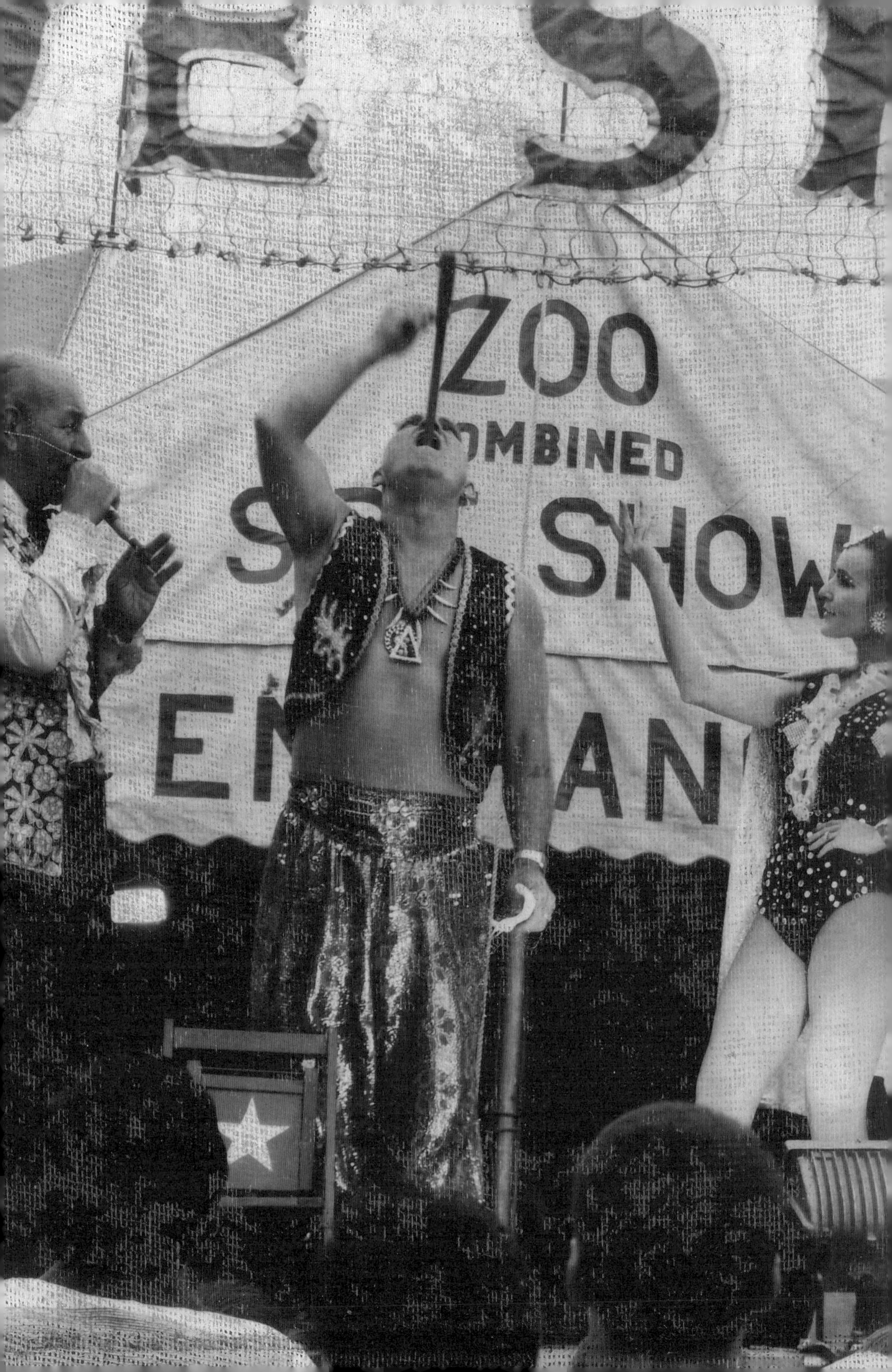
ZOO
OMBINED
SHOW

Lingo

S ome of this jargon may seem well worn. Some of it, though, is deceptively familiar. If you can sit there without reading this diminutive dictionary, feeling firm in your knowledge that bag pipe bands, glass blowers and Punch & Judy shows used to be regular attractions in sideshows, you probably don't need this chapter. Otherwise, welcome to the show.

A special note: *Lingo*, like the back end itself (you can look it up!), is a compendium of elements, only disparate at first glance. The primary element is the definitions taken from *Circus Lingo*, the seminal work on the subject by old-time trouper, circus and carnival historian, and publisher Joe McKennon, "the man who was with it." Without him and his work, this chapter would be rife with error and inaccuracy. The second, italicized element of this dictionary is my own. Step right up!

AB (Amusement Business)—*The magazine of the trade. In the old days, before its name change, it was* The Billboard. *Many, if not the majority, of traveling showmen would have* Billboard *as their address; that is, they could be contacted while on the road care of the forwarding services offered to the showmen by the trade journal. See* **BILLBOARD.**

ALLIGATOR MAN/WOMAN/ETC.—*Sideshow human oddity afflicted with skin condition, commonly ictheosis, that gives the skin a scaly, reptile-like appearance.*

ANATOMICAL WONDER—*A sideshow performer, usually perceived by the public as a human oddity, but more a working act. The performer would do stunts such as "the man without a stomach" (pulling the gut in until the backbone shows), pulling themselves through a coat hanger or tennis racket, and other Indian Rubber Man stunts.*

ANNEX—*In the case of a sideshow, another name for the area where the blow-off is located.*

BABY SHOW—*Also known as "unborn," "life," "bottle," "freak baby" and "pickled punk show," though these last terms are strictly carnival insider lingo and were not used around the general public. See **PICKLED PUNK**.*

BACK END—Inside the big top at opposite end of tent from the front door or the "connection" between the menagerie and the big top. The "back end" of a carnival consists of the shows and riding devices. Concessions, no matter where located, are part of the "front end."

BALLY, BALLYHOO—A free show given outside a side show to attract a crowd (a "tip") of potential patrons. Word came into being at the 1893 Columbian Exposition in Chicago. The fakirs, gun spinners and dancing girls from the Middle East spoke no English, only Arabic. The interpreters used the expression "Dehalla Hoon" to call performers outside to the show fronts. The Western ears of the talkers translated it as "ballyhoo" and so used it when the interpreters were away for lunch.

BANNER—Side Show. Pictorials on canvas hung in front of circus side shows and carnival midway shows depicting the wonders to be found inside.

BEARDED LADY—*Woman with a beard appearing in a show. They were most often genuine, though there were the occasional gaffs.*

BEEF—A complaint from a patron, a law officer or others concerning anything about the show.

BILLBOARD—*See **AB**.*

BLADE BOX—*Act where performer (usually a woman) lies in box while steel blades are pushed through it, the impression given the crowd that the performer is contorting herself like she's made of rubber or can twist like a snake.*

BLOW-OFF—Crowds leaving a big top after a performance. Extra pay, extra added attractions in back end of both circus and carnival side shows were also called blowoffs. *Also "blow off," "blow-off," or "the blow."*

BLOW DOWN—When one or more tents or riding devices is leveled to the ground by a wind storm.

BOSS CANVASMAN—*Literally, what it says. He's the man in charge of making sure the canvas goes up properly and doesn't come down on the show short of a major blow down.*

BOUNCER—*A rubber or vinyl reproduction of a pickled punk. There were any number of reasons for using reproductions instead of genuine punks including local legal restrictions, loss of the genuine article, or easier accessibility to one than the other.*

CARNIVAL—*A cooperative business arrangement between independent showmen, ride owners and concessioners to present outdoor amusement for the public.*

CARNY—*Someone who works in a carnival. The term is also applied to the carnival itself. It's a term used by some in the business and disliked by others.*

DEVIL BABY—*A gaffed freak, usually constructed to appear mummified or otherwise preserved, often displayed in a tiny coffin. The name is pretty much self explanatory, and they often had horns, fangs, hoofed feet, claws, etc.*

DIME MUSEUM—*A collection of specimens, exotic objects and live acts and performances, usually set up in its own building though just as often set up in an old store front. They were most popular primarily in the 19th and early 20th centuries. The present day road-side museums are their descendants.*

DONIKER—A rest room or toilet wherever it is.

ELEPHANT SKIN GIRL/BOY/ETC.—*Human oddity whose skin texture resembled an elephant's and/or whose skin was baggy and loose.*

FLAT STORE—A gaming concession that really has no winning numbers, or combination of numbers. The "gentlemanly agents" sell "conversation" to their "marks."

FRAME A SHOW—To build a new show.

FREAK—A human oddity on exhibition in a museum or in a circus or carnival side show. Early day circuses also displayed some featured freaks in their menageries.

FREAK BABY SHOW—*See* **BABY SHOW**

FREAK SHOW—*A show where human oddities and freakish working acts performed. The term applies to both circus and carnival. In prac-*

tice, these shows were often 10-in-one shows and usually had a high percentage of working acts like sword swallowers and fire eaters or "made freaks" like tattooed people.

FROG MAN/GIRL/ETC.—*Human oddity whose legs and arms could be contorted so they could squat in a frog-like position. This ability was often the result of the Ehlers-Danlos Syndrome, an affliction which can result in hyper-extensible joints, skin laxity (such as that of Rubber Skin people), and other anomalies. Otis Jordan, on the other hand, often billed as the Frog Boy, was so called as his loco-motion was by hopping, necessitated by his shriveled limbs.*

FRONT—*(show front, 200' front, talking the front, "I got your money on the front," etc.) Generally, the front of a show, though its mean-ing can change depending on usage. A 200' front pretty clearly means the show takes up 200' of the midway and "I got your money on the front" obviously means the patron paid to get into the show. On the other hand, the front end consists of only the concessions in a carnival but, on a circus, consists of the midway including concessions and the sideshows. The term "front" can also apply to how someone looks, as in "putting up a front."*

GAFF—*In the broadest sense, anything controlled or "faked". A gaffed game, for example, would be one where it would be nearly impos-sible for the patron to win unless the operator let him. In the case of freak animals (and human oddities as well on occasion), for example, a gaff wouldn't be a genuine freak of nature, regardless how convincing it looked, but instead, a specimen manufactured to look freakish.*

GIRL-TO-GORILLA/GORILLA GIRL/APE GIRL SHOW—*An elaborate illu-sion show that gives the patrons the impression that a beautiful girl is being changed into a gorilla. These shows have also appeared as variations on the transformation theme; for example, skeletal corpse to a living vampire. The girl-to-gorilla show is still the all-time money maker though.*

GIRL SHOW—*In its generic sense, a show in which dancing women are the primary attraction. These could range from the revues (the Broadway revues with dancing girls or the more exotic "foreign" revues such as the Hawaiian revues) to the racier hootchie kootchie (also houchie kouchie, hoochie koochie, hootchy kootchy, kootch, cootch, etc.) shows.*

GRAB JOINT—An eating concession (with circuses a hamburger stand). The customer is served directly over the counter from the griddle, juice bowl, etc. Circus grab joints had no seating of any kind for the townspeople. Only seating for them was in the big top. Some carnival grab joints do have seating all around the stand.

GRIFT—The crooked games, short change artists, clothesline robbers, merchandise boosters, pickpockets and all other types of skull-duggery carried by some of the "fireball shows." The term was used collectively to cover any and all such activities.

GRIND—In the spiel from a show front, the rhythmic verbal conclusion that's meant to move the patrons into the show. It differs from the opening bally, which is meant to get the attention of midway strollers and sell them on the show they'll see.

GRIND SHOW—A show or attraction that never has a "bally." Front men and ticket sellers just "grind away" all day. *Most of the shows on carnival midways today are grind shows, the grind blaring over the midway from an audiotape loop and sound system.*

GRIP—Money.

HALF AND HALF—Sideshow attractions who claimed to be hermaphrodites. Some of them were.

HALF GIRL/BOY—*A human oddity born without lower limbs.*

HEADLESS/HEADLESS ILLUSION—*Illusion show where a "headless" person is displayed. They're usually pitched as "medical "miracles" following tragic accidents.*

HEAT—Problems, arguments or battles between the show, or its people, and townspeople. Most heat was caused by illegal activities of a show, but not always by the show involved. A "burn 'em up" outfit in ahead of a real "Sunday Schooler" could and did leave a lot of heat for the latter.

HOT SNAKE—*A snake show term for a poisonous snake.*

HUMAN LIVING TORSO—*Human oddity born without arms or legs.*

INDEPENDENT MIDWAY—*The midway concessions booked in separately from those with the carnival. In a fair, for example, the independent midway could consist of booths for local businesses, food stands raising money for fraternal organizations, even shows such* *as might appear on the carnival midway such as reptile shows, motordromes, etc.*

INSIDE—(money, lecturer, etc.) "Inside the show."

JACKPOTS—Troupers' stories of their former escapades, often exaggerated. *"Cuttin' up jackpots," or "jackies," are the expressions given to swapping these stories.*

ILLUSION SHOW—*Show consisting of illusions, for example, headless, Spidora, Snake Girl, etc.*

LAND OFFICE BUSINESS—*Doing so much business you almost have to turn people away.*

LECTURER—*Individual who talks inside the show, lecturing on the various acts. Often, acts lecture on themselves, especially the human oddities.*

LOT—The show grounds.

MARK—A carnival term for townspeople. Particularly, the ones who "go up against the games."

MENTALIST—*Performer, usually working with an assistant, whose act consists of "reading the minds" of the patrons.*

MIDWAY—*In its broadest sense, the location where all the concessions, rides and shows are located in a circus, fair or carnival. Of course, a carnival is basically nothing but midway; in a circus, the midway is just that: the midway between the "front door" to the circus lot itself and the "big top" where the circus performers do their acts; and in a fair, the midway will probably be a combination of the carnival and the "independent midway," amusements booked in separately from the carnival by the fair committee itself.*

MITT CAMP—A fortunetelling booth on a carnival.

MONKEY GIRL/BOY/ETC.—*Human oddity afflicted with hirsutism. Such individuals might also be called Wolf Boys, Dog Boys, etc. Their hairiness is more extreme than, say, a bearded lady's.*

MOSS-HAIRED GIRL—*A gaffed human oddity, generally Caucasian, who would bush her hair, much in the style of the 1960s–1970s "Afro" worn by African-Americans. The pitch which usually accompanied the act involved kidnaping by "Arabs" and being forced into harem life, followed by a harrowing escape culminating in refuge there in the show.*

MOTORDROME—*A daredevil show involving motorcycles and sometimes four-wheeled vehicles, such as go-carts, which race around inside small, circular wooden enclosures ("wall of death") or spherical wire mesh steel enclosures ("globe of death").*

MUSEUM SHOW—*Virtually any show where the exhibits are not alive. The show might contain specimens that are preserved, such as taxidermied or mummified freak animals, or other exotic items of interest, such as the weapons used by famous murderers. Also called a still show.*

NUT—The operating expenses of a show (daily, weekly or yearly). The story is that the word came into usage after a creditor came onto a circus grounds and took the nuts off the wagon wheels. "I will keep them until I get my money," he announced. He was paid. The nuts went back on the wheels and the show moved that night. "So a show always sought to "make the nut" and start making money above its expenses. A show that hadn't yet "made the nut" was said to be "on the nut" and one that had was said to be "off the nut"."

OFFICE—The carnival office wagon or trailer.

OSSIFIED GIRL/BOY/ETC.—*Human oddity afflicted with a condition which effectively freezes them in position, withering their limbs, etc.*

PARADE—*The procession which used to announce the arrival of the circus to town. Traditionally, circuses would make them as glorious and spectacular as possible, and they'd wind through the middle of town all the way to the lot where the big show was to occur.*

PENGUIN BOY/GIRL/ETC.—*Human oddity afflicted with foreshortened limbs, usually with hands and feet attached directly to the torso without arms or legs. See* **SEAL BOY/GIRL**.

PERCENTAGE—*That part of a showman's gross receipts that must be paid (usually in addition to other costs, too) to the carnival owner for the right to play the spot.*

PICKLED PUNK—A carnival term for human fetuses. Two-headed human babies, joined together twins, etc., etc. (also normal specimens from one to eight months). Not India rubber as many believed, these specimens were repulsive to some, but highly educational for millions of others. *See* **BABY SHOW** *as well.*

PINHEAD—*Human oddity afflicted with microcephaly, the head coming to a point, a fact which was often further emphasized by leaving a top knot of hair to emphasize the head shape.*

PITCH—Selling merchandise by lecturing and demonstrating.

PLATFORM—*The raised staging where acts perform. It can refer to those inside the show or the bally platform on the front of the show.*

POSING SHOW—*A show where the female "models" pose as they might for artists or in imitation of poses from famous artworks. In the days of the dime museums, the posers might also be male.*

PROFESSOR—*Title often taken by any showman considered "expert" in their chosen field. It was seldom a true indicator of academic pedigree, though it could well represent a wealth of knowledge about the public at large.*

PUNK—A young person or animal. A child or an unusually immature young person. Also a type of sexual pervert.

RAILROAD SHOW—A show which travels by railroad on its own train of specially built railroad cars.

RANGY—*Worked up, often in a vulgar way. Typically, a show could be rangy (say, a kootch show; usually, though, this would be termed a "strong" show) or a lot of rangy patrons (drunken, disorderly, disruptive) could be in a show. Pronounced like what you did to the bell.*

ROUSTABOUTS—Circus working men on the lot, particularly the big top crew. Some uninformed writers just love to use "razor back" for these hands. Razor backs were always train crewmen not canvasmen, which really is the proper term to use for big top men. Men in each department had designations from the job they performed. Dog boys, pony punks, property men, skinners, bull men, cage hands, front door men, lead bar detective, honey bucket man, coffee boy, pastry cook, etc.

ROUTE—List of towns and events played each week, month or year.

RUBE—Hey Rube or a battle with the towners. *Also, a not very affectionate term for the towner himself.*

SEAL BOY/GIRL/ETC.—*Human oddity afflicted with phocomelia, or foreshortened "seal," limbs, usually with hands and feet attached directly to the torso without arms or legs. See* **PENGUIN BOY/GIRL**.

SHILL/SHILLABER—One who pretends to play a game, or to buy a ticket to an attraction, in order to entice others to join or follow him. Without a good "shill," an entire "tip" may stay perfectly still after an "opening." All with the cash in their hands, and not one of them will "break" for the ticket boxes, unless some brave soul leads the way. "Shills" fill the need for brave souls. Also, Stick.

SIDESHOW—*Essentially, any show that plays the midway, though the now more common application is to the freak shows or 10-in-one shows. Technically, however, even a menagerie on the midway of a circus is a sideshow. Also "side show."*

SIDEWALL—*The canvas wall that hangs below a canvas "top," as in "big top." What most outside the business would call a "tent" is, in reality, the canvas top with its sidewalls attached.*

SINGLE-O—*A show consisting of a single attraction.*

SLACK WIRE—*A wire act, usually performed low as opposed to high wire, in which the wire is slack and bows under the wire artist, allowing for a periodically more comic (though just as difficult) act than usually seen on the high wire.*

SPIDORA—*Illusion show in which the head of a woman appears to grow from the body of a huge spider. The illusion is a reversal of the headless illusion.*

SQUARE—To settle a dispute without use of the law or the fists. Also used by the legal adjusters for the "fixing of a town" at City Hall, and the lavish use of passes on the lot to keep the law happy.

SPIEL—*The speech made on a show front by the talker to the gathering crowd.*

STICK—*A shill. See* **SHILL**.

TABLEAU—*A grouping of figures, the term most commonly used in wax museums and their midway counterparts, the wax shows. They were usually of historical scenes, but could be literary, mythical, horrific, etc.*

TALKER—Never "barker." The man who makes the "outside openings" and "talks" in front of an attraction. If he talks inside the attraction, he is a "lecturer."

TAKE YOUR BEST HOLT—Do anything to get the money. Also "work strong."

10-IN-ONE—A carnival midway show with ten attractions inside. It is usually an "illusion" show or some other "string show." Can be either a "pit" or a "platform" show. Most of them worked on ground level, though.

TIP—The crowd gathered in front of an attraction by the "ballyhoo." They listen to the talker, watch the free exhibition on the bally platform, and if the talker is convincing enough, they buy tickets and go in to see the promised show. When entire tip has been "turned" by a talker's "opening," it is said that he has "cleaned the midway."

TOP—*See definition for* **SIDEWALL** *above.*

TORTURE SHOW—*A horrific museum show displaying implements of torture, often shown in use on mannequins or wax figures.*

TROUPER—A person who has spent at least one full season on some type of traveling amusement organization. By then, they are usually hooked.

TRUCK SHOW—*A show which travels by truck, the situation of most carnivals today.*

TURN THE TIP—The would-be patrons in front of a bally platform who have been convinced that the "talker" is truthful and his attraction must be seen are "turned" when they crowd up to the ticket boxes and purchase tickets.

WAX SHOW—A show featuring wax figures of famous people, in this case outlaws and such. These early "Law" and "Outlaw" shows later evolved into "Crime Does Not Pay" shows. Scott Younger, of the Younger Family, operated a great wax show for many years.

WIDE OPEN—*A show or carnival where anything goes, where the shows can play as "strong" as they want, (meaning raunchy in this case) and the games can take the marks for anything they can by any means possible. Such conditions never existed without the approval of the local authorities, usually after big pay-offs from the carnival people.*

WINTERQUARTERS—*Location where a show stays during its offseason, that is, the quarters in the winter. A show's (or circus's or carnival's) winterquarters need not be in a temperate climate zone, though a number of them are in the South.*

WITH IT—(as in, "with it and for it") *An expression by which one trouper may know another even though they have never met before. Warning: Do not attempt to use this word unless you have been properly instructed in the manner by which to deliver it.*

X-RAY SHOW—*A potentially lethal show that played at least one world's fair (St. Louis Exposition in 1904). Apparently, one could go into the show and look through objects, including yourself and others, by use of x-rays. Needless to say, at the turn of the century, no one was aware of the dangers inherent in such a show.*

Framing the Show

Viewings

Front Cover: Logo by Mark Frierson

Inside Front Cover, 1-3, 4-6, 8-10, 13, 18, 22-25, 46-47, 48-51, 53-79, 82, 86, 90-113, 124-127, 142-143, 199, 238, 240: SHOCKED AND AMAZED! Archive

Inside Front Cover (Zip the Pinhead), 170-185: Joe Petro III Collection

Page 7, 11-12, 14-17, 19-20, 31, 80, 85, 144, 212, 226: Photo by James Taylor

Page 26-29, 32-44: Rock Collection

Page 52: Kathleen Kotcher Collection

Page 89: Bruce Snowdon Collection

Page 114-123: Sylvia Cassidy Collection

Page 146-167: Melvin Burkhart Collection

Page 186-197, 200-202: Percilla Bejano Collection

Page 203: Photo by June Parlett

Page 204-206: Collection of Christine Quigley

Page 209: Photo reprinted with permission of John J. Dunphy

Page 211: Collection of Harvey Lee Boswell

Page 214-225, 228-234: Collection of Bobby Reynolds

Reprints

Thanks to the following for allowing us to reprint their work:

Carnival Publishers of Sarasota for excerpts from Joe McKennon's *Circus Lingo*; Wonder Book Company for *Intimate Loves and Lives of the Hilton Sisters*; McFarland and Company and Christine Quigley for *her Modern Mummies: The Preservation of the Human Body in the Twentieth Century*, an excerpt of which is reprinted here as *Mummy Dearest*; New York Press and John Strausbaugh for *City of Humbug: It's Still a P.T. Barnum Town*, an excerpt of which is reprinted here as *City of Humbug*.

Acknowledgments and Thanks

Scott Huffines, Mark Frierson, Robert Kathman, Stephen Blickenstaff, Walt Hudson, Rebecca Sleeme, Ivan Kotcher, Michele Williams, Michael Cuneo, Anne Leaver, John Trainor, Benn Ray, Rachel Wang, Sarah Boonstoppel, Christine Quigley, Joe Petro III, John Strausbaugh, June Parlett, Denny Haney, Ward Hall and Chris Christ and the ever-evolving World of Wonders troupe, Judy Rock, Sylvia Cassidy, Bobby Reynolds, Bruce Snowdon, Dorothy and Joe Hershey, Dean Jensen, Johnny Meah, Dick Flint, Billy Rogers, Joel Shipley, Gretchen Worden, Penn & Teller, Dick Flint, Jim Parker, Rob Houston, and all of the performers without whom the manic joy of being shocked and amazed would be a lot harder to come by for all of us.

Suggested Reading

Circus Lingo, Joe McKennon, Carnival Publishers of Sarasota, 1980.

Anna: A Souvenir Pitchbook, Kathleen Crawford, Dolphin-Moon Press, 1995.

Struggles and Triumphs of a Modern Day Showman, Ward Hall, Carnival Publishers of Sarasota.

In Search of the Monkey Girl, Randall Levenson, New Images, 1982.

Diet or Die—The Dolly Dimples Weight Plan, Celesta "Dolly Dimples" Geyer and Samuel Roen, Frederick Fell, Inc. 1968.

Freaks, Geeks, and Strange Girls: Sideshow Banners of the Great American Midway, R. Johnson, J. Secreto and T. Varndell, eds., Hardy Marks Publications, 1995.

P.T. Barnum: America's Greatest Showman, Philip Kunhardt, Jr., Philip B. Kunhardt III, Philip W. Kunhardt, Alfred A. Knopf, 1995.

Carnival Strippers, Susan Meiselas, Farrar Straus and Giroux, 1975.

The American Burlesque Show, Irving Zeidman, Hawthorn Books, 1967.

Freak Show: Presenting Human Oddities for Amusement and Profit, Robert Bogdan, The University of Chicago Press, 1988.

Sources

"Amazing Feets" originally appeared in *James Taylor's Shocked and Amazed!*, Volume 3, 1996; "King of the Sideshows" in Volume 1, 1995; "Kobel": Volume 1, 1995; "I Dream of Jeannie": Volume 2, 1996; "Better by Half": Volume 2, 1996; "The Intimate Lives and Loves of the Hilton Sisters": Volumes 2 and 3, 1996; "Six Gals to Hug Him": Volume 2, 1996; "The Strand": Volume 5, 1998 and Volume 6, 2001; "Eye Candy": Volume 5, 1998; "Something for Everyone": Volume 6, 2001; "In the Kingdom of the Blind": Volume 4, 1997; "I am Not a Freak": Volume 2, 1996; "The Anatomical Wonder": Volume 3, 1996; "City of Humbug": Volume 5, 1998; "Monkey Business": Volume 6, 2001; "Mummy Dearest": Volume 5, 1998; "Two Heads Are Better than One": Volume 4, 1997, "Freda-Fred": Volume 6, 2001.

Index

R

railroad shows, 20, 247

Randian, Prince, 53

ranginess, 247

rat shows, 213, 226

razor backs, 247–48

Reagan, Dolly, 11, 166

Reed, Billy, 87

Reed, Doreen, 132

Reed, Sandra (Lady Sandra), 16, 132, 137

Reeder, Tyrone, 14

revues, 115, 117–18

Reynolds, Bobby, 131, 213–14, 216, 218,
    230, 235
    animal acts, 227–32
    baby shows, 227
    ballying, 214, 217
    with Fiji mermaid, 212, 234
    as Greatest Showman in the World, 213, 228
    interview with, 215–34
    magic acts, 220
    pitches of, 236–37
    sideshows and, 223
    with snakes, 225

Reynolds, Charles, 113

Rice, Madame, 105, 105

rides, at carnivals, 19, 20, 30, 150–51, 201

ring-necked Burmese women, 234

Ringling Brothers Circus, 13, 32, 154,
    156–57, 187, 223

Ripley's Believe It or Not!, 149, 154–55, 156

road-side museums, 243

Robbins, Milt, 14

Robbins, Todd, 225

Robinson, Pete, 165

rodents, giant, 230

Rogers, Joe, 77

Rose, Ike, 53

Rosen sideshow, 130–31

roustabouts, 247–48

routes, 248

Royal American show, 118, 119–20, 121, 130

rubber men, 132

rubes, 29, 116, 248

S

Sabin, Thomas, 93, 93–94

Sadi Alfarabi, 100–101, 101

Saidor, Indian Snake Charmer, 111, 111

St. Louis Exposition (1904), 250

Saunders, Doc, 13

Sawyer, Buddy, 78

Saxon, A. H., 171, 172, 178

Schlitzie the Pinhead, 13

Scudder's American Museum, 174–75

seal boys/girls/etc., 248

Sealo. See Berent, Stanley "Sealo"

Serpentina, 23, 221

"serving lunch," 115

She Freak (film), 205

shills/shillabers, 21, 162, 190, 248

showmen, xiii, 29, 92, 99–100

Showmen's Club, 16

Siamese twins, 13, 94, 165, 179
    See also Hilton, Daisy and Violet

sideshows, 88, 193, 248
    as American invention, 91–94
    disappearance of, xii, 18, 38
    history of, 19–20

Sideshows by the Seashore (Coney Island),
    145, 214

sidewalls, 21, 248

Sindel, Freddie, 223

Sindel sideshow, 130–31

single-o girl shows, 32, 117, 248

"Sitting Bull's Log Cabin," 30

skeleton men, 94, 95

T

X

X-ray shows, 250

Y

York Fair (Pennsylvania), 21, 123, 140

Younger, Scott, 249

Yvonne and Yvette, 165

Z

Zazel, 96, 96

Zigun, Dick, 214

Zip the Pinhead, 166, 177, 181

zoological parks, 178

Zurm, Patricia (Lady Patricia), 15, 132